The Role of Theory
in Policy Analysis

Also from Westphalia Press

westphaliapress.org

The Role of Theory in Policy Analysis

Volume 2, Number 1 of European Policy Analysis

Edited by Nils Bandelow, Peter
Biegelbauer, Fritz Sager
& Klaus Schubert

WESTPHALIA PRESS
An imprint of Policy Studies Organization

The Role of Theory in Policy Analysis: Volume 2, Number 1 of European Policy Analysis
All Rights Reserved © 2015 by Policy Studies Organization

Westphalia Press
An imprint of Policy Studies Organization
1527 New Hampshire Ave., NW
Washington, D.C. 20036
info@ipsonet.org

ISBN-13: 978-1-63391-756-9
ISBN-10: 1-63391-756-8

Cover design by Jeffrey Barnes:
www.jbarnesbook.design

Daniel Gutierrez-Sandoval, Executive Director
PSO and Westphalia Press

Updated material and comments on this edition
can be found at the Westphalia Press website:
www.westphaliapress.org

Table of Contents

Editorial Introduction to the Third Issue of
European Policy Analysis (EPA)

*E*PA begins its second year of publication with a fresh new format. We have widened our range by adding two new sections: the "Forum" and "Why you should read my book" and hope you'll enjoy the new EPA spring 2016 edition.

Following this Editorial Introduction, you will now find the **Forum**, a section that gives invited colleagues the opportunity to express their views on very topical European policy issues. The currently dominating dispute on the high number of refugees and its impact on the European Union opens this section. We are grateful to **Klaus von Beyme** (Uo Heidelberg) and **Randall Hansen** (Uo Toronto) who agreed to set standards.

The next section—**Contributions**—brings together single articles that passed our thorough double-blind review process.

On the basis of a network approach **Karin Ingold** (Uo Bern) and **Géraldine Pflieger** analyze "the potential difference between a nation's domestic climate policy and its position in the international climate regime" and argue not only "that it is crucial to identify actors who participate in both the national and foreign policy making... but point on the importance of political actors who "should play a central role in both processes, and defend similar policy interests on the two levels, in order for them to be able to coordinate actions and produce coherent outputs in overlapping subsystems."

Frieder Wolf (Uo Heidelberg) and **Georg Wenzelburger** (Uo Kaiserslautern) ask "Why it turns out to be so difficult for" the newly established European Insurance and Occupational Pensions Authority(EIOPA) "to create a single market for private pensions." On the basis of the complete feedback on the EIOPA discussion paper, they found "Unlocking potential economies of scale is attractive to certain large providers, yet it is hindered by member states' widely differing tax rules and raises various distributional questions." On the other side, analyzing the position of EIOPA "vis-à-vis both the Commission and national regulators" they discovered a "strategic shift towards consumer protection."

Daiva Skučiene and **Julija Moskvina** (both Lithuanian Social Research Center) address the complex situation for older workers in East and Central European countries to decide whether to leave or to stay on in the labor market. On the basis of different sources and statistics as well as a multimethod approach, they found a variety of influencing factors. "The analysis revealed the demand for effective policies in the fields of promoting productivity and fighting discrimination."

doi: 10.18278/epa.2.1.1

Simon Hegelich (TUo Munich/Bavarian School of Public Policy) "introduces machine learning algorithms for political scientists." His argu¬ment is that machine learning should be seen as a new approach, where computers are used to analyze data "without theoretical assumptions about possible causalities" and optimize models "according to their accuracy and robustness." His contribution aims at providing "an example, how these methods can be used in political science and to highlight possible pitfalls as well as advantages of machine learning."

A regular feature of EPA is the **Special Focus**. In this issue, we present four articles that focus on "**The Role of Theory in Policy Analysis.**"

Robert Hoppe (UoTwente) and **Hal Colebatch** (Uo New South Wales) address the gap between academic and practical work. They argue that academics use the policy process in a representative mode and differentiate between "three major branches: policy as reasoned authoritative choice, policy as association in policy networks, and policy as problematization and joint meaning making." But in practice—the authors argue—these approaches "also serve performative functions," that is, "they are also mental maps and discursive vehicles for shaping and sometimes changing policy practices." "The purpose of this article is to contribute to policy theorists' and policy workers' awareness of these often tacit and 'underground' selective affinities between the representative and performative roles of policy process theorizing."

The contribution of **Holger Straßheim** (HUo Berlin) "focuses on theories of time in policy analysis." It "gives a brief overview on concepts of time in policy analysis and, more specifically, the concept of 'political time' as a common denominator in current debates." It is based on two central assumptions: the various ways time is conceptualized are closely related to underlying understandings of politics and political action." And, "theories of time are also always political theories. Debating time is thus not only of analytic value. It also has large implications on how power, rationality, and collectivity are related to each other. Moreover and probably less obvious, theories of time as political theories can be highly influential in practice. When they find their way into policy making ... they may realign the time horizons of political action."

Basil Bornemann (Uo Basel) directs our attention towards a "type of policymaking that practitioners regularly qualify as 'integrative' and 'strategic'" where "policymaking transgresses the boundaries of established policy fields and integrates differentiated policy areas." He argues "that existing ... studies of 'integrative political strategies' ... rest on problematic functional presumptions and do not consider the analytical implications of "integration" and "strategy" as practical cornerstones." Therefore, he puts forward "a 'new' type of policy field that emerges from countermovements to two dominant trends that have shaped contemporary policy systems: integration as a countermovement to the continuing differentiation of policies ... and strategy as a flexible form of boundary work that contrasts with the pattern of institutionalization."

Interlacing multiple networks with multiple streams **Evelyne de Leeuw** (Uo New South Wales), **Marjan Hoeijmakers** (Public Health Limburg, The Netherlands), and **Dorothee T.I.M. Peter** (Uo Amsterdam) "discovered that dynamic interactions between actors in the different (policy, problem, and politics) streams … produce different network configurations in each stream." They "therefore postulate that hybridization of policy network theory with multiple streams theory would create a more powerful conceptual toolbox." Moreover, they put up "criticism that has been voiced of the stages heuristic and propose that a more useful metaphor is that of juggling: policy processes may appear chaotic, but keen discipline, coordination, and acuity are required for policy analysts to keep all balls in the air."

The second new section of EPA: **Why You Should Read My Book**. The idea behind this is that EPA would like to give selected authors or editors of exciting new books in the field of public policy an opportunity to state in a few words why it should be read.

In this issue, we start this section with the book The European Public Servant: A Shared Administrative Identity? by Patrick Overeem and Fritz Sager (eds.) and the book Decision-Making Under Ambiguity and Time Constraints: Assessing the Multiple Streams Framework by Friedbert Rüb and ReimutZohlnhöfer (eds.).

Last but not least, we editors have to thank—first of all our authors for their patience and willingness to sometimes considerably revise and rework their contributions and, of course, our many reviewers—sometimes three and more per contribution—which allow EPA to meet the high publication standards and develop them further. Every second year, we will express our gratitude by publishing the names.

Those who have had an opportunity to assemble highly complex products like academic journals will know that even four editors are not enough to handle the work, to avoid or resolve problems, and to keep the machine running. This is why we are particularly grateful that Kate Backhaus (Uo Muenster) and Johanna Hornung (TUoBraunschweig) are with us and—seemingly light handedly—handle the hard work.

April 2016   Nils C. Bandelow, Peter Biegelbauer, Fritz Sager, and Klaus Schubert

Refugees and Migration in Europe

Klaus von Beyme[A]

1. Postcolonial Policies and Their Consequences in the Field of Migration

The year 2015 for most European countries seemed to be the year of a historical disaster. Around 60 million migrants were forcibly displaced worldwide, with most of them approaching Europe and not the United States, the country which, by its unwise interventions in the Third World, had caused the collapse of some of the artificial states as products of colonialism and post-colonialism. This awful intervention started more than half a century ago by the toppling of Mosaddegh in Iran in 1953 with the help of the Central Intelligence Agency (CIA). In the long run, it contributed to the establishment of a religious dogmatic system under Khomeini. The Islamic Revolution in Iran was a belated answer to the coup d'état of 1953 (Lüders 2015, 20).

The politics of intervention in the Near East was based on two problems:

1) *To support democracy and security.* The propaganda for the legal state (Rechtsstaat) and democratic anti-authoritarian politics among Western politicians frequently obscured the economic interests of securing the supply with oil and gas.

2) *To protect Israel.* It was the second target, the protection of Israel, which caused a permanent priority over the Palestinian Arabs and a decline of reputation for Europe and the United States in the whole Arab world. Maybe Daniel Barenboim's statement "the USA could solve the conflicts between Israelis and Palestinians in three days if they wanted to do so" is probably a political exaggeration of an artist. But certainly pressure from the United States and Europe could contribute to smooth down the conflict which was one of the problems in the Arab world and which caused mass emigration. The West had forgotten that Syria had turned to the Soviet Union for friendship when the Golan Heights were conquered by Israel in the Six-Day War in 1967, and the United States as well as the European States were not ready to put pressure on Israel to give back the annexed area to the Syrian State. In the long run, this became one of the reasons for supporting Israel against Assad's system which contributed to the mass emigration of Syrians. Only recently, a compromise with Russia concerning the toleration of Assad's regime became possible. Unfortunately, this chance has been abandoned because of new conflicts between Russia and the West. The conflict between Western Europe and Putin's Russia has some influence

[A] University of Bielefeld, Germany

doi: 10.18278/epa.2.1.2

on the background of migration. In Germany and other European countries, the Leftist post-communist parties blur the differences of party ideologies and are basically at one with many right-wing populist and neo-fascist groups in the assumption that cooperation with Russia, Iran, or Syria is necessary.

The failures of Western interventions from Afghanistan and Iraq to Libya contributed to the disintegration of statehood in Iraq and Syria. Sometimes this process is compared with the collapse of Yugoslavia. There is, however, one important difference: in Yugoslavia, even during Communist times, there existed "national communities" on the basis of federal structures, with integrating elements, such as language and religion. In the states of the Arab and Near East, which British and French colonialism left after the First World War, on the other hand—in spite of a certain unity of language with the exception of Curds—there were no political institutional frames and no established churches and party systems. Especially in Syria, a clear division between the followers of President Assad and the "Islamic State" (IS) was not even feasible. Many intermittent groups fight the President and at the same time occasionally collaborate with the system of his arch enemy IS. Sometimes these groups are the target of Russian bombs, meant to fight the IS in support of Assad.

Cooperation between Arab groups became increasingly difficult because of the dominance of clans and tribal groups in various Arab countries suffering from civil war. These unclear divisions in the civil wars contribute to the exile and emigration of many uncommitted

citizens who were sacrificed between the front lines and escaped terror and the threat to life. Thus, the United States as the "universal policeman" caused the rise of new enemies, such as "Al Qaida" and the "Islamic State," which ardent critics (Lüders 2015, 62, 170) referred to as "made in the USA." Turkey followed the West in political miscalculation when Erdogan broke relations with Assad. As a result, about 2.3 million immigrants arrived in Turkey which the West has recently tried to reduce by accepting certain numbers of them in Europe in exchange for another risky concession: the renewal of negotiations with Turkey for access to the European Community. The states in the European Union (EU) are still fighting about the redistribution of refugees, Cyprus has already refused to contribute money, and the envisaged redistribution of 160,000 refugees within two years has so far made little progress (figures in FAZ.7.1.2016:15).

2. The Concept of Power in the Near East

Sometimes the propaganda of the IS that "Islamism is fighting the West" is taken literally by frightened Western commentators. This hypothesis overlooks the fact that Islamism predominantly is not fighting the West—except for some terrorist incidents—but is fighting itself in civil wars, not only between Sunnitism and Shiism. The situation in the Near East in the meantime is compared to the disruptions of the Thirty Years War in Germany (1618–1648). "Confessionalism" and thinking in terms of tribes created growing intolerance. The Alawites support Assad for their survival as a minority group and even some Christians in Syria do so too. The Christians in Lebanon are also divided in groups cooperating with Iran or with the West. Western countries sometimes chose the wrong partners among Islamic groups: the *Muslim Brothers* were not accepted, but *Wahhabism*, one of the most dogmatic groups, was tolerated to keep up cooperation with the Saudi dynasty. Power in the Near East is not understood in terms of the "legal state" of the West as a possibility of mediating among groups, but rather as an instrument of preserving power. In this respect, secular despots, such as Saddam Hussein or Assad, are similar to radical Islamists. Both versions created migrations in large numbers.

The IS in the West is frequently understood as a traditional religious group. This perception overlooks the fact that IS agents, in spite of their fundamentalism, are good capitalists with their oil business and with many stolen works of art which they sell. They are quite modernized in their way of organizing military and bureaucratic power in their conquered territories which reach from the suburbs of Aleppo close to Bagdad. Modernism is, however, despised when it argues against "*Sharia*." In the universities under the domination of the IS, whole faculties in the fields of law, political science, and the arts have been closed down.

Although Western politicians recognized with secret pleasure that the Soviet Union had failed to regulate politics in Afghanistan—with many more soldiers than the United States ever mobilized in that area—they dared to intervene. Even Germany—so prudent in the Iraq War—followed this operation with little knowledge of the heterogeneous society which it wanted to influence. Recently, the

Western countries had to renounce the complete withdrawal from Afghanistan when they recognized that the central government in Kabul was no longer in control of many marginal areas of the country—a poor picture of the support for democracy. Western propaganda for democracy and market society was meaningless in countries with archaic tribal and clan structures. The West had little understanding of historical continuities in political ideologies, even in East European countries. The West needed Russia for its struggle against radical Islamists which violated Russian interests in the North Caucasian and Central Asian areas. Although Putin was open to close contacts to Western democracies until 2004, the United States and the North Atlantic Treaty Organization (NATO) extended their influence to the Russian borders. This was at least against certain cautious Western declarations in the negotiations with Gorbachev on the reunification of Germany (von Beyme 2016, 116f).

3. Immigration Policies

The collapse of the former *dualistic world system* in 1990 put an end to the old clarity of ideological borders and created *multi-polarity* alien to American perceptions that were based on the American feeling of having survived as the only world power. The Indian writer Pankaj Mishra (2012) and other essayists developed—in combination of Asian religious ideas and Western anti-capitalistic Leftist concepts—the hope that the Western way of life, with emphasis on capitalism and nation-building, is doomed to failure in the future, and, especially,

Asian religious and political ideas will get a chance to dominate the world society in the future. Even in Europe, the migration issue has created a certain alliance of Leftist parties with the nativism of Asian and African countries which was contrary to the still predominant beliefs in European values. Max Weber once emphasized the difference between "the ethics of conviction" (*Gesinnungsethik*) and the "ethics of responsibility" (*Verantwortungsethik*). Western values threaten to be abused by unrealistic emphasizers of the "ethics of conviction" as well as by Asian and African ideologues. Many of them refuse the Western concept of universal human values, although they recently proved their value in the widespread help for refugees from Asia and Africa by normal citizens in Europe.

Immigration is rediscovered as a phenomenon which existed in many periods of European history. When after 200 years, Germans in Brazil still speak a German dialect, this was praised by some observers, in a time when the obligation of immigrants to learn German is widely discussed among German Democrats. One of the most disputed topics on migration is the assessment whether immigrants are useful for the economy of a guest country. Frequently wrong comparisons are offered, such as the Russian Jews immigrating to Israel, who generally had a much higher level of education than the Jewish immigrants from Ethiopia. The 14 million German speakers who came from Eastern Europe and had to be accepted by the two Germanys after 1945 are also hardly comparable to Arabs in Scandinavia or Germany since they knew German, were well educated, and had the stubborn will to be economically successful. By about 1960, they had almost reached the income levels of West German citizens.

In German politics, the main targets of policies in the field of migration mentioned by leading politicians (Klöckner 2016, 21) are as follows:

- Facilitating the integration of refugees
- Securing the outer borders of Europe
- Distribution of refugees amongst the European countries and the German Laender
- Fighting against the military and economic causes of emigration
- Allaying civil war in Syria.

In these five areas a lot has been done. But Europe is far from succeeding.

1) The *integration of refugees* depends on how long most of them stay in Europe. Certainly, in the future, many will go back, partly disappointed with the living conditions in the camps and other accommodation facilities in the European area, partly because the conditions at home will improve—whether economically, politically, or otherwise. The older generation of migrants endorsed this assumption. Last year, more Turks, living under decent conditions in Germany, moved back to Turkey than the numbers of those Turks who came to Germany. Most of the parties agree that the refugees have to accept the values of Western democracy and to learn the language of the country. Sometimes there are, however, strange controversies when Leftists are so committed to "understanding foreign citizens" that they accept, for example, masking women with *Burkas* in public—widely not accepted by the citizens' home country.

2) For *securing the outer borders of Europe*, the members of the EU had many problems with Greece and Turkey, and also with some East European countries, especially Poland. There is the hope of some politicians that if Britain pulls out, the rules of the EU will be changed into more rigid provisions.

3) The *distribution of refugees among the members of the EU* does not function at all. The German Chancellor, Merkel, has alienated many EU members by her optimism and the slogan "We'll make it." These goals were honorable but not at all negotiated with the neighbors of Germany. Poland and other East European members accept only tiny numbers of refugees. Poland even wants to restrict this to "Christians"—a position not in tune with European democratic values. Even the distribution of refugees among the German Laender is already quite difficult, and the Federal State has many quarrels with Bavaria with regard to various forms of refugee policies.

4) *Fighting against the military and economic causes of emigration* is certainly the most complicated task. Cooperation in bombarding strongholds of the IS remains highly controversial even in Germany which did not follow the United States, Britain, and France in direct military attacks on IS strongholds in Syria. Germany did not contribute to the Iraq War but had to accept negative consequences of its participation in Afghanistan which even after the declaration of the withdrawal of troops led to new cumbersome commitments. The economic causes

are especially important in the case of African refugees, since not only colonialism but also recent dominance of Western economies, which weakened African economic performance, has to be changed.

5) *Allaying the civil war in Syria* led first to new cooperation between Russia and the West. But soon the conflict of whether Assad should be accepted as the President of Syria and the Russian bombs against other oppositional forces fighting Assad led to new disagreements. It is becoming increasingly clear that the civil war cannot be ended by bombs, and even the direct intervention of Western troops on the ground would create new hostilities among the populations in the Near East. But there is no visible coalition of IS, especially since new hostilities between Iran and Saudi Arabia began after the attack on the Saudi Embassy in Teheran.

Recently, integration policies in many European countries have improved, but they nevertheless suffer from incompatible developments that include:

1) *The closing of borders for refugees* in many European countries, even in Sweden, which so far had accepted the highest number of immigrants in proportion to its own population. An unofficial "Nordic competition" has asked: Which of the Scandinavian countries is creating the most unattractive conditions for refugees? (Wyssuwa 2016, 2). The European Community tries to mitigate the differences, but it failed in the case of Hungary, a country that even renounced

subsidies from Brussels which were meant to put pressure on. In the case of Poland, the EU hopes to have more success. Poland needs the EU much more than Hungary with its many Right-wing populist and neo-Fascist groups, and, moreover, the country has a greater pro-European proportion in its population as recent rallies against the conservative government in Warsaw showed.

2) *The tendency to leave the European Community* is becoming a major issue in some countries, such as Britain. In order to avoid a British exit, called "Brexit," the EU has to offer some concessions, such as

- the exemption of immigrants from social transfers for several years
- the preservation of national sovereignty and abandoning closer European
- policies, and guarantees for the preservation of national states
- de-bureaucratization and liberalization of commerce.

Conclusions

*I*ntegration policies increasingly aim at four areas:

1) *To limit the number of refugees per year.* In Germany, the Bavarian Christian Social Union (CSU) has asked for a limit of 200,000. These limits are differentiated from fixed quotas for all European countries.

2) *Furthering integration courses* which one million immigrants in Germany

have taken part in since 2005. Until 2013, the largest group to take part in integration courses was Polish migrants. However, there are increasingly more participants of Arab origin (Der Spiegel Nr.1 2016,30).

3) *Cutting down social subsidies for immigrants.* Even in Germany, leading Sozialdemokratische Partei Deutschland (SPD) politicians, such as Andrea Nahles and Olaf Scholz, not to mention the CSU, are in favor of restricting social subsidies which should be dependent on wages and contributions of the refugees at least for one year; Britain even demands a four-year period. The problem is, however, that in the past year only about 10% of asylum seekers in Germany have found employment. Even the German Constitutional Court was criticized by some scholars for claiming that the social benefits for asylum seekers are too low (Müller 2015, 8). There is also contention about the question whether asylum seekers have the right to invite their families to join them in Europe.

4) A new *law of integration* is increasingly demanded, which Chancellor Schröderhad already tried to introduce in 2005.

The immigration policies have changed the ideological European climate in several respects:

1) The development toward less state intervention will change into *more commitment of states* in immigration policies and questions connected with them. Increasing violence against the homes of asylum seekers requires

increasing investment in police and immigration bureaucracy. Repressive measures will be increasingly demanded, for instance, to send refugees who participate in acts of violence, such as recently in Cologne, more quickly back to their country of origin.

2) *The patterns of development policies in the Third World will change.* It is considered as an error that more development aid will stop the exodus from countries in the Third World, as long as the native economies are undermined. These economies have to be supported in adapting to the global economic system by Western countries.

3) Certain segments of young migrants and the native youth are alienated and prone to joining the IS, in France even more so than in Germany. On the other hand, extremism is increasingly accepted. This contributes to a development in which *right-wing populism changes the party systems.* Germany so far still seems to be better off than some neighboring countries, such as France or Poland. Both processes lead to the polarization of Western societies. There is a tendency of a *"State of Fear"* (*Angststaat*) growing in many European countries (Leggewie 2016, 11).

4) *The process of European integration is slowed down and nationalism is growing again in the population.* "Balkanization" of the national states is another consequence.

References

Bartsch, Matthias et al. 2016. Und du bist raus. Der Spiegel, Nr. 1, 2016: 24-30, zitiert S. 30.

"Die Ressourcen sind irgendwann erschöpft. CDU-Vize Julia Klöckner redet über Kosten und Nutzen der Flüchtlinge und wundert sich, warum Linke für die Verschleierung der Frauen sind." *FAS* 3(1): 21.

Leggewie, Claus. 2016. "Der Weg in den Angststaat." *FAZ* 6(1). 2016, No 4: 11.

Lüders, Michael. 2015. *Wer den Wind sät. Was westliche Politik im Orient anrichtet.* Munich: Beck.

Mishra, Pankaj. 2012. *From the Ruins of Empire. Intellectuals remade Asia.* New York: Strauss and Giroux.

Müller, Reinhard. 2015. "Deutsche Sondermoral." *FAZ* 18(12): 8.

von Beyme, Klaus. 2016. *Die Russland-Kontroverse. Eine Analyse des ideologischen Konflikts zwischen Russland-Verstehern und Russland-Kritikern.* Wiesbaden: Springer VS.

Wyssuwa, Matthias. 2016. "Nordischer Wettbewerb: Wer ist am unattraktivsten?" *FAS* 3(1): 2.

Immigrants, ISIS, the Refugee Crisis, and Integration in Europe: A Response to Klaus von Beyme

Randall Hansen[A]

1. Postcolonial Policies and Their Consequences in the Field of Migration

Klaus von Beyme has written an ambitious, subtle, and provocative article on Middle Eastern, Russian/Central Asian, and refugee politics. It divides into roughly two sections: (i) a discussion of the background causes of state breakdown and refugee outflows in the Middle East and (ii) an analysis of refugee policy and its relationship to broader immigration policy in contemporary Germany and Europe.

Let me begin with von Beyme's argument: "There were [in 2015] calculated to be around 60 million migrants throughout the world, most of them approaching Europe and not the USA, the country which by its unwise interventions in the Third World had caused the collapse of some of the artificial states as products of colonialism and post-colonialism." Few would dispute that Western, and above all American, intervention in the Middle East lies at the root of most contemporary refugee outflows (though only a small minority of the total 60 million *forced* migrants are making their way to Europe). Von Beyme nonetheless paints with too broad a brush. In his analysis, both longstanding American/Western support for autocratic regimes *and* more recent Western support for democracy and democratization are at fault. I am not a Middle Eastern expert, but I would suggest that we need to distinguish clearly two periods in American policy toward the Middle East: the realist period and the neoconservative/responsibility-to-protect (R2P) period. During the former, which obtained from the end of World War II until the disastrous presidency of George W. Bush, the prevailing objectives of the US State Department were to contain Communism (the Cold War gets little mention in von Beyme's historical summary) and to ensure regime stability in the Middle East supporting authoritarian regimes with often appalling human rights records (though Jordan, for instance, is far less extreme than Saudi Arabia or Syria). The second involved active efforts to reconfigure Middle Eastern politics through the invasion of Iraq, the toppling of Ghaddafi, and the support, if at least rhetorical, for the Arab Spring.

The distinction is important because it was only the second set of interventions that caused the great refugee surge that we have seen since the middle of the 2000s. Refugee movements have long been a structural feature of the Middle East (Chatty 2010), but current outflow is greater than anything

[A] University of Toronto

doi: 10.18278/epa.2.1.3

seen since the aftermath of World War II and correlates directly with war and institutional breakdown in Iraq, Libya, and Syria. The West destroyed the first two of these states, and it encouraged a rebellion that it had no intention of materially supporting in the third. Iraq was a neoconservative intervention, Libya an R2P one, but they both resulted in mass death and displacement. There was little to admire in the pre-2011 Syrian, Libyan, and Egyptian regimes, but fewer, in the first two many fewer, people died (though, of course, we will not know how many Libyans would have died had Gadhafi made good on his threats).

The Afghani case is more complicated. Afghanistan was not Iraq, and the current confusion of the two in the public, and to a degree academic mind, does violence to recent history. The Iraqi regime, though an abominable one in its human rights record and its treatment of minorities, notably the Kurds, posed no threat to the United States and the West. Containment was working. Afghanistan—or, more specifically, al Qaeda, which Afghanistan housed and tolerated—launched a direct attack on American soil. The Iraqi venture was purely voluntary, the Afghan one largely necessary, even if with the benefit of hindsight we can agree that the United States and NATO might have approached it differently. In a wider sense, the United States, of course, bears responsibility for developments in Afghanistan, in that it provided the arms and training to the Mujahedeen in the 1980s, and some of these fighters became, weapons in hand, the Taliban in the 1990s. And the United States also launched its own attacks on Afghan soil—the August 1998 bombings of al-Qaeda bases in Afghanistan—

though, of course, less brutal ones. It nonetheless remains important to distinguish the two operations.

The current military intervention against ISIS is different again. Although the Americans helped create ISIS by needlessly disbanding the Iraqi army (many of whose officers were opportunists who gladly would have worked for the new regime), it is a collection of marauding vandals that have launched direct military assaults on one ally—Iraq—and three NATO member states—Belgium, Turkey, and France. There is every moral and strategic argument in favor of its destruction, though there is naturally much debate on how best to achieve these aims.

Von Beyme's generally negative view of the United States and the West is matched by a generally positive view of Russia. Indeed, we meet in his pages the Putin of the *Versteher* lobby that is particularly vocal in Germany: a politician willing to work with the West until the latter's provocative NATO encirclement pushed him into confrontation. Von Beyme writes, "Though Putin was open for close contacts to Western democracies until 2004, the United States and NATO extended their influence [to] the Russian borders. This was at least against certain cautious Western declarations in the negotiations about the reunification of Germany with Gorbachev." The debate about which promises were made to Gorbachev in 1989–1990 rolls on, but the claim made in the first sentence is difficult to reconcile with chronology. If NATO expansion pushed Putin to the extreme, then Putin's turn to extremism should have occurred in 1999, when former Soviet client states of Poland, the Czech Republic, and Hungary joined, or in 2004, when Bulgaria, Estonia, Latvia, Lithuania, Romania, Slovakia, and Slovenia joined. It, in fact, occurred after 2008, despite several efforts by Obama to improve the relationship. The most recent NATO enlargement involved countries—Albania and Croatia—that are not on Russia's borders.

It is true or at least arguable that, with hindsight, the Europe and the United States might have taken a more consultative and inclusive position vis à vis Russia during most recent NATO expansions and during Ukraine's European Union association negotiations. But these mistakes, if that is what they were, cannot possibly justify Putin's behavior since then: his 2008 war against Georgia and, above all, his 2014 annexation of Crimea, an invasion (as Putin eventually admitted) and border alteration of the sort not seen in Europe since World War II. Von Beyme, rather incredibly, does not mention Crimea at all. Perhaps more importantly, neither Putin nor anyone else in Russia can tell sovereign states which associations they may or may not join. Moreover, Russia's treatment of Georgia and Crimea suggest that the fears of Eastern European countries that sought NATO membership were entirely justified. That so many in Germany, a country that has gone to such great lengths to repudiate its own history of militarism and imperialism, should indulge Russian militarism and imperialism is as mystifying as it is unconscionable.

There are further factors worth mentioning, none of which is flattering toward Putin or reassuring for his German sympathizers. All evidence suggests that Putin is utterly hostile to the idea that countries he regards as within the Russian sphere of influence—Georgia, Ukraine, and Moldova, along with the rest of the Caucasus and Central Asia—might determine their own future, and he likes destabilized states that he can draw into his sphere of influence. Domestic politics also play a role here: Putin's turn to extremism—his closing down of the free press, the exile and poisoning of his critics, the murder of journalists—correlates with his overwhelming fear of a domestic reaction against his corrupt and autocratic regime, above all since 2008. For Putin, power is a zero-sum game: when others have it, he does not, and when others are weak, he is strong. It is possible, and horrifying, that what Putin wants in Syria is not so much an Assad victory—bad enough, but one with which a tough realist could live *if* it brought stability—but permanent conflict and a flow of militarized refugees to a Europe that he will never forgive for applying sanctions on Russia. Putin is particularly incensed by Germany, a country he flattered himself into believing he understood because of his KGB résumé and knowledge of the language, as it was Chancellor Merkel who anchored the sanctions agreements. Again, it is odd that von Beyme adopts such a critical stance toward Western neoimperialism while remaining seemingly indifferent to Russian neoimperialism.

Von Beyme's discussion of immigration and refugees is equally ambitious and thought-provoking. Von Beyme is absolutely right that efforts to achieve responsibility sharing the distribution of refugees have resulted in absolute failure. I am doubtful, though, that better negotiation would have changed the result. There partly was not sufficient time—hundreds of thousands of refugees were on their way—and little in the behavior of Hungary, Poland, Slovakia, and the Czech Republic suggests that they would have softened their stand toward refugees had they been afforded additional time to think it over. Their governments have succumbed to and indeed fan an ugly nativism that opposes refugees because they are foreigners and above all Muslim foreigners. Their stance is a rejection of European solidarity and a repudiation of their international legal obligations. It is also willfully blind to three rather obvious facts: their own citizens were welcomed into the West as refugees; their obstinacy is staggeringly ungrateful to old EU members states who admitted them over the concerns of Western European electorates and who transfer large amounts of money to them; and if Germany behaved as they did, then hundreds of thousands of refugees would be stranded in Eastern Europe and would be their problem.

Across Europe, immigration certainly is feeding populism, as all far right parties in Europe—the Front National in France, the United Kingdom Independence Party, Jobbik in Hungary, Golden Dawn in Greece, True Finns in Finland, and the Alternative for Germany, among many others—make lower levels of migration, economic and/or refugee, a basic part of their platform. Indeed, it was one of the few points on which the far-right agrees across Europe. By contrast, the alliance between the left and nativist elements suggested by von Beyme is a limited one—most opposition to immigration emerges from the right—and is found in the countries with the most generous welfare states, reflecting both chauvinism and a reasonable concern that migrants are attracted by Scandinavian or Dutch welfare systems rather than labor markets (Favell 2014).

The obvious question is whether one can do anything about all of this. Von Beyme is also correct that the securing of the EU's outer borders is essential to preserving the Schengen system and, more broadly, free movement within the EU. The United Kingdom's exit, if it occurs, will make little difference as the one area on which it is an active participant in European cooperation is in restrictive immigration policy, and the country has always been outside the Schengen zone. The real obstacle to secure borders is weak border capacity in Bulgaria, Romania, Italy, and, above all, Greece; overcoming it will depend on whether European border policy can be truly communitarized by concentrating member resources, equipment, and personnel on the southern border. The sending and transit countries themselves will play an important role, as they always do, which is what makes the EU deal with Turkey so essential to restoring order to European migration policy. Indeed, for all the understandable opposition on human rights grounds, there was really no other way to manage flows after Austria, Serbia, Croatia, and Macedonia closed their borders, leading directly to a refugee bottleneck in Greece. Now that the Balkan and Aegean routes are closed, smugglers and traffickers may well shift their focus back to the Mediterranean and even the Black Sea, making Italy, Romania, and Bulgaria the new focuses of migrant and refugee pressure.

On immigration policy, von Beyme rightly focusses on the two issues that matter more than culture: language and work. The aside regarding praise bestowed on Germans in Brazil who speak German 200 years after their ancestors arrived, is not relevant, as they presumably speak Portuguese as well. It is essential that all immigrants, including refugees, master the language of their new country; if they also speak their home language, and perhaps several more, that is only to their advantage. I was unsure if von Beyme was criticizing or endorsing the move to limit social subsidies, but it is in any case advisable (indeed, if a figure such as Andrea Nahles endorses this measure, the argument is clearly overwhelming). Excessively high income support can serve as a magnet effect and can encourage incorporate into the welfare state rather than the labor market. The "welfare wage," as the founder of the British social state, William Beveridge, recognized, cannot be above the working wage. Public resources should not be spent on keeping young people idle (the average age of refugees is 30) but, rather, on giving them training and educational opportunities. Here the Germans are getting it right: the emphasis in discussions of refugee integration has been on work, and the *Arbeitsagentur* has rolled out a program in some federal *Länder* that allows refugees to demonstrate their skills through a few weeks' work in German firms; if they can do the job, they get the job without the formal qualifications. It is a clever move and an unusual innovation in the otherwise overly bureaucratized German labor market (Koschnitzke 2016). The Ministry of Education had already rolled out a program allowing refugees to demonstrate their credentials when they had no documentation on their qualifications, which was often destroyed in war or lost on the refugee trek, or even knowledge of German (Böse, Tusarinow, and Wünsche 2016). In this context, the

unrelated decision, designed to appease the British, to reduce benefits to the rate applicable where an EU migrant worker's family is residing is another step in the right direction: free movement within the EU, like migration (though not refugee flows) to the EU, should be about work.

The issue of jihadist radicalization mentioned by von Beyme is a real one, but it has little to do with current immigration flows, refugees included. Those radicalizing are longstanding migrants and often citizens of European societies who turn, for reasons that are not fully comprehended, to an ideology that understands nothing but fear, death, violence, and theocratic slavery. They have more to do with the Red Army Fraction than they do with refugees. The latter, above all the Syrians, know all too well what ISIS is and what it stands for.

The institutional and statist developments that von Beyme highlights—a fragmentation of the European party system, a slowing of the European integration process, and an expansion of state power in the face of terrorism—are indisputably underway, with some variation between the member states. Some of these trends, such as an expansion in repressive state powers, will be hard to check given the very real jihadist threat, which is not to say that no effort should be made. For the EU, the slowing of integration is only inevitable if we maintain the fiction that all ships must move at the same speed. The refugee crisis made it clear that the commitment of some member states to the Union—Britain (no surprise there) and Eastern European states—is largely instrumental, or at least deeply constrained by nationalism and/ or nativism. There is a strong case for a multispeed Europe in which Germany and, to borrow from Peer Steinbrück, a 'coalition of willing' (which will need to include France) moves toward a full integration of refugee and border control policy.

References

Böse, C., D. Tusarinow, and T. Wünsche, 2016. "Recognizing Vocational Qualifications of Refugees—Examples from 'Prototyping Transfer." Bonn: Federal Institute for Vocational Education and Training. https://www.bibb.de/en/39350.php.

Chatty, D. 2010. *Displacement and Dispossession in the Modern Middle East*. Oxford: Oxford University Press.

Favell, A, 2014. "The Fourth Freedom: Theories of Migration and Mobilities in 'Neo-Liberal' Europe." *European Journal of Social Theory* 17 (3): 275–289.

Koschnitzke, L. 2016. "Jung, Aber Wenig Qualifiziert." Die Zeit, January 16. http://www.zeit.de/wirtschaft/2016-01/ arbeitsmarkt-fluechtlinge-arbeitslo-sigkeit-lohndumping-realloehne.

Two Levels, Two Strategies: Explaining the Gap Between Swiss National and International Responses Toward Climate Change

Karin Ingold[A] & Géraldine Pflieger[B]

In a complex and multilevel regime, countries' national and international strategies to address climate change may considerably differ. Adopting an actor-centered approach, the aim of this article is to outline and understand the potential difference between a nation's domestic climate policy and its position in the international climate regime. We adopt social network analysis focusing on actors' identification, their relational profiles, interests, and resources. Through survey data and content analysis, we focus on those actors' positions within Swiss national and foreign climate policy. Results show that it is crucial to identify actors that participate in both the national and foreign policymaking. But participation on two levels seems to be a necessary but not sufficient condition. Actors should play a central role in both processes, and defend similar policy interests on the two levels, in order for them to be able to coordinate actions and produce coherent outputs in overlapping subsystems.

Keywords*: Multilevel governance; policy output; climate change; social network analysis; Switzerland; two-level game*

Introduction

In a complex and multilevel regime, countries' national and international strategies to address climate change may considerably differ. Adopting an actor-centered approach, the aim of this article is to outline and understand the potential difference between a nation's domestic climate policy and its position in the international climate regime.

Following Putnam (1988), domestic politics and international relations are often entangled and two policymaking processes may mutually influence each other. An important role is played by national actors who are also involved in foreign policymaking and thus suffer from double accountability: to their constituencies and to their peers, with the potential to shape or coordinate policy outcomes on both a national

[A] University of Bern, Institute of Political Science and Oeschger Centre for Climate Change Research, Fabrikstrasse 8, 3012 Bern, Switzerland.
Eawag, Department of Environmental Social Sciences, Dübendorf, Switzerland

[B] University of Geneva, Department of Political Science and International Relations, Av. Du Pont-d'Arve 40, 1204 Genève, Switzerland
University of Geneva, Institute of Environmental Science, Geneva, Switzerland

doi: 10.18278/epa.2.1.4

and international levels (Avery 1996). Newer studies, drawing on multilevel governance and the ecology of games, point to the fact that the same actor simultaneously participating in various processes that are shaped by different rules could produce very different actions and draw in different interests in each of those processes (Klijn, Koppenjan, and Termeer 1995; George 2004; Hoberg and Morawski 2008; Smaldino and Lubell 2011; Leifeld and Schneider 2012). This is why two embedded or overlapping subsystems have the potential to produce very divergent policy outputs or outcomes (Capano and Howlett 2009).

Here, we thus ask what might explain the different policies that are defended within the national and international sphere: is it the result of very different actors participating in both processes? Or, do actors who take part in both not have the power to coordinate actions across two levels? Or, do they defend very divergent interests in each process?

To answer those questions, we adopt social network analysis focusing on actors' identification, their relational profiles, interests, and resources. Through interviews, survey data, and content analysis, we focus on those actors' positions within national and international climate politics. Studying Switzerland constitutes an interesting case for several reasons: the unique position of Switzerland was that the content of its climate policy varied strongly between the domestic scale— with a weak commitment to mitigation policy and tools such as a CO2 tax—and the international scale—with a strong involvement in the field of mitigation and adaptation. Furthermore, the Swiss domestic climate policy followed a typical

industrial country perspective, focusing considerably on climate mitigation whilst fuel consumers (transport, energy, and industry representatives) tried to extensively influence the policy outputs. Internationally, and since 2001, Switzerland has been integrated in the Environmental Integrity Group (EIG) of the United Nations Framework Convention on Climate Change (UNFCCC)—also including Mexico, South Korea, Monaco, and Lichtenstein. The Group is unusual within the UN climate regime architecture because it mainly aimed for a strong focus on adaptation measures and stronger responsibility by developed and emerging economies in promoting new adaptation funding schemes. Switzerland was one of the driving forces within this group and thus promoted a completely different policy strategy (focusing on adaptation) toward climate change than in its domestic agenda.

Background

In the early 1990s, the proposed project of imposing a CO2 tax in Switzerland failed. Afraid of a second policy deadlock, the government adopted a different strategy in 1995: private partners were included in the design of the new CO2 act mandating a 10% CO2 emissions reduction by 2012, compared with 1990 emissions. In 2002, a report showed that the voluntary agreements planned thus far would be insufficient to achieve the necessary reduction (Prognos2002). In such a situation, the act foresaw the introduction of the incentive CO2 tax. Importantly, together with the tax, Switzerland also planned introducing tradable carbon permits. The idea was to link the Swiss carbon certificate market to the European scheme of tradable permits. Furthermore, Swiss sectors exempted from the tax should have compensated their exemption by their activity on this market.

At the same time, the Swiss Petrol Union launched the "climate penny" project to avoid the introduction of a tax on motor fuels. Under this, each liter of fuel would be "taxed"[1] with one penny, and the income generated thereby was used to finance national and international projects to reduce CO_2 emissions. As the voluntary agreements were no longer a sufficient solution, the actors had to decide between supporting the tax and the climate penny. Finally, in March 2004 the Swiss government decided in favor of an intermediate solution including a tax on combustibles and the penny on motor fuels. This policy output can be categorized as "modest" mitigation policy: Switzerland was only able to fulfill Kyoto targets taking forest sinks and international emissions' reductions into account[2].

Within the UN framework convention on climate change, Switzerland participated in the creation of the Environmental Integrity Group (EIG) with Mexico, South Korea, Monaco, and Lichtenstein. Switzerland and the EIG are not members of one of the major alliances or blocks that emerged during the UNFCCC negotiations, such as the blocks representing the European

Union or the G77. Therefore, it is argued that "Switzerland has no choice but to defend its interests with innovative ideas" (Arquit-Niederberger and Schwager 2004, 107). In relation to mitigation issues, the position of Switzerland was quite close to that of the EU. The country supported the 2 degrees goal and aimed at reducing its emissions by 20% by 2020 (level 1990), and by 30% if other industrialized countries engaged in equivalent objectives and if newly industrialized nations also undertook a legally binding commitment. The objectives of Switzerland were more innovative in the field of climate adaptation. In 2009, at the Copenhagen Conference, the mandate of the Swiss government included the proposition of a global CO_2 levy to finance adaptation. The specificity of the Swiss position was not only to promote adaptation funding, but also to finance instruments and mechanisms for the management of loss and damages related to climate change. Switzerland thus aimed at bringing in its expertise from the insurance and banking sector by defending an innovative and original position on adaptation finance.

As a result, Switzerland's position in national climate policy design differs considerably from its position on the international level. First, whereas the role of market-based instruments is highly contested on the national level, Switzerland's delegation tried to promote the introduction of incentive measures and finance mechanisms in international climate negotiations. Second, while

---

[1] The climate penny is not an incentive tax, but a promotional measure to subsidize national and international emissions' reduction projects.

[2] "Kräftiges Wirtscahftswachstumstellt Kyoto Ziel in Frage," Media Communication published 19.11.2010, Swiss Federal Office for the Environment; www. bafu.admin.ch, consulted July 2012

Switzerland's climate policy on the national level has been almost exclusively focusing on climate *mitigation* for decades, Switzerland elaborated funding scheme solutions that would incentivize the private sector to promote international *adaptation* measures with their international partners in the EIG group.

The policies and related negotiations we investigate in this article took place at two different points in time: the design of the policy on the national level occurred around the year 2005, when Switzerland first revised the CO2 act and introduced the tax in combination with the tradable permits and the climate penny. The international policy formulation during the COP in Copenhagen and Cancun happened in 2009 and 2010. Seen from a temporal perspective, the national position could have impacted the position of the Swiss delegation also in international negotiations. As this was not the case, the question arises whether the divergence in position is a consequence of divergent negotiation topics at the two levels, or of different negotiation cultures within the Swiss political elite on the national and the international levels. Below, we develop those thoughts and outline some theoretical arguments which could account for the difference between Switzerland's national and international position in climate change policy.

Theory

Regarding policy outputs, there is convincing evidence of policy learning, diffusion, and spill-over effects across policy levels, domains, and countries (Jones and Jenkins-Smith 2009; Gilardi 2010; Kay 2011). However, those influences are not limited to the products of policymaking, but also hold for political bargaining and decision-making processes. Although several theories and frameworks focus on actors and their role in order to explain such mutual influence mechanisms among different processes (Hooghe and Marks 2003; Marks, Hooghe, and Blank 1996; Sabatier and Jenkins-Smith 1993), there are two diverging views on how much actors might coordinate actions across levels. For instance, in multilevel governance and the "ecology of games", actors are involved in different "games" or "arenas" at the same time (Dutton, Schneider, and Vedel 2012; Lubell, Henry, and McCoy 2010). Those "games" can be characterized by very heterogeneous institutions and rules, which is why the same actors tend to behave differently and defend divergent interests (Moravcsik 1993; Lubell et al. 2012).

Putnam (1988) also argues that actors involved in foreign policymaking produce different policy outputs in the absence of domestic pressures and vice-versa; *but* this is not true in two-level games where both spheres are entangled. In such "overlapping or nested subsystems" actors are functionally interdependent, which might result in coordination and feedback from one system to the other (Jones and Jenkins-Smith 2009; Zafonte and Sabatier 1998). Finally, also Lisowski (2002) applies the two-level games metaphor for US climate politics and its repudiation of the Kyoto Protocol and convincingly demonstrates how President George Bush Jr. legitimizes his international approach with domestic evidences.

All of the authors emphasize the crucial role of actors participating in several processes and on different levels. Thus, the absence of such actors might be one explanatory factor for the production of divergent outcomes and outputs of two-level games. From this, we deduce our first hypothesis:

> H1: The difference in policy outputs between the national policy formulation and the position within international negotiations stems from the fact that hardly any actors simultaneously participate in both policy processes.

However, if we did find evidence of actors participating in both processes, they might suffer from the burden of two-level accountability: toward both domestic citizens and international peers (Papadopoulos 2010). Actors that are capable of harmonizing domestic and foreign policy outputs may thus possess high levels of power in order to do this. In their seminal work, Stokman and Zeggelink (1996) differentiate between two dimensions to be taken into account when assessing policy actors' political power: their ability to influence and access decision making, as well as the resources at their disposal. Diverging outputs on both levels thus allow us to assume that there are no such actors holding sufficient political power to coordinate policy outputs on both levels. From those insights, we deduce our second hypothesis.

> H2: The difference in policy outputs between the national policy formulation and the position within international negotiations stems

from the fact that very few actors have the power and ability to link both processes and thus influence coordinated policy outputs on the two levels.

A political subsystem or domain is characterized by actors who defend their preferences or interests in order to impact policy outputs (Knoke and Laumann 1982; Sabatier and Weible 2007). From a game theoretical point of view, however, actors may adapt their action decisions and preferences depending on the interest they have in the game-related issue, as well as the institutional and contextual settings at stake (Dutton, Schneider, and Vedel 2012). We thus conclude with our third hypothesis stating that:

> H3: The difference in policy outputs between the national policy formulation and the position within international negotiations stems from the fact that the same actor participating in both processes defends very divergent preferences and interests on the two levels.

As a first step, we thus focus on actors participating in both processes. Once we find evidence for that (and thus potentially rejected our first hypothesis), we then investigate the power structures and policy preferences of those actors.

Case and Methods

The global climate regime is characterized by horizontal and vertical fragmentations where different state and nonstate actors intervene on different decisional levels (Ingold 2014; Ingold and Fischer 2014; Ingold, Balsiger, and Hirschi 2010; Prell, Hubacek, and Reed 2007). To account for this structural complexity, different policy scholars have adopted a network approach (Ingold 2010; Newig and Fritsch 2009): in order to better reconstruct decision-making processes and stakeholder intervention (Knoke et al. 1996; Krackhardt 1990; Knoke 1990; Kriesi 1980),various studies have proven that social network analysis (SNA) provides an impressive toolbox for the empirical analysis of social network structures and their relevance for opportunities and behavioral choices of persons integrated in policymaking. We apply SNA and the methods used here in a descriptive way as we are not interested in the investigation of direct causal links or chains. The aim of this article is *to explore and understand* the potential differences in policy output production across two decisional levels.

Comparable datasets on policy networks are rare, not least because gathering data at various points in time is highly demanding and resource consuming. In that sense, the dataset at our disposal is exceptional. It is comprised of comparable network data in a policy domain collected at two different periods. The first dataset covers the decision-making process on policy instruments within the context of Swiss national climate politics between 2002 and 2005. It was gathered through face-to-face interviews in 2004 and 2005 (see Ingold 2008; 2010). The second dataset on the preparatory phase of the Swiss position at the Conferences of the Parties (COP) 16 in Cancun in 2010 stems from a written survey sent out by post in the beginning of 2011.

To identify key actors involved in the respective policymaking processes, we relied on a combination of positional, decisional, and reputational approaches. In line with Knoke et al. (1996), formal organizations, rather than individuals, are the unit of analysis. Actors in this research were therefore defined as organizations participating in the policymaking processes and, following the decisional approach, actors formally implicated in climate policymaking were identified. The first list of actors was then complemented with actors holding an overall strategic position or being mentioned as very powerful during initial expert interviews. This left us with a set of 35 actors for the national decision-making process and 50 representatives of these organizations were interviewed. For the preparatory phase of the COP 16, questionnaires were sent to 22 actors and the response rate of this survey was 70% (complete actors list in appendix). Both surveys were thus based on questionnaires designed in the same way and containing batteries of questions to investigate actors' relational profiles and policy preferences.

Based on a list of all actors participating in the respective decision-making process, interviewees were asked to identify those actors with whom they *collaborated intensely* (relational profiles). Furthermore, actors were asked to rank the policy options under discussion in the respective process (policy preferences). For the national decision-making process, they ranked the following policy instruments evaluated during the preparliamentary phase of 2004: voluntary agreements, CO_2 tax, climate penny, and tradable permits. For the preparatory Cancun negotiations, they had to give their opinion on the

Table 1: Clusters of Actors in Swiss National and Foreign CC Policy Based on Beliefs

Process Involvement		Belief MDS National CC Policy	Belief MDS Foreign CC Policy
Process Involvement		**Belief MDS National CC Policy**	**Belief MDS Foreign CC Policy**
Both processes	Ecosuisse	−0.226674199	0.65
	SGCI	0.552091241	1
	PU	−0.321665198	0.66
	Proclim	0.554830492	0.31
	OcCC	0.511774123	0.31
	NCCR	0.22452797	
	GP	0.451409727	0.23
	WWF	0.178739235	0.18
	FOEN	0.361067593	0.34
	SFOE	0.124492967	
	SECO	−0.026673712	0.34
	UVEK GS	0.51202029	
Only national CC Policy	Swissmem	−0.157758623	
	Cemsuisse	−0.119442351	
	HEV	−0.272213846	
	TCS	−0.322696537	
	FRS	−0.271957397	
	Energieforum	−0.225837544	
	FDP	−0.321427166	
	SVP	−0.270329297	
	Factor	−0.227479041	
	EFV	0.158581719	
	OEBU	0.221499845	
	VCS	0.11928343	
	SGB	0.370335549	
	TravailSuisse	0.509672701	
	EnAw	0.243292451	
	AEE	0.610045612	
	PDC	0.183548647	
	SP	0.371871144	
	Grüne	0.511299551	
	Infras	0.511382699	
	Prognos	0.177863672	
	equiterre	0.153671488	
Only international CC Policy	BAZL		1
	SwissRE		0.44
	No belief indications for the following actors: DEZA; SPBA; BLW; ETHZ; BFM; EDA; MeteoCH		

different adaptation (fast-start finance, green climate fund, and insurance mechanisms) and mitigation (global CO_2 tax, involvement of emerging economies in mitigation, expansion of clean development mechanisms and carbon markets, and prevention of deforestation) mechanisms proposed by Switzerland.

Results

Before concentrating on actors' collaboration, power, and preferences, we focus on the question of who participated in both processes. As illustrated in Table 1, only 12 actors participated in both, Swiss national and foreign climate policymaking. This corresponds to half of the actors involved in international negotiations and one third of the actors involved in national decision making. Three of them are industry and private sector representatives; three are scientific institutions; two are green NGOs; and four are federal agencies (see appendix).

Collaboration Within and Across Networks

In both networks, we asked actors to indicate with whom they collaborated strongly during the respective decision-making processes. Furthermore, and for the second survey about the preparatory phase of the Cancun negotiations, we asked actors to also indicate with whom they shared collaboration links in the former national decision-making process about the CO_2 law between 2002 and 2005. Even though those two processes happened at two different times, we could identify which actors were involved in both domestic and foreign policymaking.

In sum, we had three different policy networks: first, the domestic decision making about policy instruments to be introduced under the CO_2 law between 2002 and 2005; second, the preparatory phase of the Cancun negotiations; and third, a combined network of actors involved in both processes through collaboration relations.

For the latter (see Figures 1 and 2), there are three sets of actors worth mentioning at this stage: First, one category of actors involved in both processes seemed to be strongly integrated, but linked to their peers only: the green NGOs WWF and Greenpeace (GP) to pro-ecology actors; and the two business representatives Economiesuisse and the Petrol Union (PU) to pro-economy actors. These actors thus demonstrate the link between the national and the international policy processes, but were however only closely linked to members representing the same actor type on the national level. Inputs from international negotiations may thus only be shared with national actors having the same policy preferences.

Second, one group of actors was only formally involved in the international preparatory phase, and had very few links to national decision making. This group consists of science and insurance representatives dispatched at the left end of the graph, such as Swiss RE, Meteo CH, or ETHZ.

Third, the most important role was played by the Federal Office for the Environment (FOEN), which seems to hold both networks together. The FOEN could thus be a potential policy broker within both networks, what will be elaborated below.

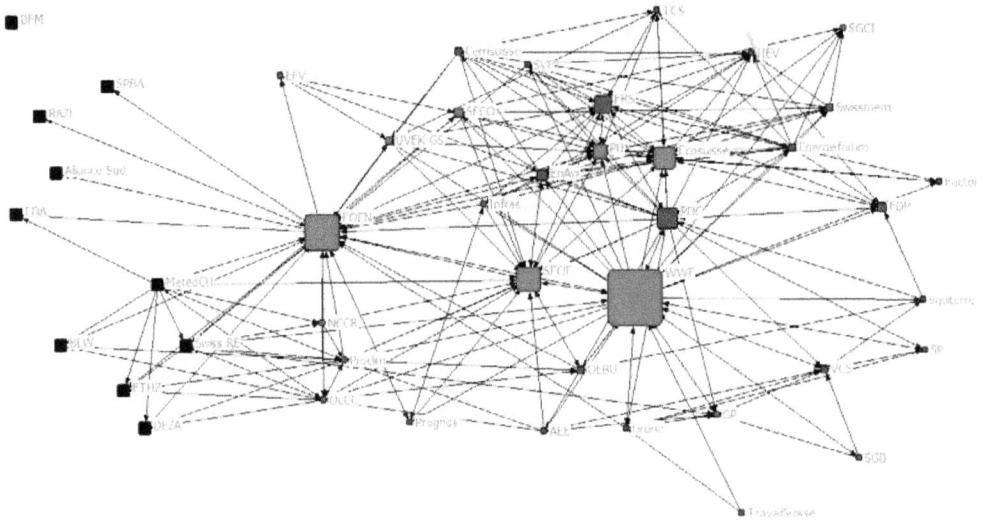

Node size: Betweenness centrality in national collaboration network (black nodes indicate actors only internationally; blue nodes actors only nationally active; red nodes are actors integrated in both processes)

Figure 1: Joint Collaboration Network of National and Foreign CC Policy—Centralities in National Network

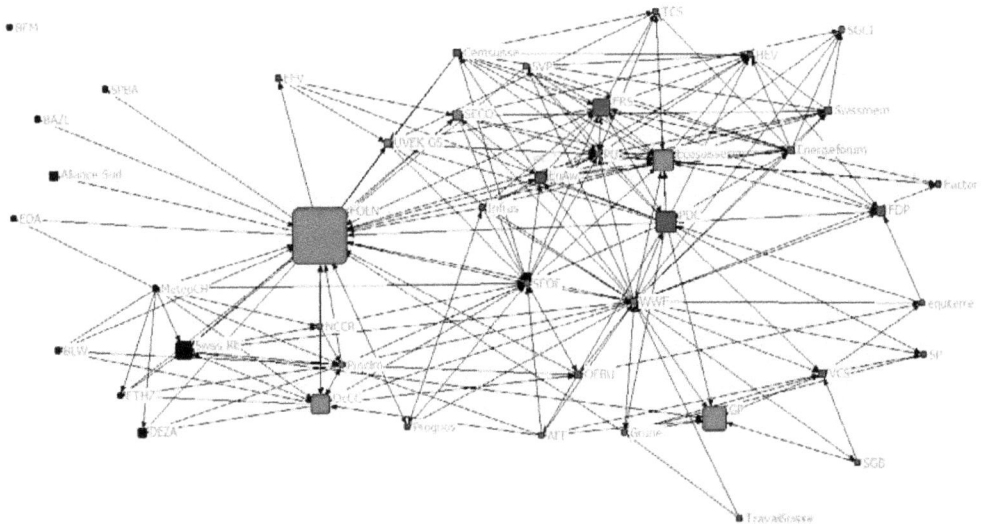

Node size: Betweenness centrality in national collaboration network (black nodes indicate actors only internationally; blue nodes actors only nationally active; red nodes are actors integrated in both processes)

Figure 2: Joint Collaboration Network of National and Foreign CC Policy—Centralities in Foreign Network

Structural Power and Reputational Resources

"Betweenness centrality" is the most prominent centrality measure used to study power and dominance, as it indicates an actor's strategic position between other actors in the network. It shows the structural advantage of an actor in the network and is thus in line with what Stokman and Zeggelink (1996) defined as access relations within policy formulation. Betweenness centrality measures the number of times an actor is on the shortest path between two other actors within the collaboration network. Concretely, this means that actors with high betweenness centrality scores have the potential to link other actors which would otherwise not be connected. Actors with high betweenness centralities thus have the opportunity to gate keep, control information flow among otherwise disconnected others, and potentially impact decision making.[3]

Only few actors in the national process had a betweenness centrality above the mean (see Table 2). Most of them, and particularly Economiesuisse, the Petrol Union, and the Agencies for the Environment (FOEN) and for Energy (SFOE), were also present in the second international policy process. Those organizations thus link different unrelated actors through collaboration ties and do this in both the national and the international settings.

In contrast to betweenness centrality, *reputational power* is not a network measure and reflects a cognitive approach to power and resource analysis. Here it constitutes the second power dimension defined by Stokman and Zeggelink (1996), namely resources enabling actors to act and influence policymaking. Participants to the survey evaluated the general reputational power of all actors integrated in the corresponding process when answering the question: "Considering the list of all actors integrated in the respective policy process, who are, following you the three most important actors?" Reputational power scores then reflect the number of times an actor was mentioned as most important, expressed in percentages (see Table 2).

The analysis of reputational power shows a different picture to that of centralities: actors having a rather weak betweenness centrality (such as HEV, TCS, EnAW, and SVP nationally; DEZA and EDA internationally), and thus being poorly interlinked within the collaboration network, may nonetheless be seen to be important by the other actors (indicated by a high reputational power score). Nationally, the actors being seen as most relevant for climate policy design include the business association Economiesuisse, the Swiss Agency of Energy (SFOE), and the Christian-Democratic People's party (CVP). Internationally, the Swiss Agency for Development and Cooperation (DEZA) and the State Secretariat for Economic Affairs (Seco) are perceived as powerful. The Swiss Agency for the Environment (FOEN) is the only actor being perceived as important in both processes and at the two levels.

---

[3] The two measures are complementary: reputational power indicates in a subjective manner which institutions are seen as powerful by the other actors in the network, while the centrality measure shows which actors hold a control position over others (Scott 2000).

Table 2: Betweenness and Reputational Power Analysis

Process Involvement		Betweenness National	Betweenness Foreign	Reputation National (%)	Reputation Foreign (%)
Both processes	*Ecosuisse*	**11.7**	**7.3**	**94**	36
	SGCI	0.1	0.1	45	0
	Proclim	0.4	0	27	7
	OcCC	0.1	**7.1**	18	7
	NCCR	0	0	0	0
	GP	0.1	**9.4**	24	0
	PU	**5.2**	0	**100**	
	WWF	**34**	0	**70**	43
	FOEN	**20.6**	**25.4**	**79**	**100**
	SFOE	**12.2**	0.1	**70**	7
	SECO	2.6	1.4	21	**79**
	UVEK GS	1.2	1.2	**61**	36
Only national CC policy	Swissmem	1.2		39	
	Cemsuisse	1.6		36	
	HEV	0.4		**57**	
	TCS	0.1		**60**	
	VCS	1.2		30	
	FRS	**7.5**		48	
	EnAw	2.9		**66**	
	AEE	0.5		18	
	Energieforum	1.5		33	
	PDC	**9.9**		**60**	
	FDP	2.3		**54**	
	SVP	0.1		**57**	
	Infras	0.5		39	
	OEBU	1		18	
	SGB	0		3	
	TravailSuisse	0		0	
	SP	0		**51**	
	Grüne	0.3		24	
	Prognos	0.1		42	
	Factor	0		33	
	Equiterre	0.2		3	
	EFV	0.1		0	
Only International CC policy	DEZA		1.7		**71**
	BAZL		0.2		7
	BLW		0		14
	ETHZ		0		14
	BFM		0		0
	EDA		0.1		**64**
	MeteoCH		1.7		14
	SwissRE		**6.1**		21
	SPBA		0		0

Note: numbers in bold indicate scores above average.

Policy Preferences

Through the following steps, actors' preferences about the different policy options were aggregated (Nohrstedt and Ingold 2011; Nownes 2000). First, we calculated the Manhattan distance measure by creating a matrix with actors in the first column and the respective preference for each policy option (on a four-point Likert scale) in the first row[4]. Manhattan distance then transforms this matrix into an actor × actor matrix, where every cell indicates the overall preference distance between two actors. The minimum distance in the matrices is 0, the maximum is 16 for the national, and is 32 for the international process among every pair of actor. A multidimensional scaling (MDS) then attributes a relative preference distance to every actor in the space. Table 1 summarizes the relative distances for all three categories of actors: those integrated in the national climate change process, those integrated in the Swiss position on international climate change policy and, finally, those actors integrated in both.

In Swiss national climate policy, industry representatives and center-right parties seem to prefer the climate penny, which is expressed through an alignment on the belief continuum toward –1 (Table 1). Green NGOs, left parties, and some federal agencies however are in favor of a strong national mitigation policy and the introduction of a CO2 tax (represented with a position toward +1 on the belief

scale in Table 1).

The results for the preparatory phase of the COP16 in Cancun are very different: first of all, one notices that the distances are not as extreme as in the national process. All survey participants who evaluated the policy options for the Swiss position in international climate negotiations seem to agree that international mitigation as well as adaptation policies are relevant and necessary. No strong opposition to any of those international measures can be identified. Positions toward 0 simply indicate that those actors (typically green NGOs) emphasize—besides climate adaptation—a stronger commitment toward effective mitigation measures.

Discussion

In our *first hypothesis*, we test if the discrepancies of policy outputs on both levels stem from the fact that barely any actor participate in both, national and international climate decision making. We have to reject this hypothesis: 12 actors representing four different organizational types (industry, science, NGOs, and administration) are involved in both processes and would thus have the formal potential to coordinate actions on both levels. But mere participation in several processes does not guarantee that those actors have the power, interest, and capacity to impact upon decision making on both levels in an integrative way.

---

[4] For the national decision-making process, we had four different policy instruments (voluntary agreements, tax, penny, and permits) that could be ranked and that could thus receive a value between 1 and 4. The same is true for the eight policy preferences evaluated for the international level.

As shown by the analysis of the collaboration networks, for instance, most actors involved in both processes only seem to be related to their peers (same actor type) in the respective process. This is already one strong indicator that they do not hold enough structural power to link actions and actors across one or more subsystems. Typically Economiesuisse, the SFOE, and the WWF are very central in the domestic process, but not in the foreign policy process. In the foreign process, no actor has significantly high centralities; and, in general, no actor seems to be central in both processes (Figures 1 and 2). There is however, one exception: the FOEN holds a key position in both processes. The strong weight of the federal administration in foreign policy processes has already been confirmed by former research (Ingold and Fischer 2014; Sciarini1995), and also here, and in the case of Copenhagen and Cancun, the consultation process was rapid and was heavily controlled by the FOEN. It is the Minister of the Environment who arbitrates with the agreement of the Federal council (government), which is why the Swiss position remains quite close to that of FOEN and is characterized by pro-climate commitments. But even if FOEN plays the key role in Swiss foreign climate policy, this cannot be confirmed for domestic policymaking where other actors were seen as more powerful.

The international climate change debate is—mainly through the impact of the Intergovernmental Panel for Climate Change (IPCC)—strongly influenced and designed by scientific actors. Swiss researchers are well involved within the IPCC and one would expect that this would also be reflected in the preparation phase for the Swiss position in international climate negotiations. The re-insurance industry is also greatly interested in policy outcomes on the foreign policy level: as an international economic sector strongly affected by climate change impacts and natural hazards such as floods and heat waves, insurance companies have a stake in the development of international climate change adaptation measures and funding. But a strong position of science and insurance representatives in the production of the Swiss foreign climate policy is not visible in our two-level reputational analysis; and it moreover seems that neither science nor insurance industries would be able to bring the knowledge back into the national climate policy, as they have, so far, played a rather peripheral function in the national decision-making network (see again, Figures 1 and 2).

We can thus confirm our *second hypothesis* and conclude that no actor has the power or ability to influence coordinated policy outputs on both levels.

For the test of our *third hypothesis*, we investigated whether the same actor displays different preferences when acting on two levels. This hypothesis can also be confirmed. On the national level, actors were very clear in their preferences: they were in favor of one set of policy instruments (incentives) or the other (voluntary measures). In Swiss foreign climate policy, preferences seem harmonized: even actors nationally against strong mitigation or adaptation commitments largely supported the instrument mix suggested by the Swiss government. In national policymaking, conflict about policy design is high, because of potential target groups, that is, actors who have to pay or to implement future policy instruments, lobby against the latter. More generally speaking, as soon as potential policy change threatens some actors or actor groups, they start opposing these measures. Policy formulation at the international level follows other rules: the Swiss delegation's choices about what position to defend in international negotiations does not have direct policy consequences for any of the delegation's members. In sum, the difference in the degree of belief conflict at both levels might be heavily influenced by different negotiation cultures, as well as divergent degrees in bindingness of the policy solutions adopted at either level.

Conclusion

This analysis has shown that investigating policy processes on two different levels and over time constitutes a challenge (see also Pralle 2009). Adopting a multilevel perspective, considering that domestic structures matter in such multisphere setting, we investigated national and foreign policymaking.

Overall, we observed a *large difference* among both levels in the structure of the policy process, actors' arrangements, and in the (power) position specific actors represent. Those structural and individual differences are very strong, leading to the conclusion that they serve as an explanation for the policy output discrepancies between national and foreign policy formulation. Domestic structures thus also matter in foreign policymaking (Avery1996), but are not replicated "telquel" on the higher level. In addition to Madden (2014), who convincingly demonstrated the relevance of national institutions and veto-points

for the explanation of policy outputs and the adoption of policy tools (see also Pralle 2009 and the relevance of agenda-setting and issue attention over time), the here presented study has shown how crucial it is to identify actors that participate in both spheres, also taking into account their political power and resources (see Putnam 1988, 445). Participation on two levels seems to be a necessary but not sufficient condition. Actors should play a central role in both processes, and defend similar policy interests on the two levels in order for them to be able to coordinate actions and produce coherent outputs in overlapping subsystems. We are aware, however, that this is a descriptive analysis and that the causal link between structures and outputs should still be systematically proven.

Furthermore, social network analysis (SNA) has proven to be an appropriate method to be applied to such a multilevel decisional setting, as it gives the researcher the possibility of drawing relations among time and space and to identify actors located within two or more networks. The aim of this research was to understand and lay-out structural and attribute-based factors in overlapping subsystems. In future research, and when focusing on causal links, social network analysis would also provide tools and models for doing so.

The case of Swiss climate policy and the discrepancy between the national and international position and strategy is rather special. In future research, it would thus be of particular interest to investigate actors' configuration and a single actors impact upon national and foreign policymaking within the same multilevel regime *in a different context*, for example, that of countries with more homogenous approaches on both levels. Besides from predominantly concentrating on negotiators' strategies and domestic structures, such an analysis would then account for country-specific institutions, this being the third element put forward by Putnam (1988) when investigating the creation of large win-sets in two-level games. This would then allow for the testing of hypotheses in a comparative setting; allowing for further confirmation of the added value of policy process theories and formal network analysis for multilevel policy investigations.

Acknowledgment

Data on Swiss national climate policy decision making was gathered within the framework of the following project and funding body: "NCCR-Climate," supported by the Swiss National Science Foundation. The authors would like to thank the two anonymous reviewers and Manuel Fischer for helpful comments about content and format of this manuscript.

References

Arquit-Niederberger, A., and S. Schwager. 2004. "Swiss Environmental Foreign Policy and Sustainable Development." *Swiss Political Science Review* 10 (4): 93–123.

Avery, W. 1996. "American Agriculture and Trade Policymaking: Two-Level Bargaining in the North American Free Trade Agreement." *Policy Sciences* 29: 113–136.

Capano, G., and M. Howlett. 2009. "Introduction: The Determinants of Policy Change: Advancing the Debate." *Journal of Comparative Policy Analysis: Research and Practice* 11 (1): 1–5.

Dutton, W., V. Schneider, and T. Vedel. 2012. *Ecologies of Games Shaping Large Technical Systems: Cases from Telecommunications to the Internet.* Berlin/Heidelberg: Springer, 49–68.

George, S. 2004. "Multi-Level Governance and the European Union." In *Multilevel Governance*, eds. I. Bache, and M. Finders. Oxford: Oxford University Press, 107–126.

Gilardi, F. 2010. "Who Learns from what in Policy Diffusion Processes?" *American Journal of Political Science* 54: 650–666.

Hoberg, G., and E. Morawski. 2008. "Policy Change through Sector Intersection: Forest and Aboriginal Policy in Clayoquot Sound." *Canadian Public Administration* 40 (3): 387–414.

Hooghe, L., and G. Marks. 2003. "Unraveling the Central State, but how? Types of Multilevel Governance." *The American Political Science Review* 97 (2): 233–243.

Ingold, K. 2008. *Les mécanismes de décision: Le cas de la politique climatique Suisse.* Zürich: Politikanalysen, Rüegger Verlag.

Ingold, K.2010. "Apprendre Pour le Future: Une Analyse de la politique Climatique Suisse." *Swiss Political Science Review* 16 (1): 43–76.

Ingold, K. 2014. "How Involved are they Really? A Comparative Network Analysis of the Institutional Drivers of Local Actor Inclusion." *Land Use Policy.* 39: 376-387. Doi: 10.1016/j.landusepol.2014.01.013

Ingold, K., and M. Fischer. 2014. "Drivers of Collaboration to Mitigate Climate Change: An Illustration of Swiss Climate Policy over 15 Years." *Global Environmental Change* (24): 88–98.

Ingold, K., J. Balsiger, and C. Hirschi. 2010. "Climate Change in Mountain Regions: How Local Communities Adapt to Extreme Events." *Local Environment* 15 (7): 651–661.

Jones, M., and H.C. Jenkins-Smith. 2009. "Trans-Subsystem Dynamics: Policy Topography, Mass Opinion, and Policy Change." *The Policy Studies Journal* 37 (1): 37–58.

Kay, A. 2011. "UK Monetary Policy Change during the Financial Crisis: Paradigms, Spillovers, and Goal Co-ordination." *Journal of Public Policy* 31 (2): 143–161.

Klijn, E.H., J. Koppenjan, and K. Termeer. 1995. "Managing Networks in the Public Sector: A Theoretical Study of Management Strategies in Policy Networks." *Public Administration* 73 (3): 437–454.

Knoke, D. 1990. *Political Networks: The Structural Perspective*. Cambridge: Cambridge University Press.

Knoke, D., and E. Laumann. 1982. "The Social Organization of National Policy Domains: An Exploration of some Structural Hypotheses." In *Social Structure and Network Analysis*, eds. P. Marsden, and N. Lin. Beverly Hills: Sage, 255–270.

Knoke, D., F. Pappi, J. Broadbent, and Y. Tsujinaka. 1996. *Comparing Policy Networks–labour Politics in the US, Germany and Japan*. Cambridge: Cambridge University Press.

Krackhardt, D. 1990. "Assessing the Political Landscape: Structure, Cognition, and Power in Organizations." *Administrative Science Quarterly* 35: 342–369.

Kriesi, H.P. 1980. *Entscheidungsstrukturen und Entscheidungsprozesse in der Schweizer Politik*. Frankfurt: Campus.

Leifeld, P., and V. Schneider. 2012. "Information Exchange in Policy Networks." *American Journal of Political Science* 53 (3): 731–744.

Lisowski, M. 2002. "Playing the Two-level Game: Us President Bush's Decision to Repudiate the Kyoto Protocol." *Environmental Politics* 11 (4): 101–119.

Lubell, M., A. Henry, and M. McCoy. 2010. "Collaborative Institutions in an Ecology of Games." *American Journal of Political Science* 54 (2): 287–300.

Lubell, M., J. Scholz, R. Berardo, and G. Robins. 2012. "Testing Policy Theory with Statistical Models of Networks." *The Policy Studies Journal* 40 (3): 351–374.

Madden, N. 2014. "Green Means Stop: Veto Players and their Impact on Climate-Change Policy Outputs." *Environmental Politics* 23 (4): 570–589.

Marks, G., L. Hooghe, and K. Blank. 1996. "European Integration from the 1980s: State-Centric vs. Multi-Level Governance." *Journal of Common Market Studies* 34 (3).

Moravcsik, A. 1993. "Preferences and Power in the European Community: A Liberal Intergovernmentalist Approach." *Journal of Common Market Studies* 31: 473–524.

Newig, J., and O. Fritsch. 2009. "Environmental Governance: Participatory, Multi-Level—and Effective?" *Environmental Policy and Governance* 19: 197–214.

Nohrstedt, D., and K. Ingold. 2011. "Venue Access and Policy Conflict: Belief System Alignment in Swiss and Swedish Energy Policy Subsystems." Presented at the Midwest Conference, Chicago, April 2011.

Nownes, A. 2000. "Policy Conflict and the Structure of Interest Communities." *American Politics Quarterly* 28 (3): 309–327.

Papadopoulos, Y. 2010. "Accountability and Multi-level Governance: More Accountability, Less Democracy?" *West European Politics* 33 (5): 1030–1049.

Pralle, S. 2009. "Agenda-Setting and Climate Change." *Environmental Politics* 18 (5): 781–799.

Prell, C., K. Hubacek, and M. Reed.2007. "Stakeholder Analysis and Social Network Analysis in Natural Resource Management." *Society and Natural Resources* 22 (6): 501–518.

Prognos. 2002. *Standortbestimmung CO2-Gesetz*. Basel: Prognos.

Putnam, R. 1988. "Diplomacy and Domestic Politics: The Logic of Two-Level Games." *International Organization* 42 (3): 427–460.

Sabatier, P., and H.C. Jenkins-Smith. 1993. *Policy Change and Learning. An Advocacy Coalition Approach*. Boulder, CO: Westview.

Sabatier, P., and C. Weible. 2007. "The Advocacy Coalition Framework. Innovations and Clarifications." In *Policy Process Theories*, ed. P. Sabatier. Boulder, CO: Westview.

Sciarini, P. 1995. "Reseau politique interne etnegociations internationales: le GATT, levier de la reforme agricole suisse." *Swiss Political Science Review* 1: 228–257.

Scott, J. 2000. *Social Network Analysis*. London: Sage.

Smaldino, P., and M. Lubell. 2011. "An Institutional Mechanism for Assortment in an Ecology of Games." *PLoS One* 6 (8).

Stokman, F., and E. Zeggelink. 1996. "Is Politics Power or Policy Driven? A Comparative Analysis of Dynamic Access Models in Policy Networks." *Journal of Mathematical Sociology* 21: 77–111.

Zafonte, M., and P. Sabatier. 1998. "Shared Beliefs and Imposed Interdependencies as Determinants of Ally Networks in Overlapping Subsystems." *Journal of Theoretical Politics* 10 (4): 473–505.

Appendix: Actors' List

Full Name	Abbreviation	Actor Type	Involvement in Processes
Economiesuisse, Swiss Business Federation	**Ecosuisse**	1	2
Swiss Association of Chemical and Pharmaceutical Industry	**SGCI**	1	2
Swiss Mechanical and Electrical Engineering Industries	**Swissmem**	1	1
Assoc. of the Swiss Cement Industry	**Cemsuisse**	1	1
Swiss House Owner Association	**HEV**	1	1
Association for Ecological Integration in Business Management	**OEBU**	1	1
Swiss Touring Club	**TCS**	2	1
Association for Transport and Environment	**VCS**	2	1
Road Traffic Assoc.	**FRS**	2	1
Swiss Federation of Trade Unions	**SGB**	3	1
Association of Trade Unions	**TravailSuisse**	3	1
Energy Agency for the Economy	**EnAw**	2	1
Agency for Renewable Energy	**AEE**	2	1
Petrol Union	**PU**	2	2
	Energieforum	2	1
Christian Democratic People's Party	**PDC**	5	1
Free Democratic Party	**FDP**	5	1
Social Democratic Party of Switzerland	**SP**	5	1
Swiss People's Party	**SVP**	5	1
Green Party of Switzerland	**Grüne**	5	1
Private Scientific Organization	**Infras**	6	1
Private Scientific Organization	**Prognos**	6	1
Factor AG, Private consultant firm	**Factor**	1	1
Forum for Global and Climate Change	**Proclim**	6	2
Advisory Board on Climate Change	**OcCC**	6	2
Swiss National Science Foundation Competence Centre on Climate Change	**NCCR**	6	2
Greenpeace	**GP**	7	2
World Wildlife Fund Switzerland	**WWF**	7	2
Green NGO	**Equiterre**	7	1
Swiss Federal Office for the Environment	**FOEN**	4	2
Swiss Federal Office of Energy	**SFOE**	4	2
State Secretariat for Economic Affairs	**SECO**	4	2
Federal Department of the Environment, Transport, Energy and Communications	**UVEK GS**	4	2
Federal Finance Administration	**EFV**	4	1
Swiss Agency for Development and Cooperation	**DEZA**	4	3
Swiss Private Bank Union	**SPBA**	1	3
Federal Office for Migration	**BFM**	4	3
Federal Office for Agriculture	**BLW**	4	3
Federal Office for Meteorology and Climatology	**MeteoCH**	4	3
Swiss Federal Office for Civil Aviation	**BAZL**	4	3
Federal Department of Foreign Affairs	**EDA**	4	3
Swiss Federal Institute of Technology	**ETHZ**	6	3
Swiss Alliance of Development Organizations	**Alliance Sud**	7	3
Swiss Reinsurance Company	**Swiss RE**	1	3

Legend to Appendix: Column Actor Type

1= Industry and Private Sector Representatives
2= Transport and Energy Representatives
3= Trade Unions and Consumer Protection
4= Federal Administration and Confederation
5= Political Parties
6= Science
7= Green NGOs

Column Involvement in Processes

1= Only National
2= Both
3= Only Swiss Foreign Climate Policy

European Policy Analysis - Volume 2, Number 1 - Spring 2016

Second Tier, Second Thoughts—Why it Turns out to be so Difficult for EIOPA to Create a Single Market for Private Pensions

Frieder Wolf[A] & Georg Wenzelburger[B]

In the context of the completion of the common financial market and historically low real interest rates, the recently founded European Insurance and Occupational Pensions Authority (EIOPA) has been assigned the task to develop a regulatory "2nd regime" for private pensions. Issuing a detailed discussion paper, EIOPA invited feedback from stakeholders and received more than 1,300 comments. Based on an analysis of these positions, our paper examines arguments justifying or criticizing the creation of such a single market and on the—sometimes surprising—emergent advocacy coalitions. Unlocking potential economies of scale is attractive to certain large providers; yet it is hindered by member states' widely differing tax rules and raises various distributional questions. Furthermore, we assess EIOPA's own emerging position vis-à-vis both the Commission and national regulators, especially its strategic shift toward consumer protection. 2nd regime regulation as one of EIOPA's first and foremost tasks proves formative regarding its institutional role perception and the legitimacy of its activities.

Keywords: private pensions, EIOPA, common financial market, 2ndregime, European social policy

1. Introduction

Low real interest rates, apparently here to stay for quite a while in the context of the euro crisis, challenge European Union (EU) member states' pension policies regarding both their central aims: avoiding poverty among the elderly and maintaining their living standards. Occupational and personal pension plans are unlikely to perform as advertised, and their administrative costs have been identified by the German government (Bundesministerium für Arbeit und Soziales 2014) as a major target in the most recent National Social Report (which is part of the EU's open method of co-ordination). In this context, the newly founded European Insurance and Occupational Pensions Authority (EIOPA) has been assigned the task to develop a regulatory "2nd tier," also

[A] University of Heidelberg/Germany
[B] University of Kaiserslautern/Germany

doi: 10.18278/epa.2.1.5

called "2nd regime," by the European Commission. This "2nd regime" is intended to trigger economies of scale by defining highly standardized products that should be attractive across the EU, thereby creating a single market for private pensions and stabilizing private pensions as an ever more important pillar of pension systems. Arguments raised against this endeavor highlight questionable demand, taxation problems, regulatory challenges at the borderline between EU member states' jurisdictions, distributional consequences, and the broader normative framework of the role of the state and private actors in pension policies.

Initiated by a call for advice from the Commission, EIOPA drafted a discussion paper and asked any interested stakeholders active in the sector to answer a catalog of 70 questions following from it. Our paper analyzes the resulting stakeholder positions and EIPOA's as well as the Commission's handling of them. We focus on arguments justifying or criticizing the creation of such a single market and on the—sometimes surprising—emergent advocacy coalitions. The paper pursues to main goals. First, we aim at identifying the stakeholders involved in the consultation process and their positions and coalitions; second, we investigate the reaction of EIOPA and the European Commission vis-à-vis the results of the consultation process. Additionally, we discuss some wider political implications, since the consequences of EIOPA's decisions regarding the 2nd tier touch upon the substance and legitimacy of European policymaking in general.

The following section sketches the current state of the single market for private pensions, illustrates the link between the euro crisis and the EU's looming pension crisis, and highlights a number of distributional and regulatory problems. Although this article is not meant to be theory testing, it has a distinct theoretical background which we will sketch in Section 3. Findings are laid out in Section 4, the first part of which deals with three analytical topics (taxation, distributional issues between different providers, and the balance between the three pillars of member states' pension systems) derived from our reading of the political and regulatory contexts in Section 2. The second part of Section 4 is concerned with the position EIOPA adopted in the advisory process toward the Commission and national regulators, in terms of both policy content and defining EIOPA's institutional role. In the conclusion, we also briefly touch upon the repercussions of European regulation on member states' public pension policies, especially the need to adjust minimum pensions, guarantee schemes, and taxation rules.

2. The Single Market for Private Pensions in Perspective—From Euro Crisis to Pension Crisis

The future of private pension politics in the EU lies at the vortex of three major policy streams that figure highly on the European Commission's agenda: completion of the common capital market, regulation of systemic risks, and sustaining pension adequacy. In turn, this leads to potential ambiguities (and thus potential for power struggles) between supranational competencies, intergovernmental powers, and responsibilities that remain in the remit of individual member states. In general, pension policy—including tax treatment—counts among the latter. Yet in as much cross-border movements or substantial investment vehicles come into play, the former become ever more relevant. As will become apparent, some European actors actively try to frame the issue as one of consumer protection (falling under Article 153 of the Treaty of the European Union) in order to overcome this conflict.

Ever since the World Bank's (1994) report on "Averting the old age crisis," complementing public pensions with capital-based occupational and/or private pensions has been the received wisdom of policymakers concerned with future pensioners' living standards. Under pressure from demographics and globalization (as filtered by party competition), 1st pillar replacement rates[1] have been cut throughout the developed world; the expansion of occupational and private schemes was noticeable, but more uneven (Ebbinghaus 2015; Wolf, Zohlnhöfer, and Wenzelburger 2014). Underperformance of the latter, 2nd and 3rd pillars, is especially dangerous for those earning less than average, or with working biographies interspersed with

phases of unemployment.[2] Since it is highly unlikely that they could afford to compensate for lower returns by increasing their contribution sustainedly,[3] they are not only facing falling living standards, but straight-out poverty. Some studies suggest a need for doubling contributions for a 40-year old facing a drop of two percentage points in real interest.[4]

Providers of private pension plans—especially insurance corporations and pension funds—receive less public attention than banks; yet, they contain a similar amount of systemic risks for financial markets (cf., e.g., Shin 2013). The creation of EIOPA as one of the three new European supervisory authorities, which were part of the crisis-induced 2010 "supervision package" of EU legislation (Buckley and Howarth 2011), bears witness to European policymaker's awareness of these risks. While the specific impact of EIOPA and her sisters, and foremost their mode of interaction with national institutions in member states, remained open at the time, there were already suspicions that the big players might be able to use at least parts of the rearranged playing field to their advantage (Buckley and Howarth 2011). Regarding occupational and private pension plans,

---

[1] Replacement rates refer to the percentage of former earnings which pensioners receive once they retire.

[2] Kluth and Gasche (2013) highlight how actual replacement rates for these workers are significantly lower than average figures for the so-called standard workers suggest.

[3] According to Gunkel and Swyter (2011), marginal households in Germany have been quicker than those further up the earnings scale to take up the tax subsidy for private (so-called Riester) pensions. Yet, Necker and Ziegelmeyer (2014) found that households taking a hit to their savings in the crisis were most likely to change their investment behavior afterward—toward safer products with even lower yields.

[4] Minimum pensions have so far been adapted only in a small minority of OECD member states (cf. Wolf, Zohlnhöfer, and Wenzelburger 2014).

they could tie in with the second Barroso Commission's discontentedness with the fragmented nature of the market for these products. The bulk of the latter remain to be highly specific to the member states' regulatory environment, tax rules, and customer preferences—and thus niches for comparatively smallish providers. The Juncker Commission recently pinpointed this fact with renewed zeal (European Commission 2015a; 2015b). Moreover, in a public consultation on the Green Paper "Building a Capital Markets Union" much like the stakeholder feedback exercise analyzed here, one of the stakeholders commenting favorably was the European Stability Mechanism (European Commission 2015c, 35–36).

In the name of consumer protection,[5] rather high administrative costs of many 1st pillar bis,[6] 2nd, and 3rd pillar pension plans had plausibly been criticized for a while. With the very low or even negative real interest rates brought about by the financial repression which is meant to safe the disbalanced currency union, a crackdown on these costs moved center-stage, and it was paired by the Commission with the promise of additional profits reapable via economies of scale in a completed single market.

This attack on administrative costs appears to be at odds with governments' requirements for tax balance sheets. Austrian and German employers, for instance, who accumulate a pension pot

for their workforce are still required to assume a return of 6% p.a. on these assets at a time when Berthon et al. (2013) report negative real returns over the last five years for 10 out of 12 EU member states analyzed, and even over 10 years for two of them—before taxation. The German Ministry of Finance plainly stated in February 2014 (Schäfers 2015) that it had no plans to lower this hypothetical rate of interest below 6%, arguing that long-term rates usually were much higher than the current short-term ones. (At the time of writing, German 30-year government bonds yield less than 1%.) Squeezed in between low interest rates and more demanding regulatory requirements, experts calculate that employers will have to double their reserves for occupational pensions by 2018 (Schäfers 2015).

Meanwhile, Solvency II (which is the insurance sector's equivalent to Basle II in banking, that is, the EU's major effort in risk regulation) obliges insurers to fulfill more demanding capital requirements, and a conflict has arisen within the Commission and the European Parliament as to which providers of occupational pensions these requirements also ought to apply to under the principle of "same risk—same rules—same capital." German Pensionskassen, for example, which at the same time pay into a quite sophisticated national insolvency insurance pool, would quite probably be priced out of the market by such a decision (Fischer

---

[5] EIOPA's mandate, among various other aspects, includes a leading role in consumer protection (cf. Görgen 2011). In this context, the widespread ignorance of employees about their opportunities regarding occupational pensions (cf. Lamla and Coppola 2013) is striking.

[6] 1st pillar bis refers to elements of state pensions in the form of mandatory capital-based (defined-contribution) plans that are privately managed. These schemes are especially prominent in Central Eastern Europe.

2012), and move their share of the market closer to larger, more innovative vessels closer aligned with investment banking (Schmidt-Narischkin and Thiesen 2012).

Regarding investment strategies for pension funds and insurers, the current regulatory environment effectively enforces a potentially dangerous dichotomy. A growing share of assets has to be invested into the safest of bonds. This is politically welcome as it further lowers the borrowing costs of certain European governments (especially Germany), and it plays well PR-wise as it ties in with macro-prudential stability goals. Yet, it forces investors who need to generate much higher guaranteed (or at least advertised) returns to take ever higher risks with the remaining part of their assets, crowding "alternative" investment markets (such as commodities, emerging market bonds, and so on) already saturated by cheap central bank money and potentially creating even larger bubbles there. In combination, this two-pronged approach raises the question whether capital-based pensions will really turn out to be superior in performance to the often discredited 1st pillar public pensions. Moreover, the administrative costs pinpointed by the Commission and the member states might actually be increased by the regulatory trend toward accounting at market prices. Ceteris paribus, this leads to pro-cyclical, short-term investment, and higher portfolio turnover from which the middlemen profit primarily—or even exclusively (cf. Woolley 2010 for a broader

critique). Thus, the agenda for consumer protection might, in fact, result in provider protection. Insofar as overcoming systemic risks in financial markets at its core means politically guaranteeing banks and insurers viable business models, this is more straightforward—and more ingenuous in terms of communicating with voters—than it might seem at first glance.

Undisputed as the need for additional retirement provision beyond the public 1st pillar has become for most Europeans if living standards are to be upheld, the open method of coordination (OMC) by and large failed to catalyze sustained efforts in that direction across the union (Lodge 2007; Wolf 2014).[7] Where they occurred, the benchmarking and reporting exercises under OMC remained ineffectual to them. Thus, the Commission's attempts at market making for a Europe-wide standardized private pension product can also be interpreted as an admission of OMC's inadequacies. Ironically, though, the over-optimistic belief in technical fixes that hampered OMC (Lodge 2007) might also return to haunt EIOPA and the 2nd tier. Thus, the Oxera report (Oxera 2007), commissioned by Directorate General for the Internal Market and Services (meanwhile renamed Directorate General for the Internal Market, Industry, Entrepreneurship and SMEs, or DG GROW) in order to assess the effects of investment restrictions between member states on the performance of capital-

---

[7] Only one stakeholder reacted to EIOPA's invitation by stating that the PPP issue would be served better by being further treated within the OMC (EIOPA 2014a, gen. com. 1)—in this case because European regulation is argued to act as a disincentive to citizens' saving efforts.

based 1st pillar elements, is by now widely cited as applying to 2nd and 3rd pillar products as well. The report is not without guilt in this regard, as it concluded very generally that "any restrictions to cross-border investments that impede efficient diversification impose a corresponding cost since they prevent investments that would allow higher returns for the same level of risks or lower risks for the same level of returns" (Oxera 2007). Even though this result is based on rather rigid ceteris paribus assumptions and is restricted to equity (as opposed to bond) markets (Oxera 2007), the Commission has worked toward lowering the said restrictions ever since—with little regard to the specific characteristics of national markets for occupational and private pensions (European Commission 2015a).

These latter characteristics exist in an uneasy tension with DG GROW's tendency to, while remaining rhetorically committed to the three-pillar model, divide the pension sector analytically (and politically) in only two basic categories: individual and group pensions. The latter are seen as obstacles to labor mobility, and as falling under the remit of member states' social policies. The former, to the contrary, are constructed as integral parts of the single capital market. Hence—and here the DG is in line with an influential strand of the academic literature on the topic—occupational group pensions come under pressure to align themselves with one of the above (usually the individual side). Typical policy proposals in this line are to do away with employers' direct management of pension pots, the coverage of biometrical risks, and provision for dependents (Hessling 2013). Social justice, it is argued, is to be established by the 1st pillar (and not its 1st pillar bis elements, for that matter) alone.[8]

So far, we can distinguish three major bones of contention in terms of both distributional and legitimatory conflicts regarding the establishment of a 2nd, Europe-wide regulatory regime: In how far would national taxation rules have to be adapted, that is, harmonized, in order to render such a standardized 2nd tier product reasonably attractive across member states? Which providers, for example, large insurers and pension funds, stand to profit from EU activities promoting such pension plans at whose expense? And which repercussions are to be expected for the balance of national pension systems as a whole, especially the public 1st pillars of pension systems and their tasks? The following analyses will be focused on these questions. (Furthermore, Section 4 will encompass an additional section of selected further topics.)

3. Theoretical Framework

Policymaking in times of crisis comes with some special characteristics. In crisis situations, political actors have to cope with many different challenges (cf. Wenzelburger and Wolf 2015). They face

---

[8] Ironically, provision for dependents has in several EU member states been cut, not raised, within the public 1st pillar in the name of emancipation. Spouses and parents are thus either directed toward additional (private) life insurance—an additional boost for the industry, or they are intentionally or unintentionally being nudged toward inheritable assets such as real estate.

complex problems to which ready-made solutions are not available. They are subject to high uncertainty which is created not only by the complexity of the underlying problems but also by the uniqueness of the situation in which "agents can have no conception as to what possible outcomes are likely, and hence what their interests in such a situation in fact are" (Blyth 2002). And, finally, they are often time-pressed and have to reach far-reaching decisions within rather short time periods. The topic of the present paper fits at least partly in this description. Clearly, the political actors within the COM were not particularly time-pressed when they decided to set in motion the process of enlarging the European single market to pension products. However, other features of the crisis context as portrayed earlier were clearly relevant. Uncertainty about the development of the financial market was evidently an issue, especially with regard to the development of the interest rate level and the related consequences for the turnover of private pension plans. And complexity was not only a challenge because of the multifaceted nature of the financial and euro crisis, but also because of the policy itself. The substantial complexity that comes with the structure of pension regimes and the involved variety of products was very likely an additional challenge. How do these features of the crisis situation impact on the policy process?

Drawing on Wenzelburger and Wolf's framework that weighs crisis-related aspects of policy output theories, the multiple streams approach and punctuated equilibrium theory (Wenzelburger and Wolf 2015), one can theoretically expect that the features of a crisis situation open a window of opportunity which can be used by skilled political entrepreneurs to put certain policies on top of the agenda and to put pressure on the decision maker to deal with them. However, whether a policy issue is successfully linked to the crisis depends much on the "framing contests" ('t Hart/Tindall 2009), in which some political entrepreneurs try to attach a certain policy problem to the crisis, whereas others seek to downplay the issue. If the policy issue is successfully linked to the crisis and highly politicized, it moves on the decision-making agenda of the top political level and major policy change is probable. The direction of this change depends much on which actors have access to the decision-making arena. As the crisis situation is characterized by high complexity, ambiguity, and uncertainty, political entrepreneurs such as lobbyists, interest groups, or other stakeholders who are close to the political actors have a good chance to insert their policy proposals into the decision-making process and affect the policy output. In contrast, if an issue is not politicized, it remains in the subsystem and many stakeholders in this field will move on to incrementally change the policy.

What do we learn from this theoretical argument for our empirical case at hand? First, and very clearly, the problems that were generated by the financial crisis and its consequences (low

---

[9] The goal of this framework drawing on several theories is to avoid a "particularistic variable-centered approach" as criticized by Blatter et al. (2015, 4)—and all too familiar in the literature.

interest rates, etc., see before) can be seen as an external force that set in motion the discussions about private pensions. The debate on the regulation of capital markets as well as that on the sustainability of private pension products in times of low interest rates has increased the attention to the issue of how the market of private pension plans could be liberalized throughout Europe. Second, and more importantly, the theoretical framework suggests that we are currently in the midst of the fascinating period of the policy process in which different actors try to politicize or depoliticize the issue, in which they try to advance a certain framing of the problem and in which certain policy solutions are put forward, discussed, dismissed, and re-inserted to the debate. In our case at hand, for the regulation of a pan-European market for private pensions, the European Commission has asked EIOPA to manage these discussions by inviting the stakeholders to give their views about the plans. While the behavior of the European Commission itself can be seen as a form of strategically depoliticizing the issue by creating a new agency (and delegating "away" the policy problem), the structured process of inviting comments allows us to clearly see the positions of the different stakeholders and their attempts to frame the issue in the most suitable way.

Furthermore, using the insights from the last section, our theoretical expectations about the main cleavages between the stakeholders can be refined. Providers of private pension plans will probably weigh their opportunity to gain market shares and profitability from a pan-European capital-based pension product against the risk of losing out to new competitors in a much more integrated market. The result of this calculus should vary according to the type of provider (e.g., insurers versus pension funds), according to the size of providers and last but by no means least according to the degree of specificity of their business model (i.e., how attuned they are to certain national pillar arrangement of pension policy and the respective habits of customers). Speaking of customers, the most important distinction between them ought to concern their attitude toward the trade-off between the safety of and returns on their accumulating capital. (Surprisingly often, self-appointed consumer advocates claim that there is a single optimal preference in this regard instead of a legitimate width of personal approaches.) Political stakeholders[10] can, on the one hand, be expected to broker between providers' and customers' interest in their respective member states and to focus on common ground between these, which again points to the degree of fit between the current national pillar arrangement and a prospective pan-European complement. On the other hand, their intrinsic interests in tax revenue and their normative attachment to specific policies will quite probably come into play.

The positions taken by the stakeholders in putting forward a certain understanding of the problem at stake and the roles played by EIOPA and the

---

[10] It is noteworthy that Ministries responding to the call for advice exclusively come from smaller member states. Apparently, bigger ones rely on different, more direct channels of influence.

Commission themselves in this contest will be discussed in the following section. The result of this process will, to a large extent, determine whether we shall see a far-reaching policy change in the near future or whether the change will remain incremental.

4. Findings

We have derived three analytical topics (taxation, distributional issues between different providers, and the balance between the three pillars) from our reading of the political and regulatory contexts in Section 2. Regarding these topics, we engaged in a critical qualitative content analysis of all stakeholder statements in reply to EIOPA's call that are relevant to the topics under investigation here, the findings from which are being presented in Section 4.1. Section 4.2 is concerned with the position EIOPA adopted vis-à-vis the Commission in the process, in terms of both policy content and defining EIOPA's institutional role. Our analysis is critical in the sense that we focus upon questions from the call (listed in Table 1) and respective answers with far-reaching distributional implications in Section 4.1. Furthermore, we critically assess how depoliticizing the issues at hand is normatively problematic in terms of regulatory governance's democratic accountability.

A fourth topic that emerged inductively from the Commission's call, the stakeholders' responses, and EIOPA's position analyzed in Section 4.1, namely whether sufficient demand for a standardized 2nd tier product is to be expected at all, deserves a moment's attention in advance. Some stakeholders

underscore in their general comments that consumers tend to approach the sophisticated task of choosing a personal pension product (PPP) guided by enculturated risk preferences and mental short cuts closely aligned to national markets and associated with their respective prevalent products (cf., e.g., EIOPA 2014a, gen. com. 13 and 14). Thus, it is questioned whether more than just a few customers would actually consider buying a 2nd tier product (EIOPA 2014a, gen. com. 1). Other stakeholders note that economies of scale may not only—and not the most efficiently—be realized by selling PPPs directly to cross-border customers. Alternatives mentioned (EIOPA 2014a, gen. com. 14 and 18) are either tapping into markets by buying or setting up national subsidiaries or trying to attract capital invested in nationally established products on the secondary cross-border investment market—a euro invested in a pension fund usually does not stay there, but is again invested by the fund elsewhere. Yet, the latter practice, in turn, is one of the sources of (too) high administrative costs of existing PPPs that triggered the Commission's and EIOPA's initiative in the first place.

Before we delve into the stakeholder comments themselves, some statistics on participating stakeholders are due. Two thirds of respondents to the open call for advice are based in member states, while a third operate on the European level. Sector-wide, three major blocks can be identified: overall, 28.5% represent the fund industry, 25% represent the insurance industry, and 20% work mainly in occupational pensions. On the European level, the insurance sector displays a stronger (and the strongest) showing with 44%, pointing to differences in lobbying strategies. Among, member states, Germany and the United Kingdom account for 15% of stakeholders each, while Southern Europe as well as Central Eastern Europe contribute another 20%, respectively. This is a surprisingly balanced picture, given that the aforementioned public consultation by the European Commission on the Green Paper "Building a Capital Markets Union" was clearly skewed toward the UK financial industry (European Commission 2015c, 3). A balanced distribution of respondents, however, does not guarantee a balanced representation of their views in summary documents.

4.1- What Is at Stake in the 2nd Tier?

At first glance, consultatory processes initiated by regulatory agencies may appear to be rather technical, day-to-day efforts, and, thus, rather un-political. Yet, when the European Commission in the person of Director General Jonathan Faull turned to EIOPA in July 2012 asking for "[t]echnical advice to develop an EU Single Market for personal pension schemes" (European Commission 2012), something way more exciting began. Faull recalled EIOPA's earlier input regarding the IORP[11] Directive, which had focused

on the 2nd pillar, and now requested counsel on the future regulation of the 3rd, albeit "in close connection with occupational pension schemes because the borderline between personal and occupational pensions is often blurred" (European Commission 2012).[12] In 2012, what is now called the 2nd tier was usually termed 28th regime (note that this was before Croatia's accession as a 28th member state) "whereby EU rules do not replace national rules but are an optional alternative to them" (European Commission 2012), and it was seen as only one part of the single market for personal pensions, the other one being the removal of obstacles for cross-border trade in nationally regulated pension products. By now, the relevant discourse largely centers on the 2nd tier while including major parts of the occupational (2nd pillar) territory.

In—somewhat belated, we shall come back to this in Section 4.2—reaction to Faull's letter, EIOPA published a discussion paper (EIOPA 2013)[13] in May 2013, inviting comments from stakeholders within three months and announcing that these comments were to be published. This was duly done in a massive document, EIOPA-TFPP-14-001 (EIOPA 2014a), in January 2014.[14] In February 2014, EIOPA drafted a preliminary report to

---

[11] Institutions for Occupational Retirement Provision. For its origins and related power struggles, cf. Haverland (2007), who argues that national pension policy designs account for the preferences not only of member states' governments, but also of business and members of the European Parliament. Thus, liberalization efforts had limited success here, but business pressure "was sufficient to secure liberal investment principles" (ibid., 886).

[12] Faull might have added that this border is not only blurred, but the ambiguous zone is expanding.

[13] EIOPA DP-13-001 is also known as EIOPA/13/241; as an institution just gaining its footing, EIOPA was also developing its documentation system gradually.

[14] These comments are also available separately. In order to maximize accessibility for our readers, we refer to their location in TFPP-14-001 here.

the Commission (EIOPA 2014b) on the matter, summarizing the stakeholders' views and—somewhat cautiously, yet with a subtle agenda; we shall come back to this in Section 4.2—expressing its own standpoint on controversial matters. The Commission, apparently not entirely satisfied, issued a renewed and this time very detailed call for advice (European Commission 2014) in July 2014, asking EIOPA to conclusively report in February 2016 (which it did not). Table 1 lists the relevant sections of the latter four documents as referred to in our analysis and the following presentation of our findings.

Topic 1: Taxational Issues

EIOPA's stance on the issue(s) of taxation was as clear as it was bold right from the beginning. In a statement typeset boxed so that no reader (whom EIOPA seems to expect to be potentially rather ignorant of the allocation of competencies within the EU) should miss it, taxational adaptations within the process analyzed here were ruled out: "Please note that EIOPA and its members do not exercise any powers in the area of taxation" (EIOPA 2013). And this is exactly why EIOPA seemed to favor the development of 2nd tier regulation as more promising than "passporting" national products for cross-border sale, for the key "advantage of the 2nd regime is that it might be possible to implement it without harmonization of national tax legislation" (EIOPA 2013).

Most stakeholders are either less enthused or more hopeful, with the extreme positions marked by the following two (general) comments. The Czech Ministry of Finance admonishes EIOPA not to solely focus on the relationship between sellers and buyers of PPPs, but to engage more with the intervening role of member state governments, especially through taxation (EIOPA 2014a, gen. com. 19). Furthermore, it states that the Czech Government is decidedly against the harmonization of direct taxes within the EU (EIOPA 2014a, gen. com. 19).[15] APFIPP, the Association of Portuguese Investment Funds, to the contrary, submits that the "EU PPP would be ideally totally tax free (both at the vehicle and at the participant levels)" (EIOPA 2014a, gen. com. 3). This might indeed constitute the most elegant way to create a product that is attractive in all 28 constituent parts of the common financial market and thus a significant step in completing it—yet, it is hardly conceivable that the national veto players involved would tolerate such a move, as will become apparent from the following analysis of stakeholders' answers to EIOPA's specific questions on the matter.

Additionally—(or actually: prior) to the specific questions addressing taxation issues (Q 10–15 and Q 22 in EIOPA 2013)—we considered stakeholder

---

[15] Whereas the Czech Ministry of Finance urges EIOPA to engage more with questions of taxation given the member state powers and the way they are exercised, Pensions Europe admonishes it for the same reason to hold its horses: "EIOPA should carefully consider whether it has sufficient powers to adopt effective policy actions in this field, namely due to its lack of competence in fiscal matters" (EIOPA 2014a, gen. com. 23).

comments on Question 8, which deals with the transferability of capital accumulated in PPPs, since taxation turns out to be its main obstacle (also cf. Guardiancich 2015: 80—with a rather pessimistic outlook on the feasibility of a true common market). A broad majority of stakeholders is generally in favor of such transferability, while only four (EIOPA 2014a, com. 198, 207, 212, 218) raise objections on principle, pointing to disadvantages for customers arising from high transfer costs and/or potential risks to the financial stability of the insurers involved.[16] It is noteworthy that three of the four opposing voices represent the insurance industry at the national or European level, while the fourth has its base in occupational pensions in Germany which often takes the form of insurance.

Among those stakeholders who generally favor transferability, but conceive strong obstacles to it, nearly all mention the differing tax treatment in member states.[17] Here, EIOPA at first glance seems to have been convinced by them, for, in its preliminary report, the young agency changes course: "In the case of transferability, different tax regimes applied to pensions in different MS may lead to double-taxation or nontaxation of transferred capital [...] Overcoming these obstacles seems to require harmonization of tax treatment of pensions across member states" (EIOPA 2014b). A sentence later, however, EIOPA admits that this "may be in practice difficult to achieve" (EIOPA 2014b). So once more, we are being directed toward the 2nd tier and the hope that its standardized products might fly below the radar of national tax regimes. Regarding these products, a clear-sighted stakeholder, the Association of the Luxemburg Fund Industry, asks for them to be "tax-neutral" (EIOPA 2014a, com. 201). Maybe biased by prejudice, we were inclined to read this as "tax-exempt" and thus as a variation of the demand of their Portuguese colleagues cited above, yet the Austrian Insurers' Association (EIOPA 2014a, com. 203) provides an alternative reading. They propose that the accumulation phase of a pan-European PPP be undisturbed by taxation, that is, taxation restricted to the payout phase.

In its preliminary report, EIOPA discusses two specific variants of proposed 2nd tier products, both stemming from inside the financial services industry. The latter one, the European Pensions Plan (EPP), exhibits this feature of deferred taxation (EIOPA 2014b), while its main competitor, the Officially Certified European Retirement Plan (OCERP) would completely fall under the existing national tax rules (EIOPA 2014b). Somewhat surprisingly, when comparing the two proposals, EIOPA judges that both "do no [sic!] deal with taxation" (EIOPA 2014b).

---

[16] Comments 208 and 209, whilst not expressly opposed to transferability, specify valuation problems pertaining to the accumulated capital, especially for insurance products.

[17] In an effort to create additional earnings, EFAMA (EIOPA 2014a, gen. com. 206) also points out that providers' back-offices could solve taxational problems relating to transfers of accumulated capital for their customers. It does not mention the fees this would entail, though.

EIOPA then proceeds to drop the ball—or should we say the bombshell—entirely by plainly stating: "Given its lack of tax expertise, EIOPA will not further develop any work in relation to tax issues nor will it include tax related proposals in its Final Advice to COM" (EIOPA 2014b). The Commission has been clearly underwhelmed by this attitude, as became apparent from its renewed call for advice in July 2014 (European Commission 2014) that explicitly includes specific tax-related questions (and has remained unanswered at the time of writing). The Commission's stated aim to "attain a level of harmonization where legislation does not need additional requirements at the national level" (European Commission 2014, introduction, Paragraph 12) ties in neatly with EIOPA's strategy to use consumer protection as a keyhole. We will return to the evolving sensitive relationship between EIOPA and the Commission in Section 4.2—and to the question whether it is ingenuous or insane to default on taxation whilst developing 2nd tier regulation.

The pattern of answers to Questions 10 (about four specific tax obstacles identified by EIOPA[18] and the feasibility of overcoming them) and 11 (about further obstacles identified by stakeholders themselves[19] and the same feasibility) is remarkable in the sense that a large majority of responding stakeholders give evasive or outright confrontational statements, while only a small majority believe in the success of either a passporting or a 2nd tier regulation for PPPs. Among the latter, two qualified proposals stand out: EFAMA, the European Fund and Asset Management Association, does not see 28 member states agreeing on tax harmonization, but thinks that "it is possible that a core group of member states would agree to adjust their domestic tax rules and existing tax treaties to facilitate the emergence of a single market for PPPs" (EIOPA 2014a, com. 272), thus creating yet another flavor of two-speed Europe. The German Insurance Association (GDV) holds that the "best way to develop a secure, workable, targeted, proportionate, effective, efficient, and standardized process might be to leverage existing tax information reporting that is currently in place in most jurisdictions" (EIOPA 2014a, com. 274)—irrespective of its worth a statement also not entirely free of subtle criticisms of EIOPA and the Commission.[20]

---

[18] These obstacles are the taxation of contributions or investment income paid to or benefits received from foreign PPPs, the transfer of accumulated capital (encore unefois!) and specific technical principles of taxation (EIOPA 2013).

[19] Three additional aspects came up in the stakeholder comments: deductibility of employers' and/or employees' contributions (EIOPA 2014a, com. 265 by ANASF, the Italian association of financial advisers) and the treatment of lump-sum payments and accruals (EIOPA 2014a, com. 275 by Groupe Consultatif, the European federation of actuaries' associations).

[20] Questions 12 and 13 refer to the discrimination of foreign providers and its treatment by the European Court of Justice. The picture emerging from the answers is that the CJEU is appropriately dealing with discrimination, but that nondiscrimination is not enough to remove tax barriers between the national PPP markets. Questions 14 and 15 are paraphrases of Questions 9 through 13, thus mainly leading to repetitive answers or back references.

Question 22, the last one considered relevant to the tax topic here, returns to the core of the relationship between 2nd tier regulation and differences in member states' tax policies. EIOPA asked: "How could the 2nd regime accommodate the tax differences among [member states]?" (EIOPA 2013). FSUG, the Financial Services User Group—a forum created by the European Commission which also appoints its members—had already answered this in its statement pertaining to Question 14: "Creating a 2nd regime […] might speed up the process toward full harmonization across the EU" (EIOPA 2014a, com. 330). This is clearly a minority view among stakeholders; yet, it is about the only perspective under which EIOPA's initial treatment of the tax issue might actually make sense. ANASF bluntly states how it might be done: "The second regime could arbitrarily establish univocal rates automatically, independently from the MS" (EIOPA 2014a, com. 475).

Topic 2: The Interests of Different Providers

Whereas the taxation issue primarily concerns public finances and, thus, distributional conflicts between jurisdictions (plus maybe between the public purse in general versus pensioners), the development of a 2nd tier also affects the distribution of market shares between different (types of) PPP providers. This is not just due to the questionable demand for a pan-European PPP, but more importantly because of its potential repercussion on national markets. The Association of the Luxemburg Fund Industry points out that "it should be taken into consideration that the key features of OCERPs may in due course become a model of best practice for the provision of pensions when designing national pension solutions" (EIOPA 2014a, com. 59).

Advocates of the introduction of a 2nd tier often have specific suggestions as to the nature of the product it ought to feature, apparently depending on their competitive edge and often referring to or further detailing either the OCERP or the EPP template already mentioned (cf., e.g., EIOPA 2014a, gen. com. 3, 5, 10, and 25). The broader the mantle of a stakeholder group, though, the less specific its suggestions tend to be, which reflects the more diverse interests it represents.[21]

Furthermore, the divide between insurers and basically all other types of suppliers that were already touched upon in the last section reaffirms itself regarding the topic of diverging provider interests. EIOPA asked in Question 2 of DP-13-001 whether it should focus its regulatory efforts on DB or DC products.[22] The result could not have

---

[21] Another pattern that emerges from a sorting of stakeholder comments is that the enthusiasm for a completed single financial market is higher in smaller member states. This tendency is especially noteworthy among the answers to Question 4 about the advantages of the Commission's initiative (cf. EIOPA 2014a, com. 102–109 and 111–124).

[22] Both are capital-based, yet DB (defined benefit) products guarantee a certain pay-out, DC (defined contribution) products a certain investment. Switching from DB to DC, which is a major trend in occupational pensions these days, implies a transfer of market risks to future pensioners.

been clearer, with 79% of respondents favoring DC PPPs and only 7% for DB (with the remainder of comments calling for a balanced approach). Yet, EIOPA's own Occupational Pensions Stakeholder Groups pointed out that the DB-DC dichotomy is incapable of absorbing a key distinction between products, namely "who is going to bear what risk?" (EIOPA 2014a, com. 63). It then goes on to propose to classify PPPs according to the distribution of "three main classes of risks: financial risks, mortality/survival risks, and expenses/administration risks." Insurance-based PPPs often cover substantial parts of the second and, therefore, have distinguishable actuarial characteristics as well as particular cost-benefit profiles to customers, both of which differ between national member state contexts.[23] The Slovak Insurance Association, for instance, highlights its opposition to a Europeanization of mortality tables (EIOPA 2014a, gen. com. 26). Consequently, it proposes that EIOPA should promote reinforced 3rd pillar investment, but asks it to refrain from marketing of a standardized product.[24] This relates to the question raised by the Luxembourg-based Association of International Life Offices (in EIOPA 2014a, com. 323, formally an answer to

a taxation question) what actually is to be counted as a pension in the emerging European regulatory regime. Insurance-based products significantly differ both from other PPPs and between themselves. An example for the latter within variation is the high frequency of lump-sum payoffs in some markets such as Germany and their prohibition in others like the United Kingdom (EIOPA 2014a, com. 323).

An additional type of answer to the aforementioned Question 2 (voiced in EIOPA 2014a, com. 53, 56, 68, and 71 as well as gen. com. 12—all stemming from stakeholders with a strong base in the 2nd pillar) negates the need for any regulatory initiative by EIOPA, based on the view that national regulatory agencies are fully (and/or more) capable of dealing with current concerns. Detailed regulation of numerous aspects beyond the definition of a more or less standardized product, on the other hand, is lobbied for only by a very small minority of stakeholders. This picture ties in directly with the answers to Question 3, where EIOPA inquired whether stakeholders perceive the need for additional prudential requirements, and a little more than 50% of the comments offered see no such necessity. About a quarter of comments to Question 3 raise fairly minor technical questions

---

[23] Linked to the financial risks first mentioned is the question of capital or interest guarantees below the threshold of full DB. There is also national regulatory variation as of now, and a potential area for EIOPA activities according to some stakeholders (cf., e.g., EIOPA 2014a, gen. com. 9 and com. 54).

[24] A position taken even more vehemently by the EIOPA Occupational Pensions Stakeholder Group: "It is not the task of the COM nor the Authority to support or promote direct or indirect EU-wide future product marketing campaigns [...] which might have the effect of undermining the extension of highly efficient occupational pension concepts in the MS" (EIOPA 2014a, gen. com. 11; also see Topic 3 in this regard).

like sustainability tests for group pensions or the design of disclosure documents.[25] The remainder of stakeholder comments (EIOPA 2014a, com. 81, 82, 85, 86, 89, 94, 98) admonishes EIOPA (and the Commission) about overlaps and potential contradictions between already existing regulatory strands. These are mainly an effect of the dichotomy of product and provider regulation. If, for example, a pension fund and an insurance company offered the same pan-European PPP, under existing rules, they would fall under different regulatory regimes, and the 2nd tier could add a second layer for both, possibly rendering the playing field both uneven and overly bureaucratic.[26] When directly asked (in Question 24) whether EIOPA should focus on either product or provider rules, however, surprisingly few stakeholders give an opinion. None favors a sole focus on providers, four think EIOPA should only address products, and six suggest a two-pronged approach.[27]

Sometimes different stakeholders disagree less about regulatory options than about assumed market dynamics, which can be illustrated with two examples regarding EIOPA's Question 9 (about provider-specific prudential obstacles to a more integrated market). While Groupe Consultatif urges EIOPA not to include any guarantees in a standardized PPP

(EIOPA 2014a, com. 235), the Bulgarian Association of Supplementary Pension Security Companies (EIOPA 2014a, com. 231) opines that such provisions would turn out meaningless in a more competitive market, because market forces would generate pressure toward very attractive terms for consumers. In the second example, market dynamics are argued to be much weaker or even absent by one of the stakeholders. The Luxembourg-based Association of International Life Offices (EIOPA 2014a, com. 225), on the one hand, points out that death benefits "in an insured PPP" might probably constitute "obstacles to transfer to or from a noninsurer". The Association of the Luxembourg Fund Industry, on the other hand, surmises that "insurers may not seek to offer personal pension products in a systematic manner throughout the European Union" (EIOPA 2014a, com. 226).

Were EIOPA—in the interest of nondiscrimination—to define a rather broad class of 2nd tier PPP that gives several options to customers, some stakeholders insist on the regulatory setting of a default option (EIOPA 2014a, com. 494 and 498). This would, of course, reintroduce official favoritism of certain providers through the back-door, if only in the shape of a more or less powerful

---

[25] Admittedly, though, it might be a challenge to devise unified a pan-European disclosure document, and to comply with it might be much easier for large providers with strong, internationally versed legal divisions. Thus, ironically concentration processes might be catalyzed in a market where the actual regulatory goal is to avoid cluster risks.

[26] The German Insurance Association provides a very simple, if somewhat one-sided solution: "we suggest taking the insurance regulation as a benchmark which includes PPPs provided by insurers and sufficiently reflects the true risk profiles of the providers" (EIOPA 2014a, com. 90).

[27] The numbers are nearly identical concerning question 25 about "same risk—same rules—same capital" (on this issue, see Section 2), and the main divide here is whether the risks covered by different existing PPPs are fundamentally similar or not.

nudge. A similar effect with disputable legitimacy could be expected if EIOPA indeed followed through on its ambition to put "PPP members […] in a position to select products characterized as good "value for money" (EIOPA 2014b). Here, EIOPA is apparently tempted to overburden the drive for transparency about PPPs' costs that in itself is backed by virtually all stakeholders (in their answers to questions 27, 56 and 58 from EIOPA 2013). Of course, as of today the actual costs to consumers are often hidden, especially in plans based on rather activist trading with relatively high and/or high-frequency portfolio turnover. Yet, as EIOPA acknowledges elsewhere (EIOPA 2014b), neither costs and real returns nor past returns and future returns are necessarily systematically linked. Thus EIOPA's quest for more and better customer information is in danger of losing legitimacy when it is coupled with unaccomplishable claims about naively simple recommendations to buyers.[28]

Topic 3: New (Im-)balances between the Pillars?

Nearly all general comments given by stakeholders which refer to the pillar metaphor either cling very rigidly to certain aspects of it or question its future viability altogether. Within the former group, representatives of occupational pensions tend to fend for a broad definition of the 2nd pillar and a narrow mandate that restricts EIOPA's PPP activities to few aspects of the 3rd pillar. In this mould, the German working group on occupational pensions (Arbeitsgemeinschaftbetriebliche Alters-versorgung, aba) emphasizes that the specific characteristics of prevalent PPP products in EU member states correspond with the respective designs of the 1st and 2nd pillars there. Therefore, it urges EIOPA to strictly restrict its PPP initiative to providers "who currently are not covered under any EU Directive and work to close these gaps" (EIOPA 2014a, gen. com. 4; also cf. gen. com. 14 by the German Insurance Association).[29] The UK National Association of Pension

---

[28] In the discussion of a question pertaining to our following third topic, EIOPA's strong confidence in customer information was also challenged. Question 29 reads: "What key questions identified in the area of occupational pensions ('Will my pension be sufficient for my demands and needs? If not, how much will the shortfall be and what can I do to improve the situation?') might be relevant for personal pensions?" (EIOPA 2013) Insurance Europe remarked in its answer that "the question in parentheses could not be answered by providing customer information", but required "a thorough assessment of the personal situation" (EIOPA 2014a, com. 621).

[29] Even more restrictive (and potentially self-serving) is the role Pensionskasse der Mitarbeiter der Hoechst-Gruppe, a German occupational pension provider, envisages for EIOPA. In their eyes, it should primarily advertise 2nd pillar products in markets where it is underdeveloped. The introduction of a 2nd tier PPP, "[o]n the other hand, […] would lead to a fragmentation in the area of supplementary pensions going hand in hand with an increasing confusion and insecurity of the citizens on the selection-process of one or several supplementary schemes. At worst, such confusion and insecurity will lead to a declining coverage ratio of all supplementary pension schemes and would therefore run counter to the objectives pursued by the European Commission to avoid old-age poverty and to ease the public pension sector(s)" (EIOPA 2014a, gen. com. 24). Furthermore, this stakeholder worries about potential "regulatory arbitrage at the expense of the individual/insured persons" (ibid.) if EIOPA's role as a pan-European regulator were strengthened.

Funds (NAPF), representing 400 providers, 1 trillion pound of invested capital and 16 million employee contracts, fears an irritation of the British market for occupational pensions if the relatively recent auto-enrolment products[30] were defined as being part of the 3rd pillar by EIOPA and were the Commission and regulated as PPPs accordingly (ibid., gen. com. 20). The Netherlands' Ministry of Finance, to include a voice from a third of the four big markets for occupational pensions, underscores that the 2nd pillar, which in the national definition covers all pension plans with an employer contribution accounts for 43% of total pensions paid there, and that its national regulation significantly differs from that of the 3rd pillar (EIOPA 2014a, gen. com. 21). Subtext: And we want it to stay that way. Pensions Europe, an umbrella group for occupational pension lobbyists, summarily calls for schemes "linked to a current or previous employment relationship" (EIOPA 2014a, gen. com.) to remain outside the scope of EIOPA's PPP agenda.[31]

So clearly the tussles about pillar definitions and EIOPA's mandate for a 2nd tier PPP have an element of turf war about market segments to them. Yet the second group of stakeholders just mentioned,

the one questioning the usefulness of the pillar metaphor and its associated border fences, put forward an argument phrased spot on by the (UK-based) Investment Management Association: "[T]he distinction in reality between pure DC funded arrangements (e.g., Pillar 1 bis, Pillar 2 occupational and Pillar 3 personal) lies often in governance and distribution arrangements. Fundamentally, the pension arrangements themselves may not look very different from one another." (EIOPA 2014a, gen. com. 18). This raises the question how different regimes can legitimately be applied to essentially identical pension products to be found across all three pillars. Of course, within each pillar they are combined with and/ or compete with distinct other products, but the parting clearly exhibits an artificial element. For example, if investment into a pension fund falls into 1st pillar bis, its tax treatment will often receive 1st pillar privileges, while the same product is treated less favorably in pillar three. So the axis of (non)discrimination between member states is complemented by the axis between pillars, and thus calls for harmonization (like the one by ABI for a single pensionable age, cf. EIOPA 2014a, com. 318) acquire a multidimensional character.

---

[30] "These [DC] schemes are established by the employer but take the form of a contract between the individual saver and a pension provider." (EIOPA 2014a, gen. com. 20).

[31] In Question 6, EIOPA explicitly asked stakeholders whether they believe that a "personal pension contract […] chosen by an employer" (EIOPA 2013) should be considered a PPP. Sixty per cent of those answering this question do not think so. Ten per cent have no firm view or feel that the crucial distinction is actually whether an employer involved is giving any sort of guarantee (for the latter view cf. EIOPA 2014a, com. 154). The coalition of those 30% who are in favor of including employer-chosen pension plans into EIOPA's PPP activities encompasses large pension fund and insurance associations from big national markets—and the Commission's already mentioned brainchild FSUG; an alliance that is as typical as it is problematic, since the Commission thus creates the impression of including consumer interests with a vehicle of its own creation.

In the course of answering the extensive catalogue of 71 questions, a number of stakeholders seem to have become a little annoyed with EIOPA. Question 17, for example ("How could a single market be developed for PPPs unregulated at EU level?"; EIOPA 2013,17) drew passes, back references, repetitions— and several ill-tempered one-sentence statements like the following two: "The question wrongly presumes that there are unregulated PPPs" (EIOPA 2014a, com. 383), and "A single market for unregulated PPPs should not be created" (EIOPA 2014a, com. 395). To a certain degree, EIOPA invited this sentiment with redundancies and a cloudy consultant-style[32] as in question 39 that asks "What regulation can be a source of inspiration for personal pensions?" (EIOPA 2013).[33] The ill will sparked by question 18 about the feasibility of a "passporting regime for providers of 1st pillar PPPs" (ibid., 17), though, does not concern style, but sensitive core areas of national interest. The vivid comment from the Bulgarian Association of Supplementary Pension Security Companies not only lets us glimpse the intensity of emotions involved, but also demonstrates that advocacy coalitions can have a strong regional dimension (as more generally analyzed by Ebbinghaus 2015) to them:

In the lack of 1st pillar bis type of retirement provision in Western Europe (established on the basis of diverting 1st pillar contributions) would mean for CEEC pension providers to have passports but not 1st pillar bis realm in Western Europe to identify themselves with. The relevance of such a 1st pillar bis passporting with regard to western Europe pension money looks like the relevance of a sailing-boat permission with regard to one's journey in Sahara. So cross-border management of 1st pillar bis schemes means that western EU managers of pension money would be able to manage directly an additional, easily accumulated pension capital from CEEC (without having the analogous access to such 1st pillar assets in their home countries), whereas their CEE counterparties would not have such a 1st pillar bis pot of money in western Europe to compete for. Put it briefly, cross-border management of 1st pillar bis pension money will drain the scarce pension resources of CEEC for the benefit of Western Europe. (EIOPA 2014a, com. 400)[34]

Central Eastern European voices are not alone in such resistance, however. Scandinavian stakeholders like the Finnish Pension Alliance point out that there would be absolutely no basis in the European treaties for such an initiative: "No, setting up a passporting regime for providers of 1st pillar bis is not feasible by any means. This idea is in direct violation

[32] Sometimes, moreover, the written English is simply spectacularly bad: "Do you see the need of the creation of a single market for products 1st pillar bis" (EIOPA 2013).

[33] Those few stakeholders that bothered to answer this question listed a number of acronyms which stand for other areas of EU regulation.

[34] The Czech Ministry of Finance in com. 408 is less affective, yet equally opposed.

of Member States exclusive discretion over social security design" (EIOPA 2014a, com. 412). On the opposite side, four stakeholders associated with the Western European financial industry (once more including FSUG) advocate the said 1st pillar bis passporting as part of a more closely integrated common financial market, even though two of them doubt its feasibility (EIOPA 2014a, com. 397, 401, 403, 404).[35]

Below the threshold of such actual market-making, EIOPA also asked whether PPP customer information ought to include material on the 1st and 2nd pillars (Question 44; EIOPA 2013). This touched a nerve with several stakeholders as well, since briefing customers about whole national pension systems and their future performance in restricted space and a standardized manner would necessarily entail an implicit appraisal of member states' pension policies. Some opponents do not welcome this in general, others fear that might result in biased assessments (EIOPA 2014a, com. 874, 877, 878, 879, 882, 888).[36]

4.2 - EIOPA's Position vis-à-vis the European Commission, National Regulators

As a European delegated agency, EIOPA exhibits two doubly indirect links to voters. On the one hand, it reports to the European Parliament, the European Commission and the Council of Europe with their distinct chains of democratic legitimacy. On the other hand, it relies on the expertise and co-operation of the member states' national supervisory authorities which in turn exercise powers delegated by national legislative and/or executive institutions. Additionally, EIOPA has been keen to communicate with the European public directly to increase its input legitimacy, and it clearly strives to provide services that create output legitimacy as well. Contrary to Maggetti's general claim according to which delegated regulatory agencies do "not rely on any kind of representativeness" (Maggetti 2010, 2), EIOPA is clearly interested in the impression to take on board a representative array of stakeholder positions. With good reasons: Taken verbally, EIOPA's mission is purely informational. Yet, given the specific way, it is asked or even pressured by the Commission to formulate legislative proposals, its political impact on agenda-setting (the vital importance of which in this very field is stressed by Hennessy 2011) and beyond is potentially much more powerful. Which, of course, need not be any less "disquieting in some regards" (ibid.), among other aspects since "the normative justification for legitimizing regulatory governance by independent agencies is, first and foremost, supposed

---

[35] In the financial sector trade unions, pan-European unanimity seems to be greater. Nordic Financial Unions, an association of Scandinavian trade unions speaking for 150,000 employees, pleads EIOPA to preserve member states' specific national three pillar arrangements. Furthermore, it emphasizes the need to train sales personnel adequately and to remunerate them for selling customers adequate products instead of maximizing turnover (EIOPA 2014a, gen. com. 22). UNI Finance Europe, an umbrella organization of 320 service sector unions in 50 countries with 7 million members, supports both claims (EIOPA 2014a, gen. com. 28).

[36] Interestingly, this group comprises stakeholders from both sides of the deep divide concerning the aforementioned issue.

to derive directly from the (expected) separateness of IRAs [independent regulatory agencies] from politics and organized interests" (ibid.).

According to Bauschke (2010) "[e]ven though research on agencification on the European level has expanded considerably in the last few years, it seems striking that questions of social legitimacy regarding the delegation to unelected bodies have not entered the debate" more vividly. When we now address EIOPA's positioning within the triangle of European political institutions, national regulators and the public in this early, defining phase of its existence, this is intended as a contribution to reduce the deficit Bauschke is pointing at. We argue that EIOPA has, after some initial wavering, taken a course projecting its self-image as purely technical. Whatever the merits of this strategy are in terms of the quality of its advice resp. legislative input, EIOPA thereby contributes to the continued depoliticization of the pensions issue within the Euro crisis. More precisely, to adopt the terminology proposed by Wood and Flinders (2014), we hold that this phenomenon is to be classified as belonging to the third, discursive face of depoliticization, that is, the variant that is pushing matters into the nonpolitical "realm of necessity." And this is exactly where most European leaders prefer to see the external effects of "rescuing" the Euro. Apart from the questionable effect this might have on European monetary and fiscal policy, it amplifies a wider and more virulent long-term danger, since it reduces "the motivation to pay attention to what politicians say and do and correspondingly diminish the value of participating in democratic mechanisms" (Vibert 2007).

In the following, we address all the topics raised in Section 4.1, but taxation receives a disproportionate share of attention. At one point in EIOPA's preliminary report, a lapse in copy-editing points to the fact that at least one internal faction sees it as crucial ("Taxation seems to be the a [sic!] significant hurdle that prevents the emergence of a single market for PPPs"; EIOPA 2014b, Paragraph 142) and we agree with that judgement.

In terms of its role perception, moreover, EIOPA comes across as increasingly frustrated by the tension between its lack of competencies and the Commission's expectations. At times, EIOPA reacts outright snappish. In the column titles "resolution" of the table EIOPA produced of stakeholder comments, in reaction to a particularly critical question regarding which type of contract qualifies a PPP for tax advantages, EIOPA states that "PPP is a not an EIOPA project, but a COM initiative. […] Work on this issue must be done by the competent authority" (EIOPA 2014a, resolution to com. 56)—that is, not EIOPA. In a similar vein, in its preliminary report to the Commission, EIOPA comes to the conclusion that

> [T]axation, social law, as well as difficulties in the harmonization of contract law, appear to be the most significant hurdles to developing a PPP single market. […] EIOPA therefore acknowledges that further analysis may be needed concerning the conditions (PPP characteristics) each MS sets in order for premiums/ contributions to qualify for beneficial tax treatment. EIOPA will closely follow the progress of COM and OECD on this matter. (EIOPA 2014b, Paragraphs 187–189)

The latter sentence quite clearly translates as "Don't give us any more homework as long as you did not do your own."

Staying closer to substance than to institutional emotions, EIOPA in its preliminary report mostly summarizes the landscape of stakeholder comments as being more friendly toward the Commission's initiative than it actually is (as we saw earlier). This is achieved by intentional vagueness, on the one hand, and a high tolerance for internal contradictions, on the other. Take, for example, the following quotes:

> The key outcome of the stakeholders' contributions received during the summer consultation period is the overarching conclusion that a single market for PPPs is advantageous for consumers, providers, and for the broader EU economy. [...] Stakeholders are aware of the advantages and the incentives arising from a single market. [...] However, most stakeholders seem to be satisfied with the present situation [...] More specifically, a significant number of the commenting stakeholders gave the opinion that it is neither feasible nor necessary to create or improve a single market. (EIOPA 2014b, Paragraphs 23–26)

Failure of the consultation process—measured by its initial ambitions—is admitted only implicitly and without drawing too much attention to the consequences. This is most apparent regarding to which products actually are to be covered by the single market for PPPs: "EIOPA believes an EU wide definition (in order to capture all existing and future

PPPs) should refer to national definitions of PPPs" (EIOPA 2014b, Paragraph 53). So EIOPA advises the Commission to treat as a PPP whatever product one of the 28 member states defines as such. This implies an enormous variance and could lead to either astonishing over-reach or utter ineffectiveness of European regulations. Even regarding the 2nd regime and thus a single, pan-European product EIOPA is not much the wiser, for example, concerning the term "retirement objective" ("EIOPA notes that for 2nd regime purposes, future work will be needed in order to establish a clear understanding of this concept"; EIOPA 2014b, Paragraph 58). At the very least, this would need to be discussed much more extensively and openly, since the political ramifications for member states' pension policies and the balance between their pillars are potentially very substantial.

Acknowledging the hurdles taxation and PPP definition represent, EIOPA sets out to reframe the issue at hand as one of consumer protection and advises the Commission as follows: "EIOPA believes a strong case is made for a future Directive that would establish a single market for PPPs inter alia through the *alignment across the EU of PPP holder protection measures*" (EIOPA 2014b,Paragraph 217, emphasis added by EIOPA). If EIOPA's resulting strategy can be summarized in a nutshell, it is this:

> The creation of a 2nd regime, introducing a highly standardized EU PPP, could overcome many consumer protection issues in the distribution process (e.g., by framing the decision-making process in a way that could encourage potential members to make suitable choices—e.g., through

default solutions and electronic platforms) and this way encourage more consumers to buy a PPP. This would be beneficial for reducing distribution costs and reaching the critical mass that is needed for providers to offer cost effective products and reach economies of scale. (EIOPA 2014b, Paragraph 269).

Strikingly, EIOPA even claims that while usually PPPs should not be bought without "the benefit of independent professional advice" (EIOPA 2014b,Paragraph 490), this were not the case in the 2nd regime. Here, EIOPA trusts and advises the public to trust solely in its own "generic advice suitable for the vast majority of citizens that could be disseminated through government or public agencies" (EIOPA 2014b, Paragraph 490).

Thus, while a number of details remain very cloudy, EIOPA counsels the Commission—in a very idiosyncratic reading of the stakeholder feedback it received—to use the cover of consumer protection to pre-emptively depoliticize pension policies and to channel a potentially huge segment of the market for PPPs to a limited range of large providers that are likely to be able to comply with EIOPA's regulatory demands (that are sketched in Paragraphs 271–292 of EIOPA 2014b). Furthermore, EIOPA strives to monopolize the advice citizens receive on PPP investment decisions. It is remarkable that an initiative with such far-reaching distributional consequences for both consumers and providers of PPPs and of member states' pension policies in general have so far received hardly any public or academic attention.

5. Conclusion

A close reading of the growing body of primary sources on a more integrated common market for private pension products reveals major divisions between the European Commission and certain large providers, on the one hand, and several member states as well as smaller suppliers that are more attuned to the existing particularities of national markets on the other. EIOPA as a pan-European regulatory body charged with the wider task of hedging systemic risk in the occupational and private pension sectors finds itself in a rather delicate dilemma. The Commission insistently expects it to devise a 2nd tier regulation embodied in a standardized PPP that ought to be attractive for all EU citizens. Yet, this endeavor runs the risk of unsettling the balance between the pillars of the 28 distinct national retirement provision policies, and it is hardly conceivable without far-reaching tax harmonization for which neither EIOPA nor the Commission have the necessary competence, albeit the latter's DG GROW clearly harbors a sustained ambition. While resistance against tax harmonization remains strong, a prolonged phase of close-to-zero real interest rates might present a window of opportunity, since nonexistent profits render no revenue no matter what the tax rate is.

This pattern clearly speaks to our theoretical assumptions about crisis policymaking. The fact that the Commission repeatedly urges EIOPA to generate far-reaching policy advice is in line with the expectation that experts and interest groups have considerable influence on policymaking when the complex problems have to be dealt with in a context of uncertainty and ambiguity. Moreover, the dilemma of EIOPA to deal with the very divergent interests of the member states and of different stakeholders wary their turf corroborates our expectation that the characteristics of the crisis context may also make the involved actor's resorting to their core values and interests. In the multilevel context of the EU, this puts EIOPA in a delicate position as it has to respect the opinions of the stakeholders while at the same time being pushed by the Commission toward giving clear-cut policy advice.

For the moment, EIOPA seems to solve this dilemma by retreating considerably from earlier statements on tax harmonization and by trying to establish itself as a purely technical entity now focusing on consumer protection. This framing might well ease its settling-in between the Commission and national regulators as well as member states governments, allowing it to present itself as an institution willing to listen and ready to learn. That way, challenges to the legitimacy of its actual function could be deflected successfully, and quite far-reaching policy change in terms of a pan-European 2nd tier might well be the consequence.

This strategy, however, threatens to perpetuate the illusion of straightforward technical fixes to the underlying distributional conflicts which are thereby depoliticized. Furthermore, it helps to uphold the state of denial regarding the external costs imposed by the Euro's (alleged) rescuers on retirement provision. Thus, EIOPA as an institution created to hedge systemic risks and their impact on the living standard of senior citizens paradoxically contributes to the prodigious pension pretense that is becoming an ever larger elephant in the room of EU social and fiscal policy.

References

Bauschke, R. 2010. "The Effectiveness of European Regulatory Governance: The Case of Pharmaceutical Regulation." In *Fakultät für Wirtschafts-und Sozialwissenschaften*. Heidelberg: Ruprecht-Karls-Universität Heidelberg, available at: http://archiv.ub.uni-heidelberg.de/volltextserver/12639/

Berthon, J., C. Cronin, G. Prache, K. Struwe, and J. M. Viver. 2013. "The Real Return of Private Pensions." A Research Report by EuroFinUse. In. Brussels.

Blatter, J., C. Bombach and R. Wiprächtiger 2015. "Enhancing Gender-Equity through Evidence-Based Policymaking? Theorizing and Tracing the use of Systematic Knowledge in Family and Tax Policy Reforms." *European Policy Analysis* 1 (1): 3–34.

Blyth, M. 2002. *The Great Transformations*. Cambridge: Cambridge University Press.

Buckley, J., and D. Howarth. 2011. "Internal Market: Regulating the So-Called Vultures of Capitalism." *Journal of Common Market Studies* 49, Annual Review: 123–143.

Bundesministerium für Arbeit und Soziales. 2014. "Strategische Sozialberichterstattung. Nationaler Sozialbericht 2014." In Bonn: Bundesministerium für Arbeit und Soziales, Referat Information, Publikation, Redaktion.

Ebbinghaus, B. 2015. "The Privatization and Marketization of Pensions in Europe: A Double Transformation Facing the Crisis." *European Policy Analysis* 1 (1): 56–73.

EIOPA. 2013. "Discussion Paper on a possible EU-single market for personal pension products." [EIOPA/13/241], available at: https://eiopa.europa.eu/Publica tions/Discussion%20paper/20130516_E IOPA_Discussion_Paper_Personal_Pensi ons_def.pdf (accessed date 12 April, 2016)

EIOPA. 2014a. Summary of Comments EIOPA Discussion Paper on a possible EU single market for personal pension products/DP13001

EIOPA. 2014b. Towards an EU single market for personal pensions. An EIOPA Preliminary Report to COM.

European Commission. 2012. Technical Advice to Develop an EU Single Market for Personal Pension Schemes.

European Commission. 2014. Call for advice from the European Insurance and Occupational Pensions Authority (EIOPA) on the development on an EU single market for personal pension products (PPP).

European Commission. 2015a. Green Paper. Building a Capital Markets Union In. Brussels.

European Commission. 2015b. "Aktion splan zur Schaffung einer Kapital-marktunion." COM (2015) 468 final, 30 September.

European Commission. 2015c. "Feedback Statement on the Green Paper." *Building a Capital Markets Union*. COM (2015) 184 final, 30 September.

Fischer, K. 2012. "Solvency II bei Einrichtungen der betrieblichen Alters-versorgung: eine europarechtliche Sack-gasse?" *Betriebliche Altersversorgung* 67 (8): 681–688.

Görgen, P. 2011. "Europa gibt den Takt." In *Betriebliche Altersversorgung und Recht— Festschrift für Reinhold Höfer zum 70,* eds. Peter A. Doetsch, and Peter Küpper. Geburtstag. München: Beck: 41-52.

Guardiancich, I. 2015. "Portability of Supplementary Pension Rights in Europe: A Lowest Common Denominator Solution." *European Policy Analysis* 1 (1): 74–91.

Gunkel, A., and F. Swyter. 2011. "Opting-Out-Modelle—Königsweg oder Irrtum." In *Betriebliche Altersversorgung und Recht —Festschrift für Reinhold Höfer zum 70,* edited by Peter Doetsch, and Peter Küpper. Geburtstag. München: Beck: 53-64.

Haverland, M. 2007. "When the Welfare State Meets the Regulatory State: EU Occupational Pension Policy." *Journal of European Public Policy* 14 (6): 886–904.

't Hart, P. and Tindall, K. 2009 "Understanding Crisis Exploitation: Leadership Rhetoric and Framing Contests in Response to the Economic Meltdown", in P. 't Hart and K. Tindall (eds.) Framing the Global Economic Downturn: Crisis Rhetoric and the Politics of Recession, Canberra: Australia National University E Press, pp. 21-40.

Hennessy, A. 2011. "The Role of Agenda Setting in Pension Market Integration."

Journal of European Integration 33 (5): 577–597.

Hessling, M. 2013. "Auswirkungen des Niedrigzinsumfeldes auf die betriebliche Altersversorgung." *Betriebliche Altersversorgung* 68 (4): 264–267.

Kluth, S., and M. Gasche. 2013. Ersatzraten in der Gesetzlichen Rentenversicherung. (In German)

Lamla, B., and M. Coppola. 2013. Is it all about access? Perceived access to occupational pensions in Germany. In. Munich.

Lodge, M. 2007. "Comparing Non-Hierarchical Governance in Action: The Open Method of Co-ordination in Pensions and Information Society." *Journal of Common Market Studies* 45 (2): 343–365.

Maggetti, Martino. 2010. "Legitimacy and Accountability of Independent Regulatory Agencies: A Critical Review." *Living Reviews in Democracy* 2:1–9.

Necker, S., and M. Ziegelmeyer. 2014. *Household Risk Taking after the Financial Crisis*. In. Munich.

Oxera. 2007. The effect of cross-border investment restrictions on certain pension schemes in the EU. Prepared for European Commission DG International Market and Services. In. Oxford.

Schäfers, M. 2015. "Wirtschaft ächzt wegen EZB-Politik unter Pensionslast." In *Frankfurter Allgemeine Zeitung*. Frankfurt am Main, Feb. 3.

Schmidt-Narischkin, N., and M. Thiesen. 2012. "Solvency II—regulatorischer Overkill oder sinnvoller Regulierungsrahmen für die Vermögensverwaltung eines VAG-Pensionsfonds." *Betriebliche Altersversorgung* 67 (5): 427–429.

Shin, H.S. 2013. "The Second Phase of Global Liquidity and Its Impact on Emerging Economies." In Keynote address at the Federal Reserve Bank of San Francisco Asia Economic Policy Conference. San Francisco.

Vibert, F. 2007. *The Rise of the Unelected. Democracy and the New Separation of Powers*. New York: Cambridge University Press.

Wenzelburger, G., and F. Wolf. 2015. Policy theories in the crisis? In Paper presented at the ICPP 2015, T01P08 (Theories and conceptions of the political process beyond "Policy Cycle" and "Multiple Streams"). Milan.

Wolf, F. 2014. *Gewalt, Armut und Ignoranz. Die Arbeitsteilung zwischen Staat und privatem Sektor bei der Bearbeitung ausgewählter vernachlässigter Probleme—Deutschland im intra- und internationalen Vergleich*. Baden-Baden: Nomos.

Wolf, F., R. Zohlnhöfer, and G. Wenzelburger. 2014. "The Politics of Public and Private Pension Generosity in Advanced Democracies." *Social Policy and Administration* 48 (1): 86–106.

Wood, M., and M. Flinders. 2014. "Rethinking Depoliticisation: Beyond the Governmental." *Policy and Politics* 42 (2): 151–170.

Woolley, P. 2012. "Why are Financial Markets so Inefficient and Exploitative— and a Suggested Remedy." In Betriebliche Altersversorgung, 67 (2): 135–143.

World Bank. 1994. "Averting the Old Age Crisis." *A World Bank Research Report.* New York: World Bank.

Notes to Table 1 (on following page)

[37] Note that this column, with the exception of the incipient general comments that each stakeholder had the opportunity to add and that differ rather widely in scope and intent, is not limited to a selection of statements deemed relevant by us—we consciously looked at all stakeholder comments responding to the respective questions.

[38] Whereas there is a direct correspondence between the lines in Columns 2 and 3, the passages listed in Columns 4 and 5 refer to the topics listed in Column 1 in a more general manner.

Table 1: Navigational Help through our Primary Sources

Topic	Relevant Sections and Questions in DP-13-001 (aka EIOPA/13/241) (EIOPA, 2013)	Stakeholder Statements[39] in EIOPA-TFPP-14-001 (EIOPA, 2014a)	Relevant Sections in EIOPA's preliminary report (EIOPA-BoS-14/029)[40] (EIOPA, 2014b)	Relevant Sections in the Commission's renewed Call for Advice (Ref.Ares(2014)2462119) (European Commission, 2014)
Taxational issues	Section 3.2: Question 8, Question 10, Question 11, Question 12, Question 13, Question 14, Question 15 Section 3.3: Question 22	General Comments Nr. 3, 19 Comments Nr. 195-203, 205-210, 212-218 Nr. 244-250, 252-261 Nr. 264-269, 271-275, 277-281 Nr. 283-288, 290-293, 295-297, 299 Nr. 300-305, 307-309, 311-316 Nr. 318-325, 327-331, 333-338, 341 Nr. 342-348, 350-352 Nr. 474-483, 485-487	Section 1.4: Paragraphs 23-27 Section 2.3: Paragraph 43 Paragraph 53 Paragraph 58 Section 3.1: Paragraph 105 Section 4.1: Paragraphs 139-140 Section 4.3: Paragraphs 142-174 Paragraphs 182-185 Paragraphs 187-189	Introduction Statement 12 Annex Section 3: Question 1 Question 3 Section 6: Question 6
Interests of different provider types	Section 3.1: Question 2, Question 3, Question 4 Section 3.2: Question 9 Section 3.3: Question 23, Question 24, Question 25 Section 4.1: Question 27 Section 4.2: Question 56, Question 58	General Comments Nr. 3, 5, 10, 11, 12, 18, 25, 26 Comments Nr. 53-72, Nr. 75-83, 85-91, 93-98, 101 Nr. 102-109, 111-124 Nr. 220-228, 230-235, 237-242 Nr. 489-502, 504-507 Nr. 509-521, 523-527 Nr. 529-540, 542-546 Nr. 569-581, 583-587 Nr. 1086-1099, 1101-1106, 1109 Nr. 1131-1140, 1142-1146, 1148	Section 6.2: Paragraph 201 Section 6.3: Paragraphs 216-217 Paragraph 219 Section 7.2: Paragraphs 227-228 Section 7.3: Paragraph 237 Paragraph 247 Paragraphs 255-257 Paragraph 259 Paragraph 266 Section 7.4: Paragraphs 268-270 Section 7.5: Paragraphs 271-298	Introduction Statement 6 Annex Section 2: Question 3 Section 5: Question 4 Question 7 Question 8
Pillar (im-)balance	Section 3.1: Question 6 Section 3.2: Question 17, Question 18 Section 4.1: Question 29, Question 39, Question 44	Gen. Comm. Nr. 4, 7, 14, 18, 20, 21, 22, 23, 24, 28 Comments Nr. 152-165, 167-170, 173 Nr. 376-386, 388-393, 395 Nr. 396-404, 406-410, 412 Nr. 609-619, 621-624 Nr. 792-803, 805 Nr. 874-883, 885-888	Section 8: Paragraphs 299-306 Section 10.3: Paragraph 487-500	Introduction Statement 9 Annex Section 1: Question 3 Section 6: Question 4

European Policy Analysis - Volume 2, Number 1 - Spring 2016

Policy and Decision to Retire in Central and Eastern European Countries

Daiva Skučiene[A] & Julija Moskvina[A]

The exit from the labor market in old age is a process determined by different institutional factors of the labor market. Working conditions, employment protection regulation, organizational policies and employers' attitude can either make people stop working or motivate them to work longer. The decision to stay or withdraw from the labor market in old age with regard to the employment policies in the Central and Eastern EU member states is analyzed in the paper. Central and Eastern European countries have been selected due to their similar historical development, as well as due to the advantages of comparative analysis providing more robust results based on the data from several national cases. For the literature analysis, the document meta-analysis and the analysis of data from the European Social Survey (ESS5, 2010) and Eurobarometer 76.2 (September–October 2011), including methods such as descriptive statistics, binary logistic regression was applied. The willingness to continue in paid work after retirement is influenced by the complexity of the institutional factors related to the working time, autonomy at work, work and family balance, training opportunities, adjustment of the work place, the view of the employers and antidiscrimination actions. The analysis revealed the demand for effective policies in the fields of promoting productivity and fighting discrimination in Central and Eastern European countries.

Keywords: decision to retire, Central and Eastern Europe, employment policies, working conditions, employment protection, organizational policies, productivity.

Introduction

The recent trends in the labor markets of the European Union (EU) countries with regard to the participation of the population aged 55+ show the consequent increase in the employment rates of cohorts 55–59 and 60–65. One of the reasons for the active participation of the older population is the increase of the official retirement age that most of the European countries practiced in the past decade.

However, this measure has only a moderate effect. Along with the increase of retirement age, political measures such as antidiscrimination laws, the strictness of employment protection and so on

[A] Lithuanian Social Research Centre, Vilnius, Lithuania

doi: 10.18278/epa.2.1.6

were adopted, in order to ensure a higher participation of older employees in the labor market.

Central and Eastern European countries also applied such employment measures to safeguard the higher employment of older employees.

In 2006–2014, almost in all Central and Eastern European countries, the duration of working life was lower than that in the EU27 countries on average, except Estonia. The growth of the working life duration during the past years in the analyzed countries was also slow. The average exit age from the labor market was higher only in Estonia and Latvia in 2006–2009, whereas it was lower in Hungary, Czech Republic, and Slovakia than that in EU27 countries on average. The employment rate of population aged 55–64 is traditionally higher in Baltic states and lower in Hungary, Poland and Slovenia. The shorter duration of working life than that in the EU on average, different average exit age from the labor market and the different level of employment rate of older population in Central and Eastern European countries give the challenge to determine the reasons behind the people's decisions either to continue working or to retire in order to extend the duration of older people's participation in the labor market.

The aim of the paper is to analyze the decision and the factors influencing it to withdraw from the labor market in old age with regard to the institutional features for employment policy in the Central and Eastern EU member states. To achieve this, a few objectives were set: first, to carry out an analysis of the theoretical background on the topic; secondly, to analyze the employment policy in the Central and Eastern EU

states and finally, to analyze the decision to retire or continue working after retirement and its influencing factors.

Theoretical Background

While analyzing employment policy instruments in connection with the subjective decision to stay or withdraw from the labor market, several important theoretical statements should be taken into account. For the analysis policy and public preferences or decisions, the institutional/neoinstitutional theories offer a reasonable framework.

Institutional/neoinstitutional tradition has an important role to play in the tradition of the social policy research domain (Aidukaitė 2004; 2009; Esping-Andersen 1990; Kleinman 2002; Pedersen 1999; Pierson 2001). However, for the analysis of the relation between policy and public preferences or decisions, a reasonable framework is advised in the following researches. The neoinstitutional theory states that, first and foremost the, formal structure reflects the public understanding and interpretation of social reality. Fredriksson, Pallas, and Wehmeier (2013) and Reay and Candace (2015) referred to Thornton et al.'s (2012) understanding about institutional logics, which shapes how individuals produce and reproduce their material subsistence, organize time and space, and provide meaning to their social reality. Fredriksson et al. (2013) used the concept of Lawrence and Suddaby (2006) "institutional work," which they explained as how rules, norms, ideas and practices are formed and transformed, rather than agents achieving the specific goal.

Fenger, van der Steen, and van der Torre (2014) used the idea of historical institutionalism based on the assumption that a set of institutional constraints and opportunities affects the behavior of political actors. Fenger et al. (2014) identified the three logics that might affect the development of highly institutionalized policy domains:

- *The logic of the socio-economic and societal environment.* Changes in socioeconomic and societal–cultural conditions create pressures on policy domains to adjust policies to the new conditions.
- *The logic of public preferences.* The concept of responsiveness refers to the extent to which policy decisions follow public preferences.
- *The internal institutional logic of the policy domain.* In this logic, the policy domains' internal paradigms, characteristics and administrative procedures guide institutional evolution. According to Fenger et al. (2014), institutional logic, public preferences and socio-economic and societal conditions are related with each other.

Kang (2014) stated that in recent years there has been convergence between rational choice and historical institutionalism. They distinguished one form of sociological/organizational institutionalism among other two, which has features such as: legitimating explanation; individuals and communities as cultural beings; an institution is reproduced because actors believe that it is morally just or appropriate; mimetic, normative and coercive pressures that challenge taken-for-granted cultural frameworks, cognitive schema and norms/values. Such form of institutionalism offers an analytical framework for policy as normative and coercive pressure for the people decisions.

Public confidence in the body politic can be restored by investigation that establishes the truth in a public manner, said Sulitzeanu-Kenan and Holzman-Gazit (2016). By them, institutional legitimacy is claimed to rely on the degree to which the inquiry conducts its proceedings in a public manner.

Employment protection, working conditions, organizational policies, including the measures to maintain productivity are such institutional features that have an impact on decision to work or retire.

Employment protection. The institutional characteristics of employment protection in selected countries are reflected in the different social models of selected countries (neoliberal Baltic states, embedded neoliberal Visegrád states, and neocorporatist in Slovenia). Employment protections such as the notice of termination, severance payment, difficulty of dismissal, and so on can vary in the analyzed countries. For example, the employment protection legislation in regular employment is less strict in Hungary, Bulgaria and Poland than in Estonia and even more in Czech Republic (Cazes and Nesporova 2004).

According to employment institutional features, Bukodi et al. (2006) classified Hungary and Estonia into the post-socialist or transition regime. They distinguished three important kinds of security: job security—the security of being able to stay in the same job; employment security—the security of staying employed not necessarily in the same job; income security—the security of having an income in the case of unemployment, sickness. These three securities have different combination in every country, because of different institutional employment features. For example, in Hungary mid-career men in higher level occupations definitely have a lower risk of experiencing unemployment.

As defined by Bukodi et al. (2006) in former socialist states such as Hungary and Estonia, the labor markets of these countries are less flexible; for example, in Hungary an increasing proportion of newly created jobs are temporary and this type is widespread among less educated, unskilled workers. Bukodi et al. (2006) summarized that all post-socialist countries spend significantly less on measures of active and passive labor market policies. Hungary and Estonia experience a relatively low degree of employment security.

According to Bohle and Greskovits (2007), three capitalisms emerged in CEE societies: a neoliberal type in the Baltic states, an embedded neoliberal in Visegrád states and neocorporatist in Slovenia. According to them, Hungary's social welfare system is among the most generous in the region. The Czech and Slovak Republics also have relatively encompassing systems of welfare; these countries supported a large number of enterprises and can control the dynamics of unemployment. In the Baltic states, labor markets are flexible, wages are low, work conditions are unregulated, and workers are less demanding of protectionist state intervention.

Saar, Unt, and Kogan (2008) stated that the degree of labor market regulation influences the employers' decision making when hiring workers. According to them, with respect to employment protection, there are variations within CEE countries. Hungary has the most flexible labor legislation, closely followed by Czech Republic and Slovak Republic, and then by Poland. The Baltic countries are in the middle, and Slovenia has most restrictive labor relations regulation. The common features among the CEE countries are as follows: employers do not always enact regulations, the low coverage of trade unions, and employees do not initiate individual claims against employers for fear of losing their jobs. A fixed term work is a widespread form of employment there. In the Baltic states, there are a significant proportion of employees without a written contract. Saar et al. (2008) referred to the previous analysis, which shows that the CEE countries have different employment protection models. In Slovenia, there is a strong employment protection policy, and, a relatively low mobility rate. In Czech Republic and Hungary, employment protection is quite low, whereas in Baltic states there is high employment protection.

Specific rules for workers reaching or approaching the age of retirement were distinguished by Tonin (2009) while analyzing employment protection legislation in Central and Eastern European countries. For example, in Hungary, an additional severance payment is prescribed for older workers, while no payment is due to workers already qualifying as pensioners. Bulgaria has particularly favorable conditions for these workers, while separate rules on the severance pay policy exist in Slovakia. A peculiarity of the Slovak labor code is that entitlement to severance allowance develops only if the employee agrees with the termination of the employment relationship prior to the commencement of the notice period, thus making notice and severance pay substitutes rather than complementary for each other, unlike other countries. A notice period is longer in Croatia for workers who are over 50 and 55. In Lithuania, workers within five years before old age pension also have a longer notice. Besides a longer notice period, older workers can usually get a higher severance payment. Cheron, Hairault, and Langot (2011) also noted that older workers are usually more protected than younger ones by tenure-related provisions: workers with a longer tenure (more likely to be older workers) are often required to be given longer notice periods in the case of dismissals and higher severance payment.

It should be noted that despite favorable employment protection legislation, the official position toward retirement may have an influence on the decision of withdrawal from the labor market. For example, Piasna (2010) while analyzing the recent changes in the Polish national social dialogue discourse found that the transition to retirement is presented in a national strategic document as highly structured and determined by the labor market policy and institutions. Piasna (2010) presents evidence that the national policy pushes elderly workers to leave the labor market at the age of retirement.

Working conditions. A number of studies focus on the influence of the working conditions while making a decision to continue or stop working in old age. Pieces of evidence from the literature on how institutional characteristics in the field of working conditions can impact preferences of retirement are presented further.

The research of Szubert and Sobala (2005) in Poland confirmed that a piecework system, overtime work, heavy lifting at work, and a self-assessment of fatigue after a workday and the amount of leisure time are the risk factors of early retirement because they lead to the inability to work. Szubert and Sobala (2005) concluded that the improvement of work organization and working conditions, mostly through the elimination of piecework systems, the reduction of physical workload, or exposure to some occupational hazards would significantly contribute to decreasing the tendency for early retirement.

Costa, Sartori, and Åkerstedt (2006) concluded that the control of the work time may improve the work–life balance (to suit the family and social commitments, to optimize the commuting hours, and to adjust

personal working capacity) of older workers in Western European countries.

The study performed by Tobiasz-Adamczyk et al. (2007) in Poland presented the evidence that the occupational status is related to the health consequences of employment in particular working environments. The analysis showed that the highest mortality risk was noted for skilled manual workers as well as workers with vocational basic education.

Siegrist et al. (2007) noted that the motivation to leave the workplace in older age in old EU member states is higher when there is a mismatch between the employee's efforts and awards. Helman et al. (2008) indicated that one of the factors that influences stop working in the age over 65 for the U.S. citizens is the lack of satisfaction with the workplace and the depreciation of the American employee's capabilities and talents.

Pietilainen et al. (2011) found that working conditions in Finland (such as shift work, temporary work contract, hazardous exposures, physical work load, computer work, low control, high demands, and social support at work) explained around 20% of the association of self-rated health with subsequent disability due to mental disorders.

Santa (2011) mentioned that other factors have an impact on the decision to continue professional activity: work-related personal satisfaction, the investment in long years and complex studies that lead to a high qualification, an appealing cost/benefit balance, the awareness of the social importance of the work.

Lahelma et al. (2012) analyzed working conditions as risk factors for disability retirement in Finland (Helsinki). The authors of the study discovered that heavy physical workload and low job control remained the primary risk factors for disability retirement. Hellemans and Closon (2013) found that, for older workers, fair acknowledgment and consideration and some psychosocial aspects such as an opportunity to participate are important.

Virtanen et al. (2014) revealed the fact that employees with a good mental health status and a high work time control are twice more likely to work longer than the employees who had both psychiatric morbidity and poor work time control. High work time control associated with extended employment similarly among those who had a somatic disease and those who did not.

Similar results were given by Robroek et al. (2015) in the study carried out in the Netherlands. Low job control was also related to unemployment and early retirement.

Organizational policies. The analysis of the organizational policy is an institutional labor market feature, which has impact on the decision to work or retire.

Harper et al. (2006) suggest that employers' attitudes toward older workers are importantly influenced by the level of country development. It was indicated that the less developed countries have a stable supply of younger workers which makes their actual and perceived need for older workers obsolete. Davey (2008) also argues that employers' attitude toward an older employer is the one of the most influential factors of early withdrawal from the labor market. The studies from Central and Eastern European countries show examples of the engagement of the employers into the elongation of working life of older employers. Domadenik, Redek, and Ograjenšek (2008) discovered that more than half of the Slovenian employers would like to keep their male and female employees over the legal retirement age under a regular job contract where legally possible.

The organizational policies toward older people usually lay on the employers' attitudes and stereotypes. These issues were widely analyzed by Western authors. Ulrich (2003) noticed that the discriminatory phrase about older workers stating that "you can't teach an old dog new tricks" is common among employers. While firing staff employers usually chose the less productive older and younger employees. However, the question of productivity of the older workers can be expressed differently depending on the sector. A qualitative study performed by McNair, Flynn, and Dutton (2007) revealed that in small firms the age of employee does not matter: older workers have more skills, more work experience, and they are more loyal and more concerned about the interests of the client. On the other hand, older workers also have poor health and they do not accept new methods of performing a job.

Discrimination against older workers arises due to their being stereotypes: older people are not productive and cost more for the employer than younger ones (Ghosheh 2008). Most employers do not consider the training of older people as useful, whereas the expected period of staying in the job for them is short. The findings of Armstrong-Stassen (2008) suggest that human resource practices within organizations are important for the decision to work longer, especially for the decision of retirees to return to work.

However, the relationship between age and productivity is not constant and changes over time (Ilmakunnas et al. 2010). If the individual work productivity is defined through experience, motivation, mental, and physical abilities, it is clear that these aspects are changing during different life stages. Experience is accumulated through the work career; however, the physical strength and health tend to decline. Therefore, the work productivity in older age may even increase depending on factors such as specific skills employed in the current work process, how the work is organized, how the individual interacts with other employees. As Bloom, Canning, and Fink (2010) noted, the transfer of the manual employee to a less physically demanding position improves the objective productivity indicators as well as the subjectively perceived level of work productivity. The aspect of ergonomics as a critical factor in the decision to retire as it influence employee's health and job attitudes was presented in the study of Schwerha et al. (2011). Conen, Henkens, and Schippers (2012) also noted that productivity depends on the physical and cognitive abilities. Physical strength is particularly needed for manual labor and unskilled jobs.

The human capital of an employee, which is defined as the skills to perform a job, is a direct measure of the productivity of work. Older age employees accumulate their experience and their specific human capital increases significantly (Karpinska, Henkens, and Schippers 2013).

Pagán (2013) shows that nondisabled 50+ workers have the highest levels of overall job satisfaction, whereas limited disabled workers report the lowest ones. The author stresses the fact that for the limited disabled sample, the main determinants of the overall job satisfaction are the domains "recognition," for the nondisabled sample, the domain "salary adequate".

Summarizing, the institutional employment protection and working conditions as well as organizational strategies can shape up the norms that influence the population decision in the labor market to work or retire. Among employment protection factors are: favorable employment protection legislation aspects as longer notice of termination, severance payment, additional protection form dismissal, and others. Among working condition factors are: control over work time, occupational status, (in)adequate awards, self-assessment of health and fatigue, physical workload, job control and participation, and others. And organizational strategies: employer's attitude, antidiscrimination policies, investments in human capital as a base of productivity, job adjustment measures.

Data and Methods

For the analysis of the factors influencing the decision to extend employment or to retire after the retirement age, the Central and Eastern European countries were selected because of the following reasons: first, their similar historical development as former socialist states, although as Bohle and Greskovits (2007) show, the development of capitalism forms in such countries was different, and second, due to the advantages of comparative analysis providing more robust results based on the data from several national cases.

The research question is: What are the factors that have an impact on the decision of population to work or retire with regard to the employment policy?

The meta-analysis of the documents of the European Foundation for the Improvement of Living and Working Conditions (Feifs et al. 2013) and analyses of the data ESS5 (2010), Eurobarometer 76.2 (Sept–Oct 2011) was applied.

The combined analysis the data of ESS5 and Eurobarometer 76.2 allows us to compare different sources and leads to a better understanding of the policy impact for people decision to work or retire, after the retirement age. The analysis was not carried out according to the age groups—the entire society was taken into consideration, since there was a presumption that aging is a long-term process and the attitude of all the members of the society is important since each one of them will face the necessity to take the decision to work or not after reaching a retirement age in an individual period. The secondary analysis of the statistical data of Eurostat allows us to compare real data with the subjective data from the surveys ESS5 and Eurobarometer.

For the analyses of the descriptive statistics, data from ESS5 and Eurobarometer 76.2, binary logistic regression is used.

For the binary logistic regression, "like to work after pension entitlement" was selected as a dependent variable. After the measurement of the Pearson correlation between independent (as independent were selected all variables in Eurobarometer 76.2 related to working condition, job security, employment) and dependent variables, only independent variables were selected, which correlated higher with the dependent variable. For the binary logistic regression, the selected variables as independent are as follows: aged 55+ stop working: places not adapted; aged 55+ stop working: lack of modern skills; aged 55+ stop working: exclusion from training; aged 55+ stop working: view of employers; aged 55+ work qualities: reliability; aged 55+ work qualities: experience; aged 55+ work qualities: up to date; aged 55+ work qualities: decision making; aged 55+ work qualities: teamwork ability; aged 55+ work qualities: problem solving; aged 55+ work qualities: open to new ideas; aged 55+ work qualities: cultural competence; aged 55+ work qualities: flexibility; aged 55+ work qualities: productivity; aged 55+ work qualities: stress handling; aged 55+ work qualities: creativity; age discrimination at work: experienced; age discrimination education: experienced. All independent variables in the model of binary logistic regression were statistically significant. The meaning of the coefficient B is indicated. Only those variables, whose B values are >0.5 are indicated.

The research was limited by variables selected from the Eurobarometer 76.2 survey, so the conclusions of this research can be tested by further research using different dataset. The control variables, such as age, gender, and education, were not used in this research, so their influence has to be tested in further research studies.

Employment Policies for Older Employees in Central and Eastern European Countries

*E*mployment protection. Despite the fact that older employees in selected countries enjoyed relatively high employment protection (as was described in the first section), the general institutional framework for them in the most of the analyzed countries remained "employment-unfriendly." The brief analysis of the national actions aimed at protecting the employment of the older people in the selected countries showed more employment discouraging factors. Most of the countries were applying attractive early retirement schemes during the reference period. The possibility of applying flexible work forms to the old age/pension age people was also limited.

For example, the mechanism of early retirement was preventing older people from the extension of working life in Hungary, Estonia, the Czech Republic, Slovenia, and Poland (till 2008, when the Act of 19 December 2008 on bridge pensions was adopted). In Slovenia, the existing culture of early retirement is preventing older workers from work–life extension, and also reinforced by the Pension and Disability Insurance Act (2006), there are numerous options for lowering the pensionable age limit (Feifs et al. 2013). Domadenik et al. (2009) analyzed the attitudes of the Slovenian employers toward older workers within the context of the aging process and the reforms in the labor market. Indeed, the employment rate of older workers in Slovenia has been significantly below the European levels and the EU employment guidelines, especially for women. The generally low employment of the older population is a consequence of transition in Slovenia due to the fact that early retirement was one of the mild approaches to reducing the number of employees in companies, which resulted in a large number of relatively young retired people. Older workers are also more prone to becoming long-term unemployed.

The active labor market policies (ALMP) that aimed to protect jobless population from unemployment during the analyzed period also couldn't make significant influence to the situation of older people in the labor market. First, most of the ALMP measures are not available for the people beyond the age of retirement. The analysis of the ALMP in the selected countries (Feifs et al. 2013) also showed that while applying ALMP measures in most of the analyzed cases, the older unemployed were included in the general group of the vulnerable people. Unemployed people over 50 (Bulgaria, Poland) or over 55 years old (Lithuania, Slovenia) were distinguished as a vulnerable group at the labor market during the analyzed period and were attributed to the additional measures to support their employment (such as vocational training, support of job creation/entrepreneurship, and others), though the wage subsidies and training measures are the most popular while integrating older people into the labor market.

Above-mentioned active policies should be considered under the context of unfavorable economic situation due to the 2008 crisis. First, the most of the analyzed Central and Eastern European countries (except Poland) traditionally spend less on ALMP (both in absolute and relative terms).

Second, the rapid growth of the number of unemployed has put demand for the higher public expenditure for activation measures. However, countries such as Bulgaria and Romania even cut the ALMP's funding, and scarce public resources during the crisis didn't allow considerably higher spending on ALMPs in Lithuania. The changes of ALMP funding reflected in the number of participants. For example, the higher spending on active measures allowed Estonia, Latvia, Slovenia, and Hungary to increase the share of ALMP's participants (participants per 100 persons wanting to work) during the crisis period. Anyway, the accessibility of ALMP measures in selected countries was still lower than that in old EU countries.

Although the unemployed people of the preretirement age had the right for protection against unemployment through participation in ALMP in selected countries, the increased unemployment and limited public resources for these measures during the period 2008–2010 reduced their opportunities to get such support in order to get back to the labor market. It should also be mentioned that the European Commission's and national governments' focus on fighting youth unemployment also influenced the national priorities toward participants of ALMP. However, Barbier, Rogowski, and Colomb (2015) stressed the different scale of compliance with European demands in different countries.

As the results from Czech Republic show, probably the changes in socioeconomic conditions didn't create enough pressure on such an institutional domain as public employment services as Fenger, van der Steen, and van der Torre (2014) suggested. Thus, the policies implemented by the public employment services (a) lost institutional legitimacy (if apply the concept of Sulitzeanu-Kenan and Holzman-Gazit (2016) and (b) were lagged in time with the important labor market changes (if apply the concept of Kang (2014)). As Kotrusová and Výborná (2011) indicated, despite the high level of flexibility in the implementation of active employment policies at the local level, a large part of general public and enterprises limited their expectations from them.

The contradiction in different institutional characteristics of employment policies for older people can be partly explained by the absence of fragmented employment strategies toward aging population in selected countries during the analyzed period. For example, in Estonia, the Employment Contracts Act allowed the employer terminating the employment relationship on the basis of the persons' age till 2006. In 2007, the Articles of the Public Service Act legally permitting the dismissal of public sector employees aged over 65 years on the basis of their age was declared invalid by the Estonian Supreme Court (Feifs et al. 2013). Most of the analyzed Central and Eastern European countries introduced active aging strategies much later than many of the "old-European" countries. Older people as a separate target group of national social policy were not distinguished in the official strategic documents of the analyzed countries till 2008 or even later.

The content of the strategic documents can also vary from declarative to program-like documents. Polish national strategic document (Solidarity between the Generations: Actions for Increasing Occupational Activity of People Aged 50+ (2008–2020)) is aimed at improving the working conditions, promoting employment of people over 50 and developing of age management strategies. According to Feifs et al. (2013)

the implementation of the strategy has already shown practical results in the fields of vocational training, counseling, entrepreneurship and information measures. Subsidies to the civil society organizations defending the needs of senior citizens were introduced in the Czech Republic (The National Program of Preparation for Ageing for 2008–2012).

The national strategic documents from the other countries usually focused on broad societal groups and envisage general employment and well-being aims. For example, in Hungary, the National Reform Program (2012) aimed at increasing the activity rate and improving the health status of the active population. In Estonia, strategic documents aim to support active aging through a variety of measures including lifelong learning and health promotion, and in Bulgaria, to create conditions for active and dignified life by promoting equal opportunities.

Working conditions. The new EU member states usually show poor working conditions, low job quality indicators, and low wage levels (Erhel and Guergoat-Larivière 2011). The development of job quality in 1995–2010 in Eastern European countries characterized by the low job discretion, cognitive demand, workload, and working time quality, as well as high work risks (European Foundation for the Improvement of Living and Working Conditions 2015). The job discretion characteristics are closely related with the possibility of managing family and work responsibilities as "the care for the elderly was mostly done by the family and state care would only intervene if the family could not afford it or if there was no family (European Foundation for the Improvement of Living and Working Conditions 2015a)."

The problem of reconciliation work and family responsibilities is closely related with the flexible working time. The limited access to flexible work arrangements for older people prevents them from the extension of working life. For example, this kind of barrier is unsolved in Lithuania: the Labour Code of the Republic of Lithuania does not provide opportunities for older people to work shorter hours, neither are older workers granted any special privileges in the case of setting part-time work at their workplace, neither part-time work is very common in Estonia. The main reason behind the low use of part-time work there is the taxation system. Employers, therefore, are not motivated to hire part-time workers. Flexible employment is not common also in the case of the Hungarian elderly population (Feifs 2013). In Bulgaria, the limited social security and low level of pay are the impediments to a higher flexibility of the working time, part-time, or temporary employment (Dimitrova 2007).

Organizational strategies. As was defined in the literature analysis, the organizational strategies can vary broadly from technological and managerial adjustments to the needs of older employees to their skills upgrading. However, the lack of comparable data on organizational strategies for the prolongation of working life of the older employees unable us to make a detail analysis of the situation in selected countries. On the other hand, we can see the general trends in the developments of institutional characteristics of lifelong learning where governments introduce different supportive measures to involve employers and employees into training activities.

The high gender segregation and low levels of training are among the common features of the Central and Eastern European countries (Erhel and Guergoat-Larivière 2011), though it should be stressed that during the analyzed period (2008–2010), in the majority of countries, the percentage of people in employment who are involved in training experienced a small decrease (European Foundation for the Improvement of Living and Working Conditions 2011). As the employers (especially those of SMEs) were not willing to provide training (the main reason according the survey being that "in the long term, they do not consider this as a good investment"), different state-supportive policies such as the short-time work/temporary lay-off schemes and training activities were introduced in some of the analyzed countries (the Czech Republic, Lithuania, Poland, Slovenia). However, as was showed in European Foundation for the Improvement of Living and Working Conditions report (2011), the proportion of companies benefiting from them is rather limited.

Together with the specific anticrisis lifelong policy measures the analyzed countries implementing general policies supporting training costs and/or wages for enterprises: the national EDUCA program aimed to help enterprises to carry out training activities for their employees or for employers themselves in some selected National Association of Corrosion Engineers (NACE) sectors in the Czech Republic (since 2009), the Estonian national program "Support for development of knowledge and skills" aimed to promote the participation of enterprises in job-related training activities, use of consultancy services for training purposes, and participation in professional conferences (since 2008), the Lithuanian national support measure to subsidize enterprises carrying out in-house training activities for employees affected by the notice of dismissal or for the temporary secondment of these employees to other enterprises to acquire missing skills, and national support for training activities carried out by enterprises regulated by the Law on Employment Services in Slovakia.

To summarize, the active aging policy in Central and Eastern European countries started later than in Western European countries. The active aging policy instruments in the region are lifelong learning, wage subsidies, vocational training, higher protection from dismissal, healthy working life, and so on.

The next chapter provides the analysis of the reasons that are important to make decisions to work and to retire after the retirement age.

Decision to Work or Retire in Central and Eastern European Countries

Employment Protection

Job security issues can hamper or promote the longer performance in the labor market. As can be noticed from ESS5 data, the respondents who gave higher preferences to job security (variable "important if choosing a job: secure job") more often belong to the groups that are willing to retire in Lithuania, the Czech Republic, Slovenia, and Poland. However, an opposite situation (when people for whom a secure job is important more often decide to stay in the labor market) is noticed in Bulgaria, Estonia, Slovakia, and Hungary. Probably the preferences for the secure job are related to the higher employment insecurity in the mentioned countries and prevent to continue in paid work after the official age of retirement.

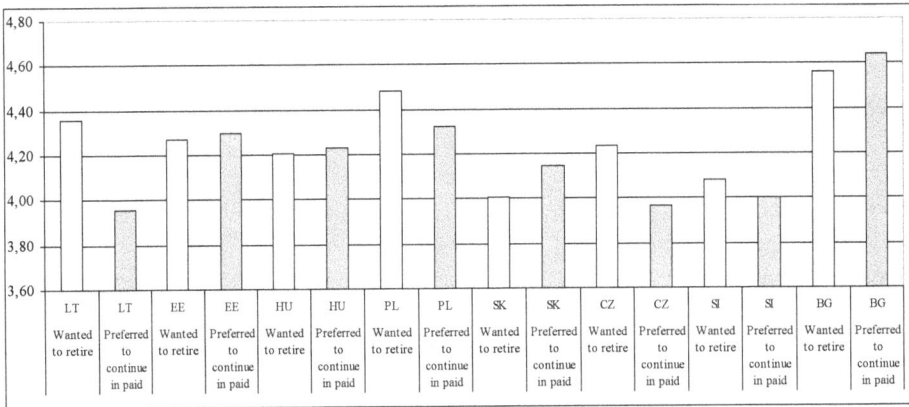

Figure 1. Wanted to retire and preferred to continue in paid work by the variable "important if choosing job: secure job" (mean value, 5 original categories from "not important at all" (1) to "very important" (5); ESS 5)

The data also showed that among hired people (employees), there is the highest proportion of those who would like to stop working after the official retirement age. It can be closely related to the flexible working arrangements that are more acceptable for the people who want to continue in employment and usually unavailable within employee position.

The opinions of the self-employed were distributed equally, that is, they want to both work and to retire, except Poland where a greater number of the self-employed want to retire, probably because these persons are mostly agricultural workers. Occupation in the agricultural sector is usually related to the heavy physical workload that increases the probability of retiring.

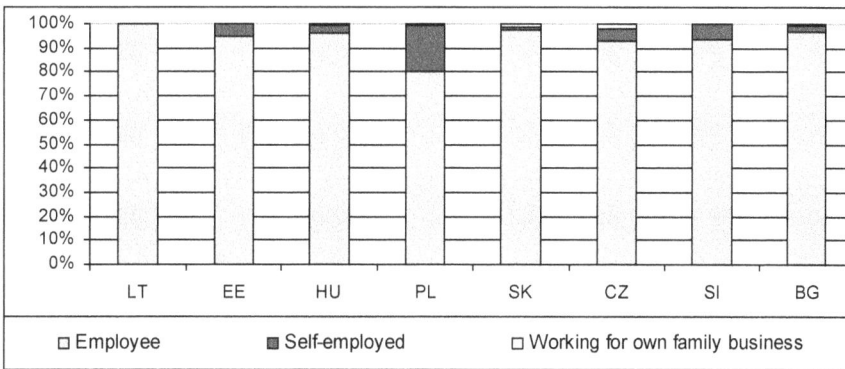

Figure 2. Wanted to retire by the type of employment relation (%, ESS5)

The major differences noticeable in the countries according to the variable "what type of organization work/worked for" were between the representatives of the public and private sectors. In Lithuania, the public sector employment is more than 30% of total employment, whereas in Bulgaria, as well as in Hungary, Slovenia, Poland, Bulgaria, Estonia, Slovakia, it is between 20% and 30%. This share is less than 20% in the Czech Republic and Romania (Sirovátka, Greve, and Hora 2011).

Among the respondents who are willing to stay in paid work, the share of those working in the public sector and state-owned enterprises is slightly higher in Bulgaria (74% and 66%, respectively) and Lithuania (80% and 74%, respectively).

In Slovenia, Poland, Hungary, and Estonia the share of the people from the private sector who preferred to continue in paid work was higher (22%, 20%, 31% and 30% respectively)

ESS 5 data suggest that, in the Czech Republic and Slovakia, the sector (public or private) has little influence on the preference to stay or leave from employment in old age.

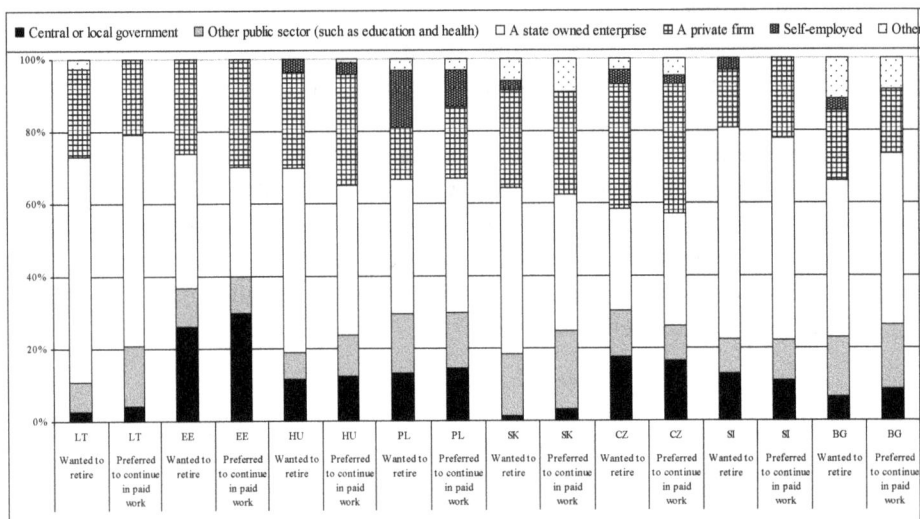

Figure 3. Wanted to retire and preferred to continue in paid work by the type of organization they work/worked for (%, ESS5)

This may be related to the possibilities of flexible working conditions: the private sector (including self-employment) allows more balancing between family and work, whereas the public sector does not. It is also likely that the higher income of people working in the public sector allows them to enjoy higher retirement pensions and, thus, they feel more secure in older age, which makes the decision to retire easier. In 2010, in most analyzed countries, the average hourly earnings in the public sector were higher than those in the private sector. The only exceptions are Slovakia where the hourly earnings in the private sector seem to be higher and Hungary where there are lower public wages, though the difference was minor (less than 3%) (de Castro, Salto, and Steiner 2013).

The limited duration of the contract can also be involuntary (insecure employment). While analyzing two groups of respondents who that wanted to retire and those who preferred to continue in paid work based on the type of the contract, the major differences are noticeable in Slovakia, Slovenia, Bulgaria, and Estonia where, among those who preferred to work, the share of people with limited contracts is higher: respectively 2% and 6% in Slovakia, 2% and 5% in Slovenia, and 3% and 5% in Bulgaria and Estonia.

Slovak and Slovenian employees in temporary employment feel more secure in the labor market. Eurostat data show the positive response of the population to the employment in the countries where social policies were implemented: 74.6% of the temporary employed Slovaks and 40.6% of Slovenians aged 55–74 didn't want a permanent job in 2010. And oppositely, the inability to find the permanent job can also influence the decision of Bulgarians and Estonians to work longer. According to Eurostat, 83.4% of temporary employed Bulgarians and 62% of Estonians in age 55–74 couldn't find permanent job. So even if the limited contract ensures more instability in the labor market, it can encourage employees to work longer after retirement.

Job security, the type of organization, and the type of employment contract show that, in the Central and Eastern European countries, there is still some space for policy instruments related to the higher employment protection of older employees.

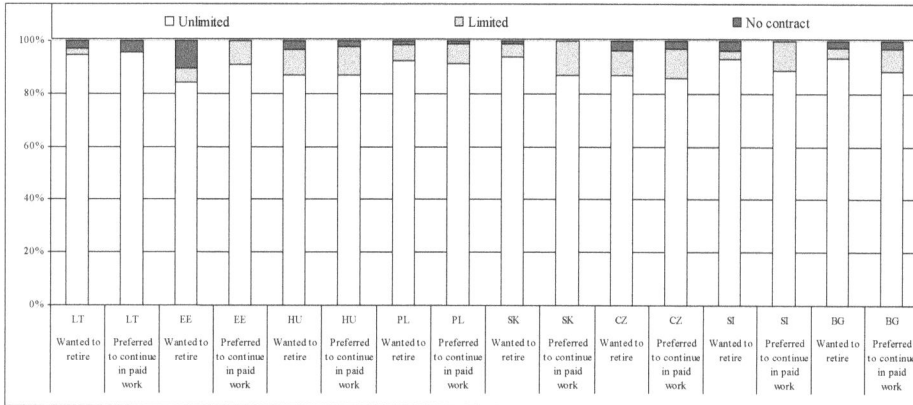

Figure 4. Wanted to retire and preferred to continue in paid work by the type of the contract (%, ESS5)

Working Conditions

Income from work. In general, the importance of high income from work is seen in all analyzed countries for both groups of respondents. The respondents from Bulgaria, Estonia, and Slovenia preferred to continue in paid work, and they pointed out that high income is important for choosing a job. Hence, low wages and also low retirement provision in these countries are the constraining obstacles for the decision to work.

Hours worked. The respondents from Poland and Slovenia work longer hours per week (more than 45). In Central and Eastern European countries, those who work overtime, in general, preferred

to retire. The results from Poland confirm the findings from Szubert and Sobala (2005) about overtime work as a risk factor for early retirement.

However, there are two exceptions—respondents who work for longer hours in Slovenia and Hungary are willing to stay in the labor market for longer duration. This may be related to the previous topic of the well-paid job as the level of the incomes from work in these countries was higher among the analyzed countries. So we assume that in order to get higher incomes, the population of these countries is ready to meet more demanding working conditions, such as slightly longer work hours.

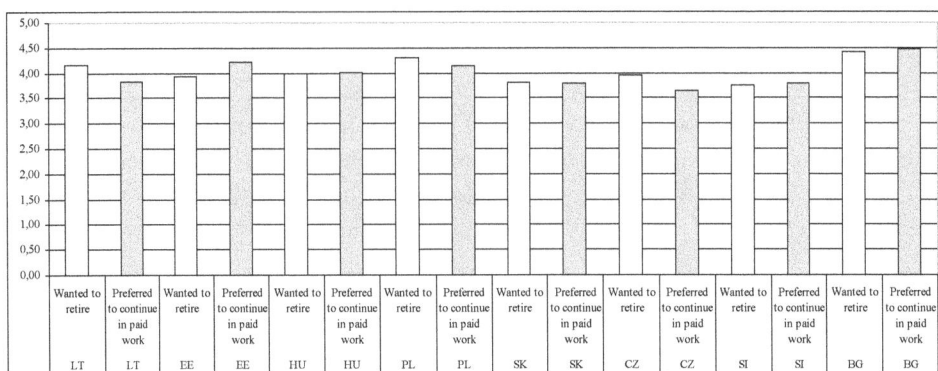

Figure 5. Wanted to retire and preferred to continue in paid work by the variable "important if choosing job: high income" (mean value, 5 original categories from "not important at all" (1) to "very important" (5); ESS5)

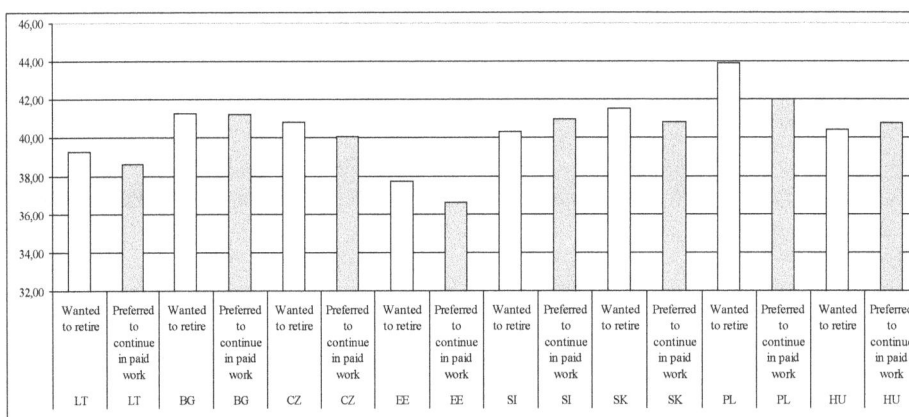

Figure 7. Wanted to retire and preferred to continue in paid work by the variable "total hours normally worked per week in main job overtime included" (hours, ESS5)

Daily work organization. Slovenians, Bulgarians, and Lithuanians who preferred to continue in paid work gave more importance to the variable "allowed to decide how daily work is organized." Seemingly, the possibility of choosing the pace of work independently can also influence the prolongation of work life in the countries in question: the respondents from Bulgaria, Slovenia, Lithuania, and Estonia who liked to work longer also chose the variable "allowed to choose/change the pace of work" more often.

The lack of flexible work arrangements that was stressed in previous sections reflected in the results from the EES5. So the broader possibilities of managing work time could rise the motivation of older people to participate in the labor market longer. This finding is closely related with the work-life management problem. Further analysis shows that in Lithuania, Estonia, and Bulgaria those issues are more pronounced.

Work/ life balance. The possibility of managing both family and work life can influence the decision to withdraw from the labor market or to stay longer in it. Seemingly, in Lithuania, Poland, Slovenia, and Bulgaria, there are fewer opportunities to reach the balance between the work and family life for those who would like to continue in paid work.

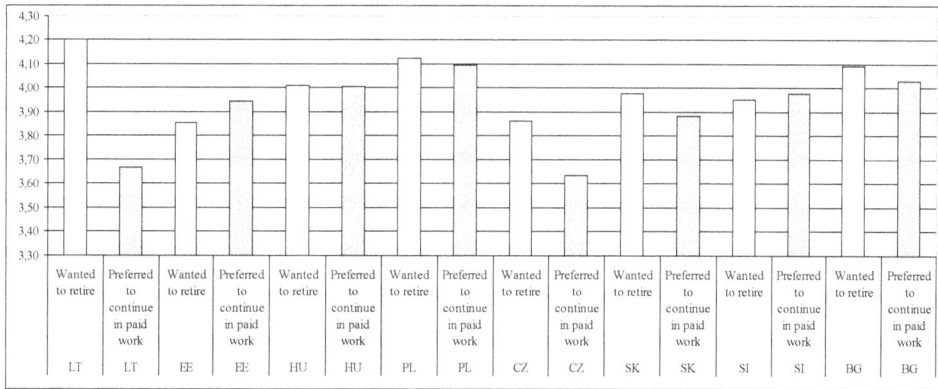

Figure 8. Wanted to retire and preferred to continue in paid work by the variable "important for choosing a job: job allowed you to combine work/family life" (mean value, 5 original categories from "not important at all" (1) to "very important" (5); ESS5)

The implementation of family–work reconciliation measures at the level of enterprises is less developed in Central and Eastern European countries. The proportion of women and men who reported their work hours fit well or very well, their demands from the private life are much less than that in EU-27 and especially less than that in Northern European countries (77.9% and 89.6%, respectively) (European Foundation for the Improvement of Living and Working Conditions 2012a).

According to Eurobarometer (76.2), family care obligations can cause withdrawal from the labor market of working people aged 55+. Family care obligations push a bigger share of older population to stop working in Romania, Bulgaria, Hungary, and Poland (this factor was very important for, respectively, 26%, 25%, 24%, and 21% of the respondents). In the case of older employees, the family care obligations are usually related to the need to take care of older parents/relatives. According to Eurostat, the expenditures on care for the elderly (2012, % of GDP) in these countries (except Hungary—0.5%) and in Baltics were the lowest: less than 0.2% of GDP, while average expenditure on care for elderly in the EU28 was 0.5%. And (as was previously mentioned) the individuals/families are mostly responsible for the care.

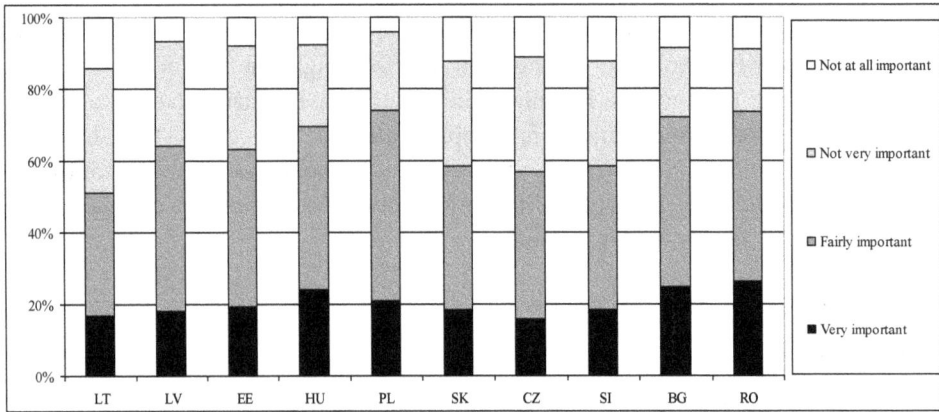

Figure 9. Respondents by the variable "aged 55+ stop working: family care obligations" (%, Eurobarometer 76.2)

Organizational Strategies

Human resource practices. A higher level of responsibility at work has an influence on the longer working life. In almost all analyzed countries (except Slovakia, Poland, and Estonia), the share of the respondents that are responsible for supervising other employees is higher among those who are willing to continue in a paid work. The willingness is related not only to the higher autonomy at work but also to the higher salaries that people responsible for supervising get from work.

Participation in organizational activities (variable "allowed to influence policy decisions about activities of organization") is more important for working life prolongation in Slovenia, Lithuania, and Bulgaria as well. The importance of showing own initiative at work is more important for longer working life for the respondents from Bulgaria and Estonia (variable "important if choosing a job: job enabled you to use own initiative") (ESS5).

In the case of older employees, the supervision of other employees reflects the higher formal position in the organization and, respectively, higher remuneration, which increases chances to stay longer at the job. However, the other different human resource practices (e.g., the transition of the skills and knowledge to the younger colleagues, active involvement/participation activities, fair acknowledgment, and consideration) that show the positive attitude of the employer toward older employees may also positively influence the decision to prolong working life (that proves the findings from Davey 2008; Harper et al. 2006; Hellemans and Closon 2013; Santa, 2011).

An opportunity to get *training at work* can possibly influence the decision to stay or withdraw from the labor market in older age. A higher number of those, who noted that the job offered good training opportunities, preferred to continue in paid work was in Estonia, Hungary, Slovenia, Poland. However, the opposite distribution of respondents was in Lithuania, Slovakia, and the Czech Republic.

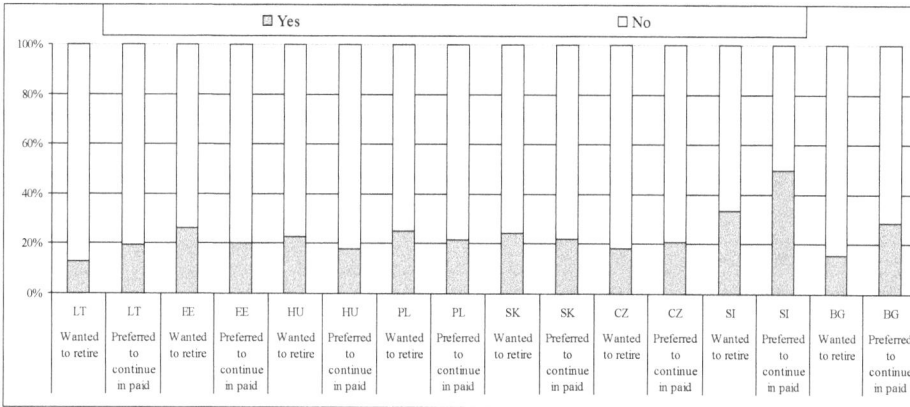

Figure 6. Wanted to retire and preferred to continue in paid work by the variable "responsible for supervising other employees" (%, ESS5)

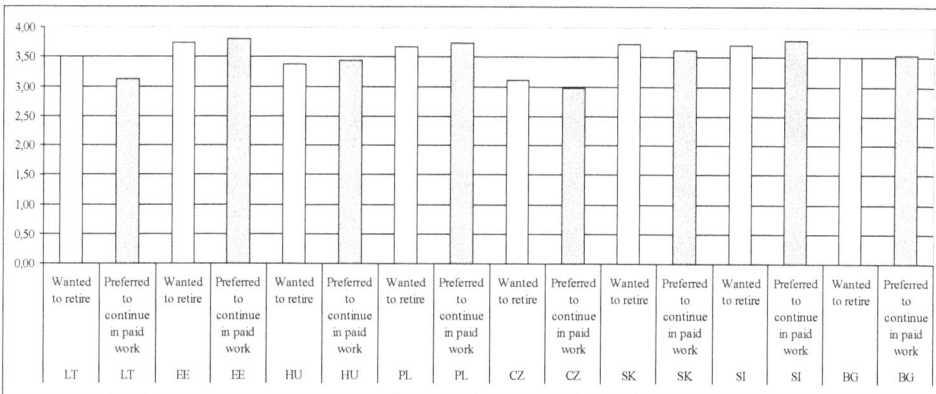

Figure 10. Wanted to retire and preferred to continue in paid work by the variable "important for choosing a job: job offered good training opportunities" (mean value, 5 original categories from "not important at all" (1) to "very important" (5); ESS5)

The actual participation in lifelong learning in selected countries is poor. Only the respondents from Slovenia reported more often that they participated in different kinds of training programs during the last 12 months.

Only in the Czech Republic and Slovakia, the respondents who received training more often belong to the group of the respondents that are willing to stay longer in the labor market. In other analyzed countries, the situation is opposite (see Table 1). We relate it to the fact that training opportunities more often are offered for the employees in the public sector, and less in the private one.

Table 1. Wanted to retire and preferred to continue in paid work by the variable "Improve knowledge/skills: course/lecture/conference, last 12 months" (ESS5)

	LT	LT	EE	EE	HU	HU	PL	PL	SK	SK	CZ	CZ	SI	SI	BG	BG
	Wanted to retire	Preferred to continue in paid work	Wanted to retire	Preferred to continue in paid work	Wanted to retire	Preferred to continue in paid work	Wanted to retire	Preferred to continue in paid work	Wanted to retire	Preferred to continue in paid work	Wanted to retire	Preferred to continue in paid work	Wanted to retire	Preferred to continue in paid work	Wanted to retire	Preferred to continue in paid work
Yes	3.5	0	3.3	1.7	0.3	1.2	3.9	0	1.8	2.4	1.7	2.5	5.3	3.8	0.6	0
No	96.5	100.0	96.7	98.3	99.7	98.8	96.1	100.0	98.2	97.6	98.3	97.5	94.7	96.3	99.4	100.0

Where: W—Wanted to retire; P—Preferred to continue in paid work

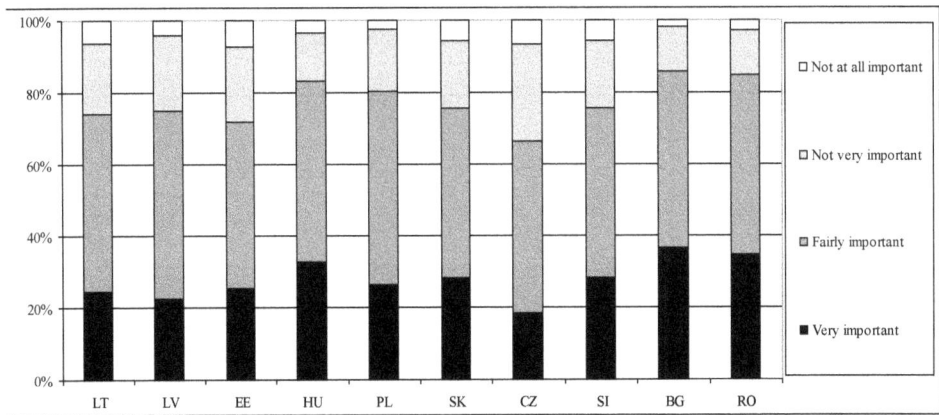

Figure 11. Respondents by the variable "aged 55+ stop working: exclusion from training" (%, Eurobarometer 76.2)

The importance of participation in training for working life prolongation is observed from the Eurobarometer 76.2 survey. Exclusion from training can push older employees from the labor market. About 80% of the respondents from the selected countries feel threatened by this (considering the answers "very important" and "fairly important"). The respondents from Bulgaria, Romania, and Hungary are especially concerned about being excluded from lifelong learning activities (the respective share of the answers "very important" is 37%, 35%, and 33%).

While comparing the two groups of the Eurobarometer survey, participants according to their willingness to work or not to work after pension entitlement, the exclusion from training in the older age can be a reason to stop working for Bulgarians, Hungarians, Slovenians, and Romanians (the answers "very important"). In these countries, the significant state supportive policies in the field of promotion of lifelong learning were absent during the analyzed period.

The recent crisis brought serious transformations to the structure of the economies in the analyzed countries. However, the structural changes in new EU member states have generally been greater than that in the majority of old EU members with broader shifts from industry toward services (Havlik 2014).

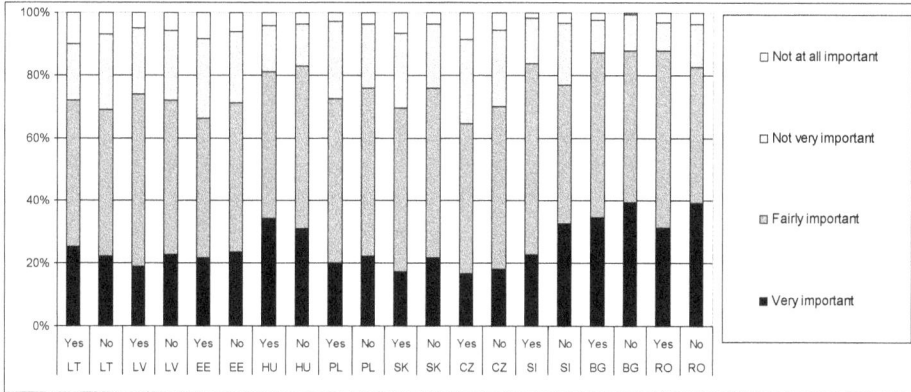

Figure 12. Respondents who like (yes) and who don't like (no) to work after pension entitlement by the variable "aged 55+ stop working: exclusion from training" (%, Eurobarometer 76.2).

With regard to the structural changes as well due to the process of technological change (including the transfer of technologies between countries and regions) (Cörvers and Meriküll 2007), the need for more qualified labor force is envisaged in the nearest future—both in Western and in Central and Eastern Europe. As CEEDEFOP (2010) indicates, most countries will show a significant reduction of the share of low-qualified people in the labor force. It is also predicted that most countries will reduce the overall share of low-skilled people mainly as a result of the age cohort effect.

The recent crisis also influenced the growing labor productivity and declining employment in manufacturing, especially in Hungary, Romania, and the Baltic states (Havlik 2014). This explained how exclusion from training/retraining can prevent a large share of low and medium skilled employed population from the participation in the labor market.

While talking about aging workforce, the *job place adjustment* appears as one of the solutions for the prolongation of working life of older employees. However, as data from Eurobarometer (76.2) show, generally the importance of the job place being adapted to the needs of aging employees seems less important than training opportunities. In addition to this, the respondents from analyzed countries have a different view on the opportunities led by the adjusted job places. Hungarians are much more concerned about how their jobs are adapted (43% chose the answer "very important" in comparison with average 24%). It can be related to the demand to continue to work after retirement and the lack of flexible employment in this country. So, the job adaptation could compensate the lack of flexible working time arrangements. Especially, in this case, the security to stay in the same job is widespread in Hungary.

While comparing those who would like and who would not like to work after pension entitlement, it is noticeable that not adapted jobs can be more important for Slovenian and Hungarian employees and, thus, can prevent them from the prolongation of working life.

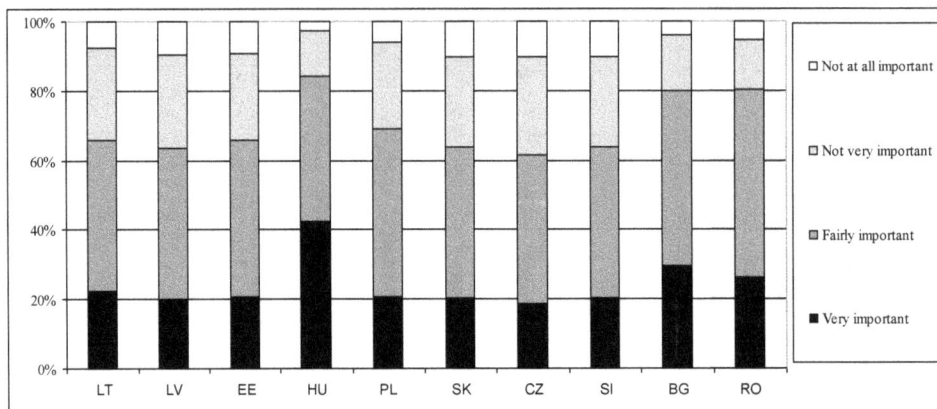

Figure 13. Respondents by the variable "aged 55+ stop working: place not adapted" (%, Eurobarometer 76.2)

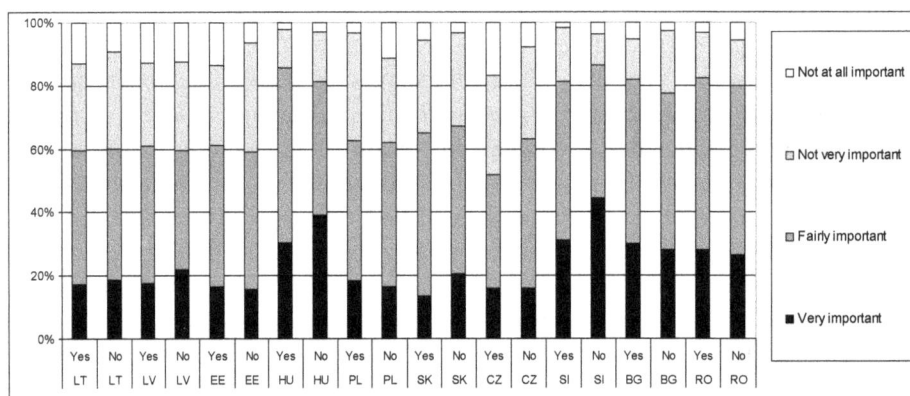

Figure 14. Respondents who like (yes) and who do not like (no) to work after pension entitlement by variable "aged 55+ stop working: place not adapted" (%, Eurobarometer)

As was mentioned in the first part of the paper, the *employers' attitudes* toward older workers can considerably improve the situation of older people in the labor market. The data from the Eurobarometer 76.2 show that the view of employers can be one of the major factors that influence withdrawal from the working life in old age. According to the opinion of the vast majority of the respondents, the view of employers is very important or fairly important while taking a decision to stop working. This factor is more important for the Hungarians, Bulgarians, and Romanians (a respective share of the answers "very important" is 48%, 44%, and 42%).

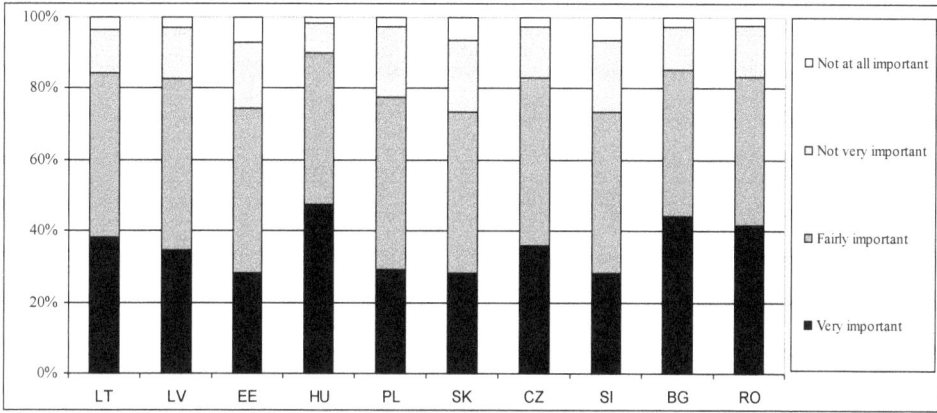

Figure 15. The respondents by the variable "aged 55+ stop working: view of employers" (%, Eurobarometer)

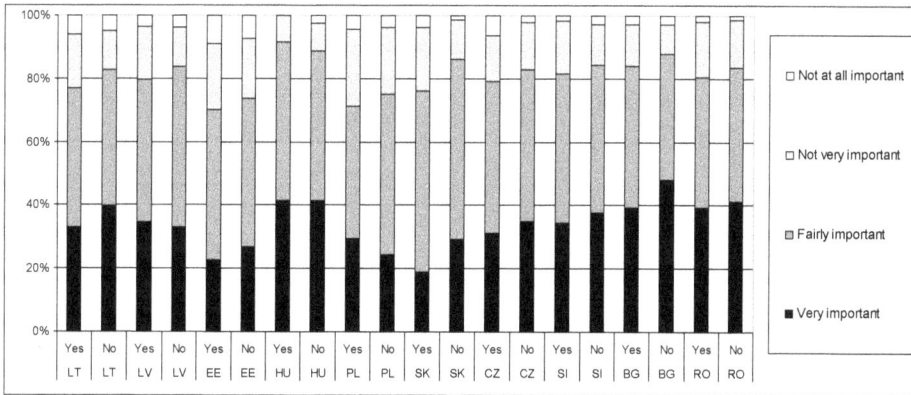

Figure 16. Respondents who like (yes) and who do not like (no) to work after pension entitlement by variable "aged 55 + stop working: view of employers" (%, Eurobarometer)

It is observed that, in general, the view of employers toward the old age employee is an influential factor in the analyzed Central and Eastern European countries. As a factor that can prevent from the prolongation of working life, it is more recognized by the respondents from Bulgaria, Lithuania, Slovakia (the difference between the shares of two groups of the respondent while choosing the answer "very important"). It can be related to the facts that employers do not always enact regulations, employees do not initiate individual claims against employers for fear of losing their jobs, and the coverage of trade unions is low. A fixed term work is a widespread form of employment. In the Lithuania, a significant proportion of employees work without a written contract. These circumstances determine that the view of the employer is important to the decision to work or retire.

Table 2. The variables influencing the decision "like to work after pension entitlement"

Country	Variable	Category	B coefficient
The probability of liking to work after pension entitlement increased if			
Bulgaria	Aged 55+ work qualities: creativity	"Somewhat less likely"	0.546
Czech Republic	Aged 55+ stop working: places not adapted"	"Very important"	0.753
		"Fairly important"	1.034
		"Not very important"	0.679
Hungary	Age discrimination at work: experienced	"Not mentioned"	0.701
Poland	Aged 55+ work qualities: decision making	"Somewhat less likely"	0.566
Romania	Age discrimination education: experienced	"Not mentioned"	1.635
Slovenia	Aged 55+ work qualities: productivity	"Somewhat more likely"	0.543
		"No difference"	1.038
		"Somewhat less likely"	0.988
Slovakia	Aged 55+ stop working: lack of modern skills	"Very important"	0.749
	Aged 55+ stop working: view of employers		1.105
		"Very important"	0.937
		"Fairly important"	0.593
		"Not very important"	
The probability of liking to work after pension entitlement decreased was respectively			
Bulgaria	Aged 55+ work qualities: up to date	"Much more likely"	−1.185
		"Somewhat more likely"	−0.909
	Aged 55+ work qualities: decision making	"Much more likely"	−1.894
		"Somewhat more likely"	−1.133
		"No difference"	−1.14
			−1.923
		"Much more likely"	−1.484
	Aged 55+ work qualities: teamwork ability	"Somewhat more likely"	−1.624
		"No difference"	
			−0.648
		"No difference"	
	Aged 55+ work qualities: cultural competence		
Estonia	Aged 55+ work qualities: experience	"Much more likely"	−0.779
	Aged 55+ work qualities: flexibility	"Much more likely"	−0.945
		"Somewhat more likely"	−1.413
		"No difference"	−1.182
		"Somewhat less likely"	−0.771
Hungary	Aged 55+ work qualities: up to date	"Somewhat more likely"	−0.604
	Aged 55+ work qualities: creativity	"Much more likely"	−1.763
		"Somewhat more likely"	−1.306
		"No difference"	−1.306
		"Somewhat less likely"	−0.924
			−0.574
	Aged 55+ work qualities: open to new ideas	"Much more likely"	
Lithuania	Aged 55+ work qualities: stress handling	"Much more likely"	−0.808
		"Somewhat more likely"	−0.663
	Aged 55+ work qualities: experience	"Much more likely"	−0.804
		"Somewhat more likely"	−0.746
Latvia	Aged 55+ stop working: lack of modern skills	"Very important"	−1.006
		"Fairly important"	−0.533
		"Not very important"	−0.582
Poland	Aged 55+ work qualities: productivity	"Much more likely"	−1.601
		"Somewhat more likely"	−0.947
		"No difference"	−0.812
Slovenia	Aged 55+ stop working: lack of modern skills		
		"Fairly important"	−0.665
		"Not very important"	−0.893
	Aged 55+ work qualities: creativity	"Much more likely"	−1.010
	Aged 55+ work qualities: decision making	"Much more likely"	−1.050
		"Somewhat more likely"	−1.174
		"No difference"	−1.076
Slovakia	Age discrimination at work: experienced	"Mentioned"	−1.090
	Aged 55+ work qualities: creativity	"Much more likely"	−0.578

Three major groups of the factors that have influence on the willingness to participate or withdraw from the labor market were highlighted from the analysis: work qualities (creativity, productivity; decision making; teamwork ability; stress handling; open to new ideas; cultural competence); stop working because of the lack of modern skills; places not adapted; discrimination (at work and in education).

Willingness to work after the age of retirement is higher when discrimination at work and education was not experienced. The low importance of such work qualities as creativity, decision making also increases the chances to work longer, while the productivity issue is distributed differently from important to not important. At the same time, the probability of stopping working career is higher when the view of the employer is very important, when there is a lack of modern skills and when the work place is not adapted.

The wish to work after official age or retirement and being entitled for old-age pension is lower when factors such as flexibility, creativity, openness to new ideas, decision making, and teamwork ability are important.

The complexities of work qualities reflect various characteristics of work productivity, which are important for the labor market: the preservation of the characteristics of work quality or work productivity as well as the lack of modern skills and inability to update professional competencies due to lifelong learning policy in the region. Hence, one can state that lifelong learning in the entire Central and Eastern European regions is insufficient for the preservation of the productivity of work. In addition to this, the statistical data on lifelong learning and

continuing vocational education present the poor performance of the Central and Eastern European countries. For example, the job quality index on skills and career development (European Trade Union Institute 2013) shows that all of these countries, except for Slovenia, in 2010 performed below the EU average. The values of Romania, Lithuania, Slovakia, and Hungary are below 0.1, and, thus, show very poor results on this subindex (in comparison to Denmark whose value is close to 0.9).

Although there is no statistical data on employers' investment into the job place adjustments, we can assume that the situation in the analyzed region is similar to the situation of lifelong learning. As Eurostat data show, the percentage of all the nontraining enterprises in selected countries is usually higher than that in other EU countries. There are two main reasons for this: the existing skills and competences of the persons employed corresponded to the current needs of the enterprise and the training is too expensive (the last reason being more important in Bulgaria, Poland, and the Baltic countries, see Table 3). Hence, the companies tried to recruit people with the required skills rather than investing in training or job-place adjustment to enhance the skills and productivity of their existing workforce.

The work places not adapted can prevent longer work life as the data of the Czech Republic show. As was mentioned in the theoretical part of the paper, the workplace adaptation is particularly needed for manual and unskilled job (Conen, Henkens, and Schippers 2012). As statistical data from Eurostat show, in the Czech Republic, as compared to the other Central and Eastern European countries, the number of people employed

Table 3. The percentage of all nontraining enterprises, according to the reasons for not providing CVT, 2010

	Total	Too expensive	Either focus on IVT than CVT	Major training effort realized in a previous year	The existing skills and competences of the persons employed corresponded to the current needs of the enterprise
European Union (28 countries)	34	31	25	12	77
Bulgaria	69	49	37	8	77
Czech Republic	28	10	2	7	72
Estonia	32	47	14	14	65
Latvia	60	47	34	16	82
Lithuania	48	68	11	11	84
Hungary	51	15	4	1	73
Poland	78	43	39	16	81
Romania	76	30	1	3	64
Slovenia	32	41	31	30	88
Slovakia	31	32	34	25	85

Source: Eurostat

is higher in such physical work demanding sectors, such as mining and quarrying, construction, transport, and storage.

The factor that reflects direct discrimination experience at work or education was significantly influential only in Hungary, Romania, and Slovakia. The discrimination experienced lowers the willingness to work in older age and, on the other hand, positive experience enhances longer participation in the labor market. However, as was noticed in the previous analysis, the respondents recognize the influential role of the employer (the view of employer) for the prolongation of working life (that coincides with Harper's et al. (2006) and Davey's (2008) conclusions). Unfortunately, the prevailing view of the employers toward older working people is still unfavorable. Hence, we can maintain that organizational policies (including the provision of training opportunities, adjustment of the work place, antidiscrimination actions) are the main fields to promote longer participation in the labor market in old age.

Conclusions

The research analyzing the decision of the persons employed to continue with their current work career after the retirement age looks into various circumstances that may influence this decision. One of the institutional features is the importance of working conditions for the willingness to work after the retirement age. It is usually stated that the organization of work and the improvement of the working conditions have not only a positive effect on the health of the persons in employment, but they also increase their willingness to continue with their working career after the retirement age. The analysis of the employment protection emphasizes the different measures applied for older age persons in employment and criticizes the limit of the established retirement age, which serves as an impetus to withdraw from the labor market. The organizational policy aiming at employees' work satisfaction, a positive employer's attitude could also encourage continuing their working career. The issue of work productivity is one of the main reasons for the prolongation of the working career of older age persons. The productivity of work is usually associated with the accessibility of lifelong learning and with the complex set of job adjustment characteristics.

Even though Central and Eastern European countries adopted the active aging strategies later than Western European countries, the policy aiming at the implementation of these strategies comprises the general mainstream: lifelong learning, wage subsidies, vocational training, flexible work arrangements, healthy working life, and higher protection of dismissal.

In the context of the aging society, to prolong the participation of older age persons in the labor market and to balance the labor force supply and demand, it is obvious that these policy means are not sufficient in Central and Eastern European countries and their application is patchy. The overall labor market policy for all persons in employment faces challenges since the decision of persons to continue with their work career after the retirement age faces a number of problems of poor work conditions, such as working overtime, lack of autonomy at work and family–work imbalance, and the view of the employer that is not yet positive. The economic situation of the countries that is overall poor is a coercive rather than motivational measure for the prolongation of working career, and work pay is one of the factors that encourage

to work. The gaps of participation and active aging policy, such as participation in lifelong learning and training opportunities as the main presumptions to preserve labor productivity, have not been filled yet. The services of supervision are not sufficient; hence, family care obligations make persons withdraw from the market. Inadequate effectiveness of the antidiscrimination policy also determines the wish to retire and discontinue the working career in Central and Eastern European countries.

References

Aidukaitė, Jolanta. 2004. "The emergence of the post-socialist welfare state—The case of the Baltic states: Estonia, Latvia and Lithuania." Doctoral dissertation. Stockholms Universitet.

Aidukaitė, Jolanta. 2009. "The Welfare System of Lithuania." In *The Handbook of European Welfare Systems, eds. Klaus Schubert, Simon Hegelich, and Ursula Bazant*. London ; New York : Routledge, 294–309.

Armstrong- Stassen, Marjorie. 2008. "Organisational Practices and the Post Retirement Employment Experience of Older Workers." *Human Resource Management Journal* 18 (1): 36–53.

Barbier, Jean-Claude, Ralf Rogowski, and Fabrive Colomb, eds. 2015. *The Sustainability of the European Social Model: EU Governance, Social Protection and Employment Policies in Europe*. Edward Elgar Publishing. Cheltenham UK, Northampton USA.

Bloom, David E., David Canning, and Günther Fink. 2010. "Implications of Population Ageing for Economic Growth." *Oxford Review of Economic Policy* 26 (4): 583–612.

Bohle, Dorothee, and Béla Greskovits. 2007. "Neoliberalism, Embedded Neoliberalism and Neocorporatism: Towards Transnational Capitalism in Central-Eastern Europe." *West European Politics* 30 (3):443–466.

Bukodi, Erzsébet, Ellen Ebralidze, Paul Schmelzer, and Ilona Relikowski. 2006. Increasing Flexibility at Labour Market Entry and in the Early Career. *Flex Career working paper.* http://www.flexcareer.de/papers/no6.pdf (accessed December 8, 2015).

Cazes, Sandrine, and Alena Nesporova. 2004. "Labour Market in Transition: Balancing Flexibility and Security in Central and Eastern Europe." *Labour Market in Transition.* Special issue: April 2004. International Labour Office.

Chéron, Arnaud, Jean-Olivier Hairault, and François Langot. 2011. "Age-Dependent Employment Protection." *The Economic Journal* 121 (557): 1477–1504. https://hal.archives-ouvertes.fr/hal-00623282/document

Conen, Wieteke S., Kène Henkens, and Joop Schippers. 2012. "Employers' Attitudes and Actions Towards the Extension of Working Lives in Europe." *International Journal of Manpower* 33 (6): 648–665.

Cörvers, Frank, and Jaanika Meriküll. 2007. "Occupational Structures across 25 EU Countries: The Importance of Industry Structure and Technology in Old and New EU Countries." *Economic Change and Restructuring* 40(4): 327–359.

Costa, Giovanni, Samantha Sartori, and Torbjorn Åkerstedt. 2006. "Influence of Flexibility and Variability of Working hours on Health and Well-Being." *Chronobiology International* 23 (6): 1125–1137.

Davey, Judith. 2008. "What Influences Retirement Decisions?" *Social Policy Journal of New Zealand* 33: 110–125.

de Castro, Francisco, Matteo Salto, and Hugo Steiner. 2013. *The Gap between Public and Private Wages: New Evidence for the EU.* No. 508. Directorate General Economic and Financial Affairs (DG ECFIN), European Commission. Brussels.

Dimitrova, Snezhanka. 2007. *"Quality in Work and Employment—Bulgaria."* European Foundation for the Improvement of Living and Working Conditions. Observatory: EurWORK.

Domadenik, Polona, Tjaša Redek, and Irena Ograjenšek. 2009. "Slovenian Employers and the Challenge of Longer Working Life." *Revija za socijalnu politiku* 16 (2): 141–158.

Erhel, Christine, and Mathilde Guergoat-Larivière. 2011. "Job Quality: A Comparative Perspective on the Basis of EU Indicators." *WISO—Wirtschafts-und Sozialpolitische Zeitschrift.* (34): 144-159.

Esping-Andersen, Gosta. 1990. *Three Worlds of Welfare Capitalism.* Princeton, New Jersey: Princeton University Press.

European Foundation for the Improvement of Living and Working Conditions. 2011. *Preparing for the Upswing: Training and Qualification during the Crisis.* Dublin. http://www.eurofound.europa.eu/sites/default/files/ef_files/docs/ewco/tn1010023s/tn1010023s.pdf.

European Foundation for the Improvement of Living and Working Conditions. 2015. *Convergence and Divergence of Job Quality in Europe 1995–2010.* Luxembourg: Publications Office of the European Union.

European Foundation for the Improvement of Living and Working Conditions. 2015a. *Working and Caring: Reconciliation Measures in Times of Demographic Change,* Luxembourg: Publications Office of the European Union.

European Trade Union Institute. 2012. "*Job Quality in the Crisis—An Update of the Job Quality Index (JQI).*"Janine Leschke, Andrew Watt and Mairéad Finn. Working Paper 2012.07. ETUI aisbl, Brussels.

Feifs, Tom, Tina Weber, Oscar Vargas, Karel Fric, Maurizio Curtarelli, and Irene Mandl. 2013. *Role of Governments and Social Partners in Keeping Older Workers in the Labour Market.* Luxembourg: Publications Office of the European Union.

Fenger, Menno, Martijn van der Steen, and Lieske van der Torre. 2014. "The Responsiveness of Social Policies. Explaining Institutional Change in Three Policy Domains." *International Review of Administrative Sciences* 80 (3): 659–680.

Fredriksson, Magnus, Josef Pallas, and Stefan Wehmeier. 2013. "Public Relations and Neo-Institutional Theory." *Public Relations Inquiry* 2 (2): 183–203.

Ghosheh, Naj. 2008. *Age Discrimination and Older Workers: Theory and Legislation in Comparative Context.* International Labour Organization, http://www.ilo.org/wcmsp5/groups/public/---ed_protect/---protrav/---travail/documents/publication/wcms_travail_pub_19.pdf.

Harper, Sarah, Hafiz T.A. Khan, Atulya Saxena, and George Leeson. 2006. "Attitudes and Practices of Employers Towards ageing Workers: Evidence from a Global Survey on the Future of the Retirement." *Ageing Horizons* 5: 31–41.

Havlik, Peter. 2014. Structural change in Europe during the crisis. No 022. *FIW Policy Brief Series,* FIW.

Hellemans, Catherine, and Caroline Closon. 2013 "Intention to Remain at Work Until Legal Retirement Age: A Comparative Analysis Among Different Age Subgroups of Employees." *Europe's Journal of Psychology* 9 (3): 623–639.

Helman, Ruth, Maria Greenwald, Craig Copeland, Jack VanDerhei, and D. Salisbury.2008. "EBRI 2008 Recent Retirees Survey: Report of Findings." *EBRI Issue Brief* 319: 24. http://www.ebri.org/pdf/briefspdf/EBRI_IB_07-2008.pdf.

Ilmakunnas, Pekka, Jan van Ours, Vegard Skirbekk, and Matthias Weiss. 2010. "Age and Productivity." In *Ageing, Health, and Productivity: The Economics of Increased Life Expectancy,* eds. P. Garibaldi, J.O. Martins, and J. van Ours. Oxford: Oxford University Press, 133-240. http://ukcatalogue.oup.com/product/9780199587131.do.

Kang, Nahee. 2014. "Towards Middle-Range Theory Building in Development Research: Comparative (Historical) Institutional

Analysis of Institutional Transplantation." *Progress in Development Studies* 14 (3): 221–235.

Karpinska, Kasia, Kène Henkens, and Joop Schippers. 2013. "Retention of Older Workers: Impact of Managers' Age Norms and Stereotypes." *European Sociological Review* 1: 1323–1335.

Kleinman, Mark. 2002. "*European Welfare State? European Union Social Policy in Context.*" Palgrave Macmillan. Basingstoke.

Kotrusová, Miriam, and Kotrusová, Miriam, and Klára Výborná. 2015. "A Policy Fiasco: The Institutional (non-) Reform of Czech Public Employment Services in 2011." *Central European Journal of Public Policy* 9(1): 148–169. http://www.cejpp.eu/index.php/ojs/article/view/224.

Lahelma, Eero, Mikko Laaksonen, Tea Lallukka, Pekka Martikainen, Olli Pietiläinen, Peppiina Saastamoinen, Raija Gould, and Ossi Rahkonen. 2012. "Working Conditions as Risk Factors for Disability Retirement: A Longitudinal Register Linkage Study." *BMC Public Health* 12(1): 309.

Thomas B. Lawrence and Roy Suddaby (2006) Institutions and institutional work. In Stewart R. Clegg, Cynthia Hardy, Thomas B. Lawrence & Walter R. Nord (Eds.) Sage Handbook of Organization Studies, 2nd Edition: 215-254. London: Sage.

McNair, Stephen, Matt Flynn, and Nina Dutton. 2007. *Employer Responses to an Ageing Workforce: A Qualitative Study.* (No. 455). Corporate Document Services, http://www.northantsobservatory.org.uk/docs/docageingworkforce070928144858.pdf.

National Reform programme 2012 of Hungary, April 2012. http://ec.europa.eu/europe2020/pdf/nd/nrp2012_hungary_en.pdf

Pagán, Ricardo. 2013. "Job Satisfaction and Domains of Job Satisfaction for Older Workers with Disabilities in Europe." *Journal of Happiness Studies* 14(3): 861–891.

Pedersen, Axel West. 1999. "The Taming of Inequality in Retirement: A Comparative Study of Pension Policy Outcomes." *Fafo Report* 317: P474.

Piasna, Agnieszka A. 2010. "Changing Images of Retirement and the 'Flexicurity' Policy: Labour Market Flexibility, Mobility and Security in Social Dialogue on Retirement in Poland." *International Journal of Interdisciplinary Social Sciences* 5 (5):121-133.

Pierson, Paul. 2001. *The New Politics of the Welfare State.* Oxford University Press.

Pietilainen, Olli, Mikko Laaksonen, Ossi Rahkonen, and Eero Lahelma. 2011. "Self-Related Health as a Predictor of Disability Retirement—The Contribution of Ill-Health and Working Conditions." *PLos ONE* 6 (9): 1–7.

Reay, Trish, and Candace Jones. 2015. "Qualitatively Capturing Institutional Logics." *Strategic Organization,* (6/2015): 1–14.

Robroek, Suzan J.W., Anne Rongen, Coos H. Arts, Ferdy W.H. Otten, Alex Burdorf, and Merel Schuring. 2015. "Educational Inequalities in Exit from Paid Employment among Dutch Workers: The Influence of Health, Lifestyle and Work." *PloS ONE* 10(8): e0134867.

Saar, Ellu, Marge Unt, and Irena Kogan. 2008. "Transition from Educational System to Labour Market in the European Union A Comparison between New and Old Members." *International Journal of Comparative Sociology* 49 (1): 31–59.

Şanta, Carmen. 2011. "The Early Retirement on Ill Health Bases: Actual Problems in EU Member Countries." *Acta Medica Transilvanica* 16(2): 202–205.

Schwerha, Diana, Charles Ritter, Sean Robinson, Rodger W. Griffeth, and David Fried. 2011. "Integration Ergonomic Factor into Decision to Retire." *Human Resource Management Review* 21 (3): 220–227.

Siegrist, Johannes, Morten Wahrendorf, Olaf Von dem Knesebeck, Hendrik Jürges, and Axel Börsch-Supan. 2007. "Quality of Work, Well-Being, and Intended Early Retirement of Older Employees—Baseline Results from the SHARE Study." *The European Journal of Public Health* 17 (1): 62–68.

Sirovátka, Tomáš, Bent Greve, and Ondřej Hora. 2011. *Public/Private Mix and Social Innovation In Service Provision, Fiscal Policy And Employment*: European Commission, NEUJOBS State of the Art Report No. 2/ November 2011. http://www.neujobs.eu/ sites/default/files/publication/2011/11/ NEUJOBS%20SoA%20Report%20No%20 2%20Deliverable%20D7.1.pdf.

Sulitzeanu-Kenan, Raanan, and Yifat Holzman-Gazit. 2016. "Form and Content: Institutional Preferences and Public Opinion in a Crisis Inquiry." *Administration and Society* 48 (1): 3–30.

Szubert, Zuzanna, and Wojciech Sobala. 2005. "Current Determinants of Early Retirement among Blue Collar Workers in Poland." *International Journal of Occupation Medicine and Environmental Health* 18 (2): 177–184.

Tobiasz-Adamczyk, Beata, Ewa Barto-szewska, Piotr Brzyski, and Marek Kopacz. 2007. "Long-Term Consequences of Education, Working Conditions, and Health-Related Behaviors on Mortality Patterns in Older Age. A 17-Year Observational Study in Krakow, Poland." *International Journal of Occupational Medicine and Environmental Health* 20(3): 247–256.

Tonin, Mirco. 2009. "Employment Protection Legislation in Central and East European Countries." *SEER-South-East Europe Review for Labour and Social Affairs* 12 (04): 477–491.

Thornton PH, Ocasio W and Lounsbury, M. 2012. *The Institutional Logics Perspective: A New Approach to Culture, Structure and Process*. Oxford: Oxford University Press.

Ulrich, Lorene Burns. 2003. Older Workers and Bridge Employment: an Exploratory Study. http://scholar.lib.vt.edu/ theses/available/etd-03262003-083517/ unrestricted/ULRICHETD.pdf.

Virtanen, Marianna, Tuula Oksanen, G. David Batty, Leena Ala-Mursula, Paula Salo, Marko Elovainio, Jaana Pentti, Katinka Lyback, Jussi Vahtera, and Mika Kivimaki. 2014. "Extending Employment Beyond the Pensionable Age: A Cohort Study of the Influence of Chronic Diseases, Health Risk Factors, and Working Conditions." *PloS ONE* 9 (2): e88695.

Decision Trees and Random Forests: Machine Learning Techniques to Classify Rare Events

Simon Hegelich[A]

The article introduces machine learning algorithms for political scientists. These approaches should not be seen as a new method for old problems. Rather, it is important to understand the different logic of the machine learning approach. Here, data is analyzed without theoretical assumptions about possible causalities. Models are optimized according to their accuracy and robustness. While the computer can do this work more or less alone, it is the researcher's duty to make sense of these models afterward. Visualization of machine learning results, therefore, becomes very important and is in the focus of this paper. The methods that are presented and compared are decision trees, bagging, and random forests. The latter are more advanced versions of the former, relying on bootstrapping procedures. To demonstrate these methods, extreme shifts in the US budget and their connection to the attention of political actors are analyzed. The paper presents a comparison of the accuracy of different models based on ROC curves and shows how to interpret random forest models with the help of visualizations. The aim of the paper is to provide an example, how these methods can be used in political science and to highlight possible pitfalls as well as advantages of machine learning.

Keywords: Machine learning, methods, punctuated equilibrium, statistics for the 21st century

Introduction

Machine learning—the usage of computer algorithms that are changing their performance with new data—is a new tool for political scientists that can be very useful, especially in analyzing "unusual" settings such as extreme events, big data problems, or classification of rare events. The main difference between machine learning and classical statistics is the way problems are formulated. Traditional approaches in political science start with the formulation of hypothesis, creation of formal models that represent the underlying causalities, and then by the test of these models on the available data. Machine learning starts with data, tries to find hidden patterns, and then comes up with formal models that can "explain" additional cases. So, both approaches follow a quite different

[A] Technical University of Munich / Bavarian School of Public Policy, Munich, Germany

doi: 10.18278/epa.2.1.7

logic. The traditional approach is closer to our ideas about how politics work. Researchers have some expectations about causalities and try to verify or falsify these expectations empirically. Most of the time, they will end up with two values: one describing the strength of the effect (e.g., R^2) and one the certainty of these results (e.g., the significance level). In this approach, data has to be carefully selected in order to allow the generalization, which is the aim of the whole procedure.

Machine learning takes data as given. Without hardly any theoretical assumptions about the relationship between different variables, the computer tries to identify patterns and transfers these findings into a computational model. The researcher is interested in the accuracy (comparison of predicted values and real values) and the robustness (performance on new data) of the model.

> With algorithmic methods, there is no statistical model in the usual sense; no effort has been made to represent how the data were generated. And no apologies are offered for the absence of a model. There is a practical data analysis problem to solve that is attacked directly with procedures designed specifically for that purpose. (Berk 2006, 263)

These differences can be seen as strengths as well as weaknesses of the two approaches. The traditional approach is more general because it is based on expected causalities. On the other hand, the approach will hardly detect any patterns that are not connected to the former expectations. In addition,

expected causalities might even bias the results because data collection, analysis, and interpretation are guided by the research interest.

Machine learning often outperforms traditional approaches in accuracy and might reveal relations that are nonintuitive. On the other hand, generalizations from machine learning can easily lead to misjudgments, especially when correlations are taken for causalities.

Machine learning, therefore, is not just a new toolbox for the same problems. It should rather be seen as a different way of thinking about political science issues which is adequate in cases where data is complex and theoretical expectations are missing or are drawn into question.

The paper is structured as follows. In the *Statistical Theory and Data Explanation* section, the applied machine learning methods will be presented. The section starts with a closer look on the idea behind machine learning and discusses why machine learning is useful in political science. To have an example on which the methods can be discussed, this paper takes a test case from the mainstream of policy studies: Federal budget of the United States and attention of Congress and President. Researchers from punctuated equilibrium theory (PET) have intensively studied budgets and attention.

Based on this, the machine learning methods—*decision trees* and *random forest*—are introduced. The section ends with an explanation of the concept of cross-validation.

The second part of the paper shows an *empirical application* in detail. The discussed methods are used to predict punctuations in annual budgets. In this *rare event classification task*, the decision trees, bagging, random forest, and logistic regression are compared and approaches to visualize the results are discussed.

The paper ends with a conclusion summing up the advantages and pitfalls of machine learning in political science.

Statistical Theory and Data Explanation

Machine Learning—A Closer Look

The term "machine learning" means that a computer program (algorithm) changes its performance when new data is provided:

> A computer program is said to learn from experience E with respect to some class of tasks T and performance measure P, if its performance at tasks in T, as measured by P, improves with experience E. (Mitchell 1997, 2)

Spam filters are a good everyday-life example for machine learning (Conway and White 2012, 73-92). If users add an email to their spam folder, the program analyzes the data of this email and will probably identify similar emails as spam from thereon.

A common subdivision of machine learning is the differentiation of *supervised* and *unsupervised learning*. Supervised learning—like in the spam-filter example—relies on a training sample with known values of the response variable, while unsupervised learning algorithms search autonomously for similarities in data like patterns or clusters.[1]

Within supervised learning techniques, it is common to differentiate between *classification* and *regression* problems. The former are the tasks where the response variable is *categorical*: like TRUE/FALSE or "American," "European," "Asian," and so on. In regression tasks, the response variable is numeric. However, many machine learning algorithms can deal with classification as well as regression problems.

One of the key advantages of machine learning is its biggest pitfall as well. Machine learning algorithms can easily handle great numbers of variables. Unlike in normal linear regression, there is even the possibility of having more predictor variables than cases in the data.[2] Of course, this makes machine learning very computational intensive, but this is not really the problem, as long as the machine is doing this work.[3] In most settings, this flexibility will lead to a situation in which machine learning is outperforming the accuracy of classical statistical approaches. But the danger is that machine learning is just too good: "These more complex models can lead to a phenomenon known as *overfitting* the data, which essentially means they follow the errors, or *noise*, too closely" (James et al. 2013, 22). Fitting *noise* instead of the *signal* (Silver 2012) means that the model will predict very accurate even those points in the data that deviate just randomly. In consequence, the model that seemed to be very sound would perform weak on new data. To overcome this problem, it is common practice to do the work twice. The original data is divided (often randomly) in a training set and a test set. Then the model is only fitted on the training data. In the second step, this model is used to predict the test data. To evaluate the model's performance, the predicted results are compared with the known values of the response of the test data. This approach is called *cross-validation*.[4]

Why is Machine Learning Useful in Political Science?

On the one hand, it is quite obvious that a society that is affected by "big data" (Mayer-Schönberger and Cukier 2013) in so many ways needs political data science capable of analyzing these processes. Wherever we have to deal with a huge amount of data that might be poorly structured, machine learning should be at hand. Network data—for example, from social media—often falls in this category. Machine learning is extremely powerful on microdata like consumer behavior or real-time sensor data (e.g., GPS data from steadily moving targets). An additional field of application that is perhaps closer to political science is social media (e.g., data from Twitter or Facebook). Finally, spoken language as data has been analyzed with machine learning algorithm very successfully (Suzuki 2009). In recent years, machine learning has gained more and more attention in social science, but this process seems to be quite slow. Seven years ago, Lazer et al. wrote in *Science*: "If one were to look at the leading disciplinary journals in economics, sociology, and political science, there would be minimal evidence of an emerging computational social science engaged in quantitative modeling of these new kinds of digital traces" (Lazer et al. 2009, 721). And, in 2012, Jim Giles complained in *Nature*: "Little data-driven work is making it into top social-science journals" (Giles 2012, 450). Although this observation is still true if compared with the overwhelming

majority of nonmachine learning articles, in the last years machine learning related work has been published in top political science journals (Cantú and Saiegh 2011; Grabau and Hegelich 2016; Grimmer and Stewart 2013; Hainmueller and Hazlett 2014; Hegelich, Fraune, and Knollmann 2015; Hill and Jones 2014; Hopkins and King 2010; Montgomery, Hollenbach, and Ward 2012). Nevertheless, up to now, machine learning is rather an exotic approach to political science and there may be multiple reasons for this. First, machine learning—as will be demonstrated on the following pages—is very different from "normal statistics." It is not about R^2 and significance levels, and it requires some effort to get familiar with these methods. Second, although more and more statistical software has integrated machine learning algorithms, state of the art in this method requires a good deal of computer science knowledge to obtain, manipulate, and analyze data (Abedin 2014; Ergül 2013). Third, political scientists do not often have to deal with data tables with more than a million rows or datasets exceeding 1 TB. Comparing voter participation in 28 European countries, for example, would probably not reveal any limits of "conventional" statistical approaches. Machine learning, therefore, is definitely no one-fits-all solution.

To demonstrate the scope of machine learning approaches, this paper takes data from the policy agenda project (PAP) (www.policyagendas.org) as a test case.[5] The paper focuses on the question which attention variables can explain dramatic shifts in annual budgets (punctuations). This is a supervised classification task in a rare event classification problem.

Data Explanation

The data from PAP has two different coding systems. Budget data uses Office of Management and Budget (OMB) functions and subfunctions, whereas attention data is coded by the coding scheme of the PAP. Eleven topics are more or less convergent in both coding schemes and, therefore, were selected for the analysis. The topics are: "National Defense," "International Affairs," "Energy," "Natural Resources and Environment," "Agriculture," "Transportation," "Education, Training, Employment, and Social Services," "Health," "Social Security," "Administration of Justice," and "General Government."

For all selected 11 topics, the annual percentage budget shifts were taken together with the corresponding year and the legislative period. Figure 1 shows the histogram of the annual percentage budget shifts for all 11 topics. It can be seen that the distribution of budget shifts is clearly not following the bell shape of the normal distribution (black line). Instead, we find far too many incremental changes and many extreme values. To decide, whether a budget shift can count as punctuation the interquartile range for each topic is calculated following the approach of Hegelich, Fraune, and Knollmann (2015). The data contains 553 cases that are no punctuations and 57 cases that are counted as punctuations.

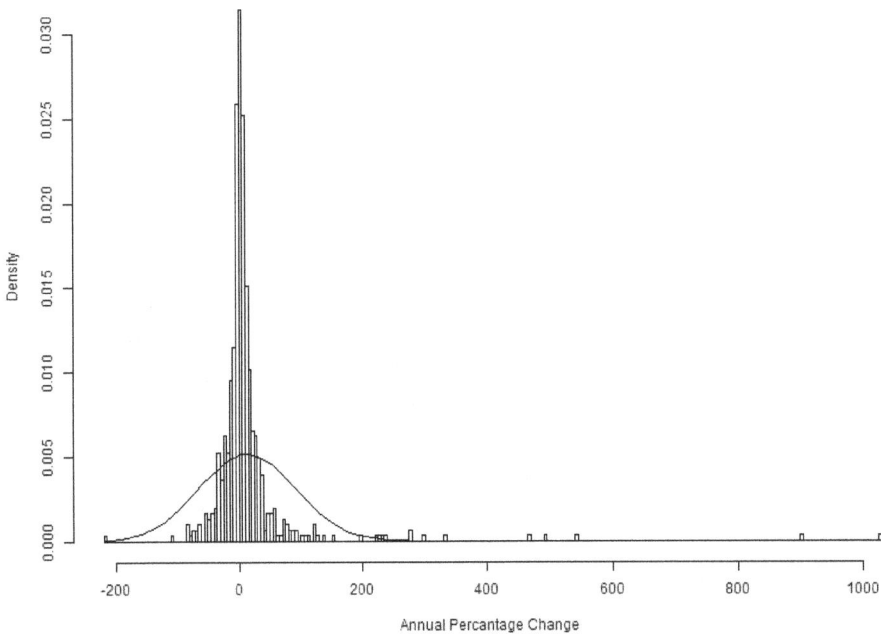

Figure 1: Annual Percentage Changes in US Budget Functions

The budget data is then linked to the attention data. The construction of this combined dataset can be studied with the attached *R*-code (see supporting information) and is, therefore, only explained in general terms here. For each topic, the following variables are calculated from the PAP data:

- the annual number of Congress' hearings on each topic (congress),
- the annual number of public laws passed by the Congress on each topic (laws),
- the annual number of executive orders issued by the President on each topic (eo),
- the annual number of State of the Union speeches by the President on each topic (sou),
- and the annual percentage, how often the topic was mentioned in Gallup's most important problems (gallup).

These variables measure the attention within the policy process on different topics at a given time. For example, if the President is relating to environmental issues six times in his annual State of the Union speech, the variable *sou* has the value 6 for the topic "Natural Resources and Environment" in this year. Time span of all variables goes from 1948 to 2014.

In addition, there are four variables derived from the budget data:

- punctuation TRUE or FALSE (Punc),
- the year, for which the budget was proposed (Year),
- and the budget function (TopicCode).

The President reports on the beginning of each year: how the budget in the last year really was (this is the data in the PAP dataset), how the budget is distributed in the actual year, and what his budget plans are for the year to come (True 2009). To catch the effect of attention on budget decisions, it is necessary to calculate a time lag of two years. Therefore, for all 610 data points, budget is compared with the attention variables from two years earlier.

As can be seen in Figure 2, there are not many punctuations compared with incremental budget shifts.

Figure 3 gives an overview of the variables at hand. In the diagonal panels, we see histograms of the variables with density plots. The other panels show the cross-wise comparisons of the variables. In the lower left panels, the variables are plotted against each other with a linear regression fit. In the upper right panels, the correlation coefficient of the cross-wise comparison is reported. For example, there is a correlation of 0.66 between *congress* and *eo*.[6] Figure 3 gives a good overview of the complexity of the dataset. We find a combination of categorical and numerical variables, of which the latter do not seem to follow a normal distribution (see histograms). There are no strong correlations with the response variable *Punc*, but some of the predictor variables are highly correlated. These features would make the analysis with conventional methods quite tricky.

This data is now the starting point for the task to predict punctuations in the annual budget with machine learning algorithms.

Distribution of Punctuations

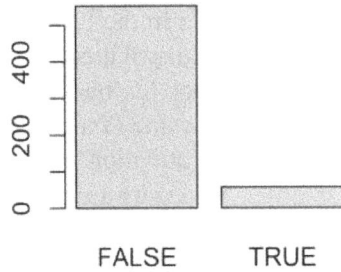

Figure 2: Bar Chart of Budget Punctuations

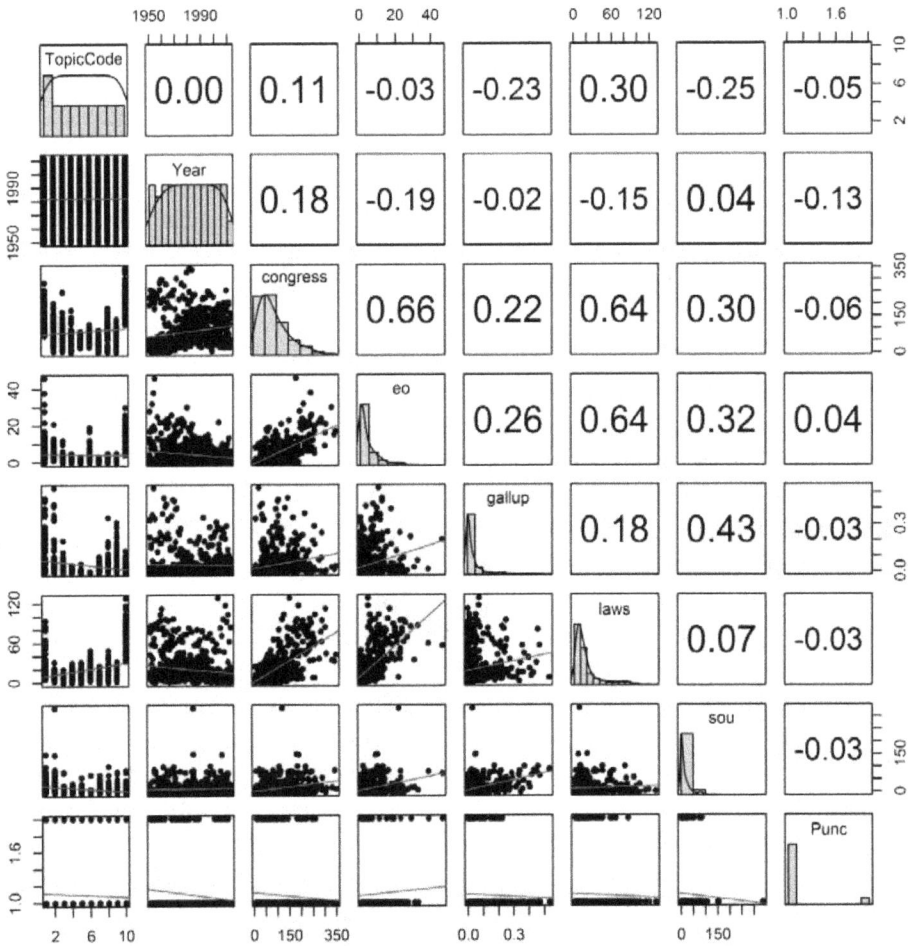

Figure 3: Correlations of Variables in Budget Data

Decision Trees

A common used class of machine learning algorithms runs under the label *decision trees*. Decision trees can be used for regression as well as for classification problems and are suitable for extreme event studies (Frohwein and Lambert 2000). In comparison to most methods in classical statistics, decision trees are not based on any probability density function. This means that there is no assumption of any underlying distribution. Decision trees, therefore, belong to the field of *nonparametric statistics*. In tree-based methods, the predictor space is segmented in a number of simpler regions. For each region, the most likely value of the

response is calculated separately.

To demonstrate this method, a simplified version of the data described earlier is used. Data is limited to a random sample of 50 data points with only the three variables *sou*, *Year*, and *Punc*.

Figure 4 shows the predictor space of this sample data with the State of the Union speeches (sou) on the x-axis and the Year on the y-axis. Punctuations are represented with triangles and incremental changes with circles. There is no eye-catching pattern. The values "Punctuation" and "Incremental" rather seem to be randomly scattered in the plot.

But this picture changes, if the predictor space is divided in several regions.

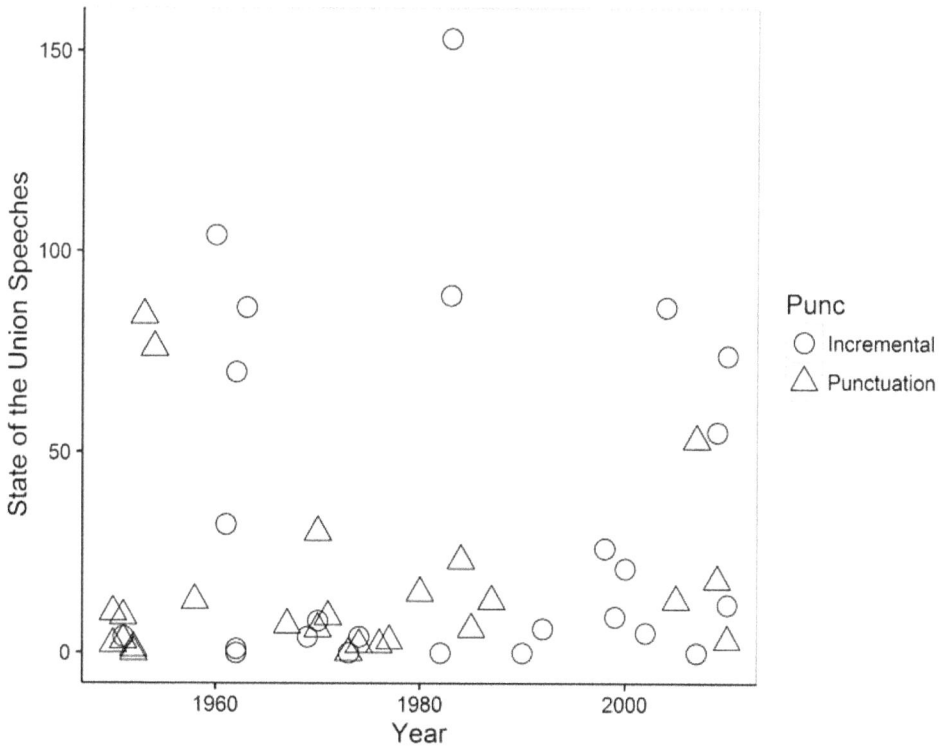

Figure 4: Predictor Space of Sample Data

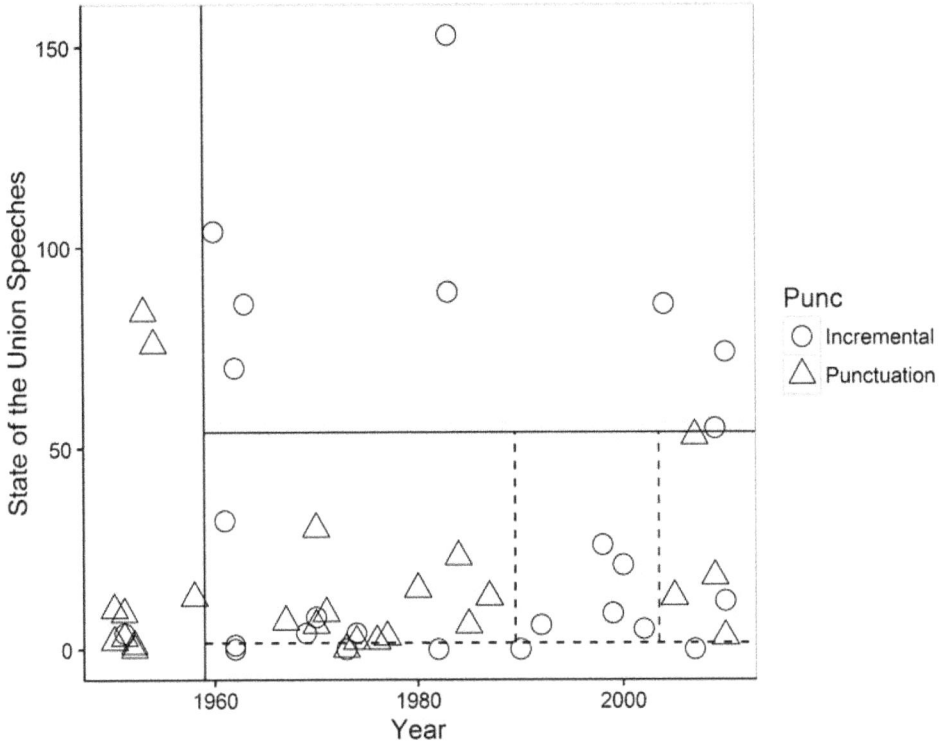

Figure 5: Divided Predictor Space

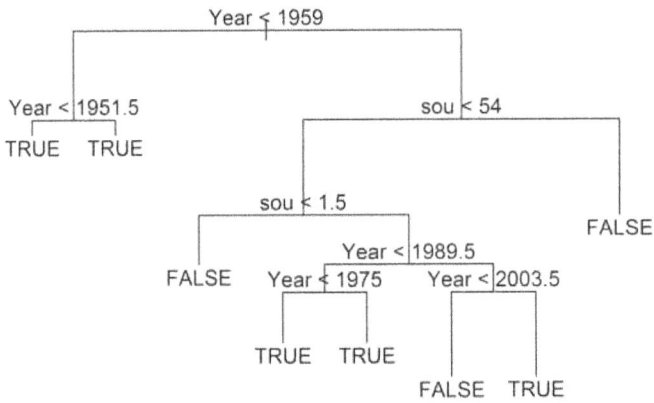

Figure 6: Decision Tree of Sample Data

In Figure 5, predictor space is now divided in a way that either more "Punctuation" or more "Incremental" values are in each region. For classification, we simply look for the dominant category in each region. For example, if *Year* is less than 1959, it is more likely that there had been a punctuation in budgets. If we split the remaining area again, we see that frequent mentioning of a topic in the State of the Union speeches of the previous years made punctuations less likely.[7]

The division of the predictor space in different regions can be visualized in a decision tree. Figure 6 shows the corresponding decision tree.

The great thing about splitting the predictor space in regions is that the direction of the predictors' influence can change. If *sou* is bigger than 1.5, this increases the chance of punctuations, but if it is above 54 punctuations are less likely.

In order to find out how the predictor space could be divided in regions, two things are necessary: a criterion to evaluate the value of a possible split and an algorithm to find splits that optimize this criterion.

In classification trees, the *classification error rate* for each region would be a compelling evaluation criterion[8]:

$$E = 1 - \max_k(\hat{p}_{mk}).$$

Here, $\hat{p}_{mk}$ represents the proportion of training observations in the mth region that are from the kth class." (James et al. 2013, 311–312).

Because the classification error is not sensitive enough for tree growing, in practice, the *Gini index* is often preferred. "The *Gini index* is defined by

$$G = \sum_{k=1}^{K} \hat{p}_{mk}(1 - \hat{p}_{mk}),$$

a measure of total variance across the K classes" (James et al. 2013, 312). The Gini index can be interpreted as a measure of *node purity*, that is, the lower the number of observations from different classes in a region, the lower the Gini index will be. For a region with only one class, the Gini index will be zero.

To find the best partition of the predictor space, *recursive binary splitting* is used, which is a *top-down, greedy* approach:

The approach is *top-down* because it begins at the top of the tree (at which point all observations belong to a single region) and then successively splits the predictor space; each split is indicated via two new branches further down on the tree. It is *greedy* because at each step of the tree-building process, the *best* split is made at that particular step, rather than looking ahead and picking a split that will lead to a better tree in some future step. (James et al. 2013, 306)

It is *recursive* because every branch of the tree could be seen as a tree on its own and the same procedure is applied again (Siroky 2009).

The algorithm can be described as follows:

1. Try all possible cutpoints for the first predictor and calculate the resulting evaluation criterion.
2. Choose the cutpoint that reduces the criterion most.

3. Do the same with all other predictors.
4. Choose the predictor and the corresponding cutpoint that reduces the criterion most.
5. Split the data in two parts according to the selected cutpoint.
6. Repeat the procedure for both parts of the data until a stopping criterion is reached; for instance, until no region contains more than five observations.

Decision trees are very prone to overfitting. In an extreme case, we could divide the predictor space in as many regions as data points. The result would be a perfect prediction of the data (unless two cases with different classes share exactly the same position). But such an overcomplex tree would perform poorly on new data (i.e., it would not be robust). Contrary, to keep the regions as big as possible (view splits) increases the robustness of the decision tree because these big regions will probably be suitable for new data points. But the tradeoff then is a higher classification error.

Random forest is an upgrade of the decision tree method that overcomes this problem.

Random Forest

The problem with decision trees is that they suffer from *high variance*. This means that slightly different data might lead to very different decision trees. Calculating the mean is a common way to reduce the variance. In a set "of n independent observations $Z_1,...,Z_n$, each with the variance σ^2, the variance of the mean $\check{Z}$ of the observations is given by σ^2/n. In other words, *averaging a set of* *observations reduces variance*" (James et al. 2013, 306). So, if we ran the decision tree algorithm on multiple training sets, we could average the models and come up with one low-variance machine learning algorithm. The problem is, of course, that we (normally) do not have multiple training sets. Splitting our data in different sets does not help because every model builtd on a subset would be strongly biased. The solution is *bootstrapping*.[9]: The procedure is quite simple. We can create multiple datasets from the original data by a sample with replacement (Mooney 1996;, Shikano 2006). The dataset is treated like a bag from which every observation can be drawn and added to the bootstrapped dataset. Then this observation is returned in the bag so that it could be drawn once again.

This method described so far— using decision trees on bootstrapped datasets—is called *bagging*. With bootstrapping, we can create hundreds or thousands of datasets that are unique representations of the distributional features of the original data. We now fit a deep decision tree (with a lot of splits) on each of the new datasets. Therefore, each tree has high variance but low bias, that is, it is one *special* representation of the *general* data.[10] Averaging these trees now reduces the variance so that we come up with a robust model with a low bias. To average the classifications of the different trees, we take the *majority vote* of all the single decision trees. For example, we created 1000 bootstrapped datasets and plant 1000 decision trees. Then we look for every observation in the original data: how the majority of trees have classified this data point.[11] This is why *bagging* (and *random forest*) is called an *ensemble* approach.

Random forest, an algorithm developed by Breiman (2001), adds one other very clever feature to the bagging procedure. At each split of the tree, the number of available predictors is reduced to a random sample of all predictors. Typically, the size of this random sample is the square root of the total number of predictors (e.g., three out of nine). "In other words, in building a random forest, at each split in the tree, the algorithm is *not even allowed to consider* a majority of the available predictors" (James et al. 2013, 320). This seems counter intuitive, because the procedure will negligently reduce the explanatory power of each single tree. For example, there is one predictor (like the *Year* in the above example) that can explain a lot of variances in the data. If this predictor is neglected in many splits, the model will get worse. On the other hand, the limitation of predictors at each split has a very advantageous effect on the *ensemble* of trees. Especially, when there is one predictor that is stronger than the others, all trees will automatically chose this predictor as a starting point with the result that all trees look more or less the same and are highly correlated. But "averaging highly correlated quantities does not lead to as large of a reduction in variance as averaging many uncorrelated quantities" (James et al. 2013, 320). As long as the number of trees is sufficiently high to guarantee that all predictors get their chance and all data points are evaluated by enough decision trees, random forest is a very robust algorithm with high accuracy.

The bootstrapping has an additional advantage. Every tree is built only on a sample of the data. The other data points are *out of bag* (OOB), that is, they are not used to fit this special tree.

Because several (100) trees are grown, every observation will be OOB in some of the models. For every data point, we can take only those trees where the point has been OOB and use these models to predict the class of the data point by averaging the predictions. This way we receive a more or less unbiased performance indicator (OOB error), because now only the prediction of trees is evaluated where the data point in question has not been considered for building the model. The OOB error can be used to find a good value for the number of trees that are grown in a random forest. In general, random forests are very robust against overfitting so the number of trees should be sufficiently high (see Hastie, Tibshirani, and Friedman 2009, 596–597 for critical analysis). A standard value is 500, but especially in huge datasets, this value might be too low. A plot of the decrease of the OOB error against the number of trees is a good way to see if more trees might lead to better results.

Random forests are very sensitive to the number of predictors tried at each split. Testing different values here might improve the model strongly.[12] The evaluation criterion for the splits depends on the type of problem (classification or regression). Besides the described Gini index, *cross-entropy* is often used for classification. Regression trees normally rely on the *residual sum of square* (RSS). Especially, for the study of rare events, changing the *ensemble rule* is very interesting (Hastie et al. 2009, 622).

As discussed above, random forest normally takes the majority vote of the classification of all trees to predict the class of an observation. The problem here is that extreme events are very rare by nature. Therefore, they are always *underrepresented* in the data and the majority vote might be too strict. In our budget example, only 57 of 610 budget shifts count as punctuation. Therefore, the random chance for any observation to be a punctuation is about 10 percent. If our model predicts 40 percent probability that an observation has the value "Punctuated," this is four times as higher than the random chance. Still the majority vote would classify the observation as "Incremental," because this decreases the classification error (Chen, Liaw, and Breiman 2004). If we instead change the ensemble rule (let's say every observation is labeled as "Punctuated" in case 30 percent or more of the single decision trees classify the observation as a major budget shift), the model will predict more punctuations which will lead to more correctly classified "Punctuated." But, of course, this will weaken the overall classification rate because more incremental changes will be wrongly labeled as "Punctuated." Whether this is desirable depends on the objectives of the model. If the model is seen as the most accurate classifier, to change majority vote often means to decrease the performance. But if the model is seen as a "detector" for rare events, it can be useful to increase the number of rightly detected punctuations even at the cost of accuracy.

Cross-validation

As discussed earlier, overfitting is a serious issue with machine learning. The algorithms are sometimes very accurate on the dataset the model is fitted to but perform poorly on new data. Random forest increases its robustness by means of the ensemble approach. Nevertheless, overfitting remains an issue. The state-of-the-art procedure to deal with this situation is *cross-validation*. The idea is to build the model on one dataset and test it on a different one:

> Ideally, there would be two random samples from the same population. One would be a training data set, and one would be a testing data set. [...] Often, there is only a single data set. An alternative strategy is to split the data up into several randomly chosen, nonoverlapping parts. (Berk 2006, 277)

For cross-validation, the dataset is split randomly in a training set containing, for example, two thirds of the data and a test set with the remaining one third. The final model is fitted on the training data only and the predictions for the test data are evaluated. This *validation set approach*, in principle, should prevent *overfitting*. An advantage of this method is that it is easy to apply, but there are two potential drawbacks that should be kept in mind:

1. The validation-set approach can lead to quite different results, depending on the actual division of training and test set. In practice, splitting the data should always be made with a "frozen" random number generator[13] so that others are able to reproduce the results.

2. "Since statistical methods tend to perform worse when trained on fewer observations, this suggests that the validation set error rate may tend to *overestimate* the test error rate for the model fit on the entire data set" (James et al. 2013, 178). The splitting of the data in a training set and a test set, therefore, leads to a lower level of accuracy.

The two-thirds approach is often seen as best practice because it takes many observations for training—which leads to high accuracy—but leaves sufficient observations for testing. But, in practice, any other proportion of test and training data is possible (e.g., two sets of equal size).

Other cross-validation approaches are more computational intensive. *Leave-one-out cross-validation* builds as many models as there are observations, each with one data point missing and then predicts the value for each missing observation. A different common approach is *k-fold cross-validation*. Here, data is divided in *k* randomly selected subsets and then each subset is used once as a validation set. Both approaches have in common that averaging the results will lead to more robust estimations of the model performance (e.g., classification errors).

To demonstrate random forests in action, the next section analyzes the whole budget data. A focus will be on visualizing the results.

Empirical Application: Predicting Punctuations in Budget Shifts

In the following example, the validation-set approach is used by dividing the PAP data in a training set containing two-thirds of the dataset (randomly selected) and a test set with the remaining third of the observations. All seven predictor variables have been used.

Comparison of Decision Trees, Bagging, and Random Forest

In this example, I will fit a decision tree on the training set, discuss the results, and then improve the performance with bagging and random forest.

First, a single decision tree is grown (Figure 7).

The bold printed statements in the tree describe the points where the predictor space is split. In the first node, for example, data is divided in two parts: those observations where *Year* is equal or bigger than 1952 and those observations that were before this time. The left branch of each node represents data that fulfills this condition (the "yes-branch"), while the right branch does not fulfill the condition. The leaves of the tree show the dominant class ("FALSE" (no punctuation) or "TRUE" (punctuation)) for the region defined by the nodes. In this visualization, the classification rate for each leaf has been added. This information is very helpful to understand the results. We see, for example, in the leaf of the first node that there have been 358 out of 384 incremental budget shifts in this branch. The next split is based on the variable *TopicCode*. In the years before 1952, budget functions with the codes 150, 300, 500, or 800 were very likely to show extreme shifts (8 of 13 cases). The importance of *Year* is a good example for nonintuitive finding. Starting with a theory in mind, the year of the budget plan might seem less relevant than the attention Congress or President is paying to a topic. But once the pattern is exposed, it is easy to think about possible interpretations. For example, it could be possible that shortly after World War II, the shift to a civil economy had led to many shifts in Federal budget, as well.

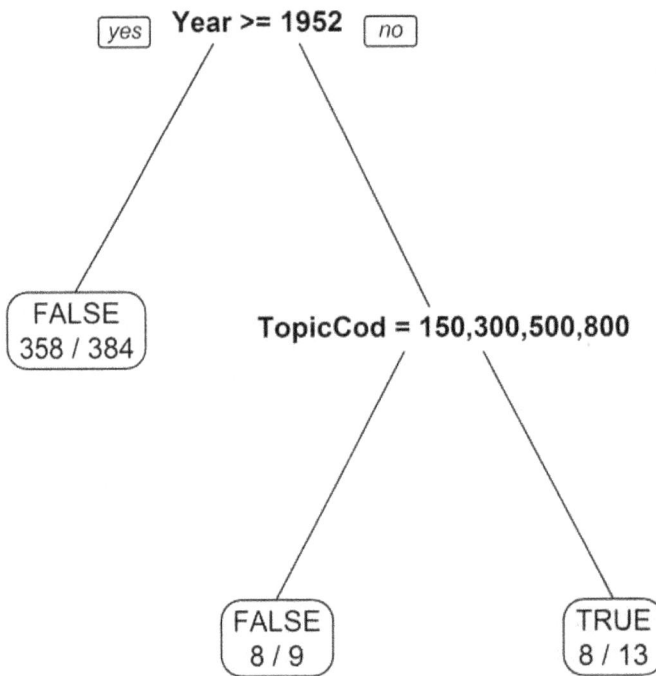

Figure 7: Decision Tree on Training Set

Table 1: Cross-table Decision Tree/Training Set

Prediction	Real		
	FALSE	TRUE	Total
FALSE	366	27	393
TRUE	5	8	13
Total	371	35	406

The cross-table of the results (Table 1) shows the predicted results in the rows and the real results in the columns. For example, the decision tree has predicted 393 times the class "FALSE". Three hundred sixty six of these cases have been correctly detected (true positives), while 27 have the real label "TRUE." We can see that the decision tree has predicted the right results in 374 (366 + 8) of 406 cases. This is the classification rate of 97 percent.

Unfortunately, these results are strongly overfitted. If the model is used to predict new data from the test set, the results are much weaker (Table 3). Now, the classification rate reaches "only" 87 percent. More dramatic: only one punctuation was rightly detected.

Table 2: Cross-table Decision Tree/Test Set

Prediction	Real		
	FALSE	TRUE	Total
FALSE	178	21	199
TRUE	4	1	5
Total	182	22	204

To find a more robust model, the described bootstrapping procedure is applied. A bagging model and a random forest model are fitted on the training set. As described earlier, both models are very similar. The random forest only selects the possible predictor variables at each split of each tree randomly, while the bagging model always takes the best predictor for each split.

First, the number of bootstrapped trees has to be defined. If the number of trees is too low, the model is underperforming. An ensemble with more trees would be more accurate.[14] To evaluate the performance with different numbers of trees, we can plot the error rates as a function of the number of trees. Figure 8 shows the classification error rates (i.e., the percentage of wrongly classified observations) for both classes "TRUE" and "FALSE." The black curve is the OOB rate. Since the bootstrapped data is not using all observations in each tree, we can predict that the classification error rate for those observations that have been randomly excluded from the sample the tree is built on. The OOB error rate, therefore, is a very good measure for the robustness of the model. If the OOB error rate is no longer decreasing when adding more trees to the ensemble, we have reached a sufficient number of trees. Figure 8 shows that the OOB error rate seems quite stable with 200 and more trees so 300 trees should be a save choice.

In the next step, the performance of the models has to be evaluated. One way would be to compare the cross-tables of the models, as has been done with the decision tree model. But this comparison is not trivial. Do we prefer a model that is highly *sensitive*, that is, it identifies a high number of the rare class "punctuation"? Or do we look for a model that is very *specific*, that is, it is only seldom wrong when predicting punctuations? But there is a way to deal with this trade-off.

The ROC curve is a popular graphic for comparing the performance of different classification models. "The name "ROC" is historic, and comes from communications theory. It is an acronym for receiver operating characteristics" (James et al. 2013, 147). As described before, the models do not only predict the most likely outcome for every observation, but they also calculate a probability for this assignment. The decision tree in Figure 7, for example, includes the proportion of right classifications for every node which can be translated into a probability value. For an ROC curve, the predictions are ordered by these probabilities. In some cases, the model "is very sure" that there was no punctuation (e.g., probability 0.1); in other cases, TRUE is a more likely prediction (e.g., probability 0.8). For every probability value, the true positives (i.e., the cases which have been *rightly* labeled "TRUE" of "FALSE", also called *sensitivity*) and the false positives (i.e., the cases which have been *wrongly* labeled— also called *specificity*) are counted. Plotting these values against each other results in an ROC curve (see Figure 9). A perfect model that predicts every observation right would be represented by an ROC curve that hugged the top-left corner of the plot. The bigger the *area under the*

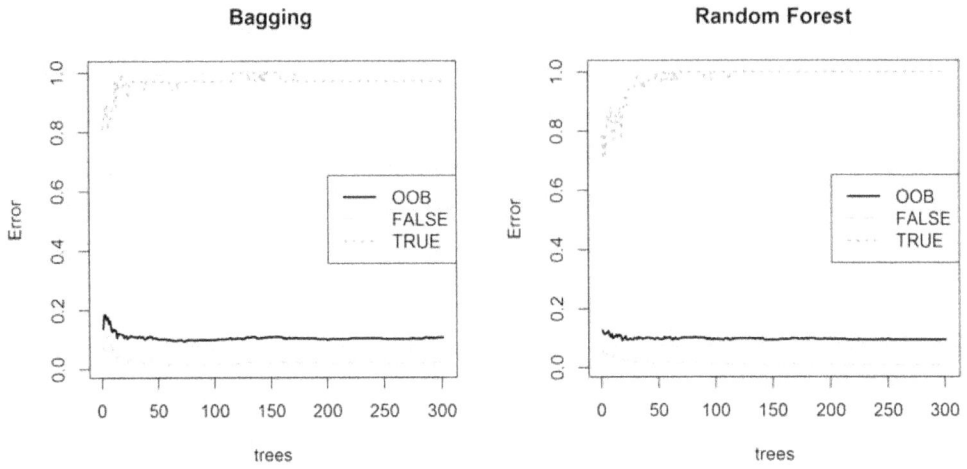

Figure 8: Error Rates of Ensemble Models/Training Set

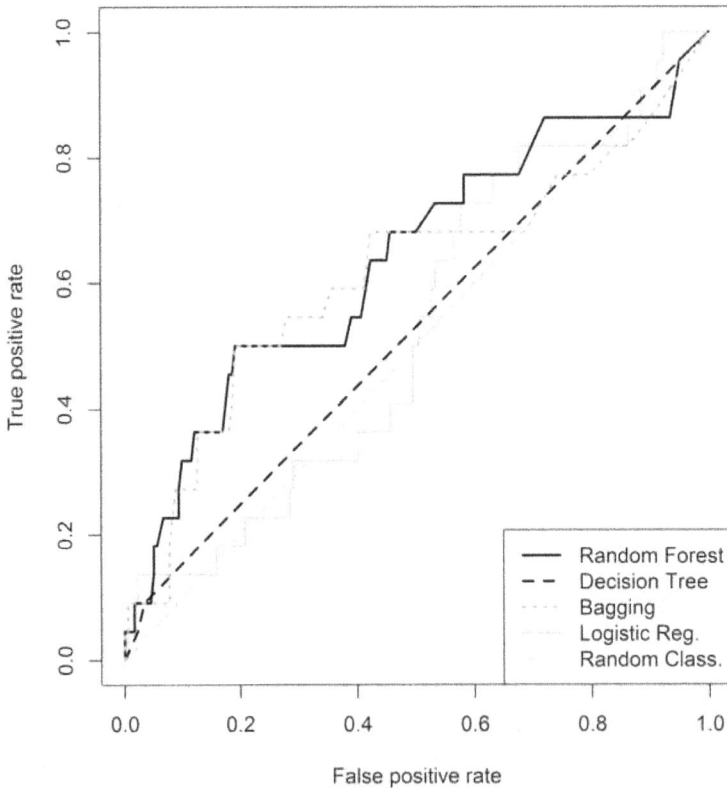

Figure 9: ROC Curves of Budget Models/Test Set

ROC curve (AUC), the better the model. A purely random classifier has an AUC of 0.5 and is presented by a straight diagonal in the plot. Because the true and false positive rates are independent from the type of classification model, we can use ROC curves to compare the performance of any classifier.

Figure 9 shows the ROC curves for all three decision tree models: single decision tree (dashed black line), bagging (dashed gray line), and random forest (black line). For comparison, a random classification is added (the dashed light gray diagonal) as well as a logistic regression model (gray line) fitted on exactly the same data. As can be seen in the plot, the ensemble methods bagging and random forest clearly outperform the logistic regression and the single decision tree.

These differences become even clearer when looking directly at the AUC. Figure 10 shows a bar plot of the different AUCs with the critical values 0.5 (random classification) and 0.75 (standard for

clinical tests) added as dashed lines.[15]

Now, we can conclude that the random forest model outperforms the other models. In data mining, this result could be the end of the analysis.[16] The best model is taken to run predictive analytics and the accuracy leads to sound predictions. But in political science, the focus is normally not foremost on the precision of predictions but on understanding relationships between variables.

A good way to interpret a random forest model is to look at the variable importance. For every predictor variable, we can calculate its influence on the final result. As described earlier, splits in decision trees result from optimizing the classification error rate or the Gini coefficient. So, each split in every tree will lead to a decrease of these two measures. Predictors that lead to stronger decreases, therefore, are more important for the model. The variable importance plot (Figure 11) shows the mean decreases for all seven predictors.

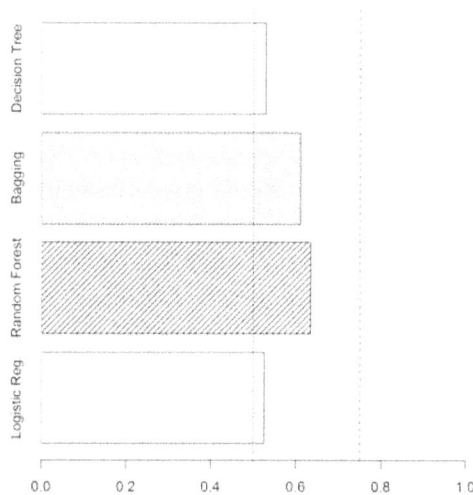

Figure 10: Bar Plot of AUCs for different Models

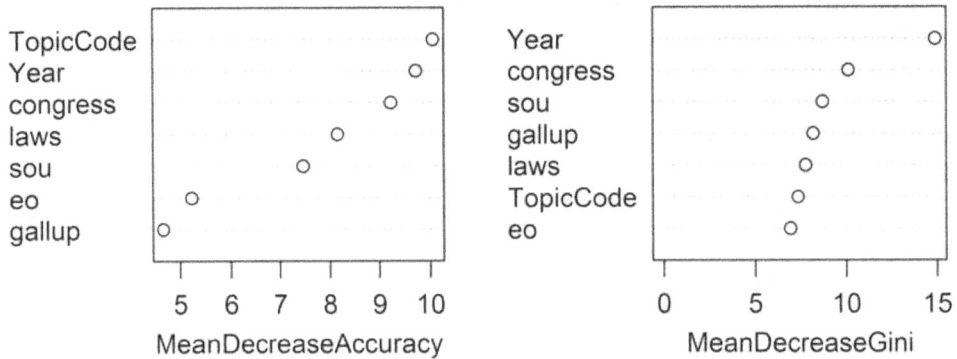

Figure 11: Variable Importance Plot

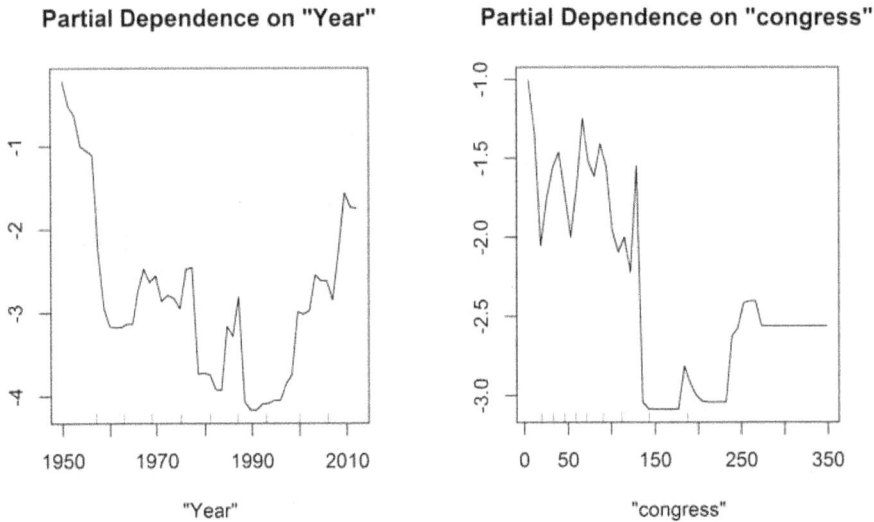

Figure 12: Partial Dependence Plots

Both measures see *Year* and *Congress* within the most important variables. For node-purity (Gini), *TopicCode* is not so important, although it is the most important variable for accuracy. In our case, where we are interested in the classification of rare events, the Gini coefficient should be preferred.

But there is more to learn from the random forest model. As described earlier, decision trees are capable of fitting truly nonlinear effects. In Figure 6, we saw already that *Year* and *sou* sometimes had a positive effect and sometimes a negative one, depending on the critical value of the split. We can now extract all these split points from the ensemble of bootstrapped trees to see how the effect of the variables changes (Figure 12). This visualization is called *partial dependence plot*.

The curve in the left partial dependence plot starts close to zero. This means that in the early 1950s, punctuations were quite likely. The chance of punctuations started decreasing then, but it rapidly rose at the end of the 1990s. The *congress* plot shows us that the attention of the Congress on a topic lowers the possibilities of dramatic budget shifts. This is absolutely in line with PET, because frequent attention on a topic prevents policy bubbles. But if attention rises too much, this can be a cause for punctuations as well. As we can see, decision trees are very good tools to deal with such nonlinear effects.

Conclusion

The results have shown that random forest is a very powerful algorithm to analyze extreme values. "Random forests are an effective tool in prediction. Because of the Law of Large Numbers they do not overfit. Injecting the right kind of randomness makes them accurate classifiers and regressors" (Breiman 2001, 29).

Taking the potential of machine learning into consideration, political science should welcome these approaches where complex data is to be analyzed. The advantages are the ability to deal with multiple—even highly correlated—predictors, the sensitivity to nonlinear effects—including contradictory effects in different regions of the predictor space—and the possibility of analyzing unbalanced data, where one class strongly outnumbers the others. But these advantages come with a price that is not limited to the extra effort necessary to learn new and complex methods: "*There is no free lunch in statistics*:

no one method dominates all others over all possible data sets" (James et al. 2013, 29). Most importantly, there is a trade-off between prediction accuracy and model interpretability. While decision trees are quite easy to explain,[17] random forests are much harder to interpret. Often, political science is more interested in inference than in accuracy, which sets a natural limit to the scenarios this approach might be implemented successfully. In addition, if applied as "black-box-algorithm" without a deeper understanding of the inner mechanism, random forests might lead to misinterpretations and false discoveries. But this should be seen as strong argument for political scientists to engage in these "new" methods. In the big data world, the machine learning algorithm will become more and more popular. Hastily conclusions from models that are accurate but lack a deeper understanding of the political context can only be criticized by scientists who are familiar with the subject as well as with the method.

Notes

[1] There are scenarios in which the distinction between supervised and unsupervised might not be as clear as indicated here, for example, when there is a response variable but only for some cases. James et al. use the term "semi-supervised learning" for those kinds of problems (James et al. 2013).
[2] A good example is the "bag of words" approach in text mining. Here, every word that is present in any of the documents of the corpus is taken as one predictor. Therefore, the number of predictors will often outnumber the number of documents.

³ Especially, in big data analytics, computation time may increase in a way that it really becomes a problem. State-of-the-art machine learning tries to overcome this situation by making the algorithms scalable, that is, several machines (computers or cores in one computer) are working parallel on the same task.

⁴ Sometimes, the division in one test set and one training set is still strongly biased. More complex approaches to cross-validation are *leave-one-out cross-validation* and *k-fold cross-validation* (James et al. 2013, 178–184).

⁵ The data used here were originally collected by Frank R. Baumgartner and Bryan D. Jones, with the support of National Science Foundation grant numbers SBR 9320922 and 0111611, and were distributed through the Department of Government at the University of Texas at Austin. Neither NSF nor the original collectors of the data bear any responsibility for the analysis reported here.

⁶ As can be seen, the predictor variables are strongly correlated (e.g., *congress* and *eo*). Unlike with conventional statistical approaches, this is not a problem for the machine learning methods that are used in this paper, because they fall in the class of nonparametric models, that is, there are no assumptions about underlying distributions.

⁷ It is obvious that the same procedure can be used for regression problems, as well. Instead of counting the elements of different classes, one would take the mean or the mode of the response for each region.

⁸ For regression trees, the residual sum of squares is used as a criterion.

⁹ In political science, bootstrapping is often used to calculate confidence intervals for unknown distributions (Jacoby and Armstrong 2014)

¹⁰ For a deeper discussion of the bias-variance problem, see Hastie et al. (2009, 219–225).

¹¹ Because of the bootstrap, not every observation is in every dataset. So the number of trees should be sufficient so that every observation is represented in the ensemble.

¹² In addition, there are optimization algorithms for this parameter like the tuneRF() function in *R*.

¹³ In the computer language *R*, this is done with the command "set.seed()."

¹⁴ Too many trees are not really a problem for the model in this case. A very high number of trees might lead to overfitting, but, in general, random forests are quite robust. In addition, the cross-validation would reveal such shortcomings. In real-world examples, computational time might be the biggest problem when growing deep random forests with a lot of trees.

¹⁵ None of the tested models is reaching an AUC of 75 percent. If compared with clinical studies, the accuracy even of the random forest model was too low to be accepted. This remark is meant to remind the reader that even the best available model might not be good enough for reliable predictions.

¹⁶ The next step in data mining would be to enhance the accuracy of the model further by tuning the variables of the algorithm. The AUC benchmark for clinical studies could easily be reached by changing parameters like the number of predictors at each split or the majority rule.

¹⁷ "Some people believe that decision trees more closely mirror human decision-making than do [other] regression and classification approaches" (James et al. 2013, 315).

References

Abedin, Jaynal. 2014. *Data Manipulation with R.* Packt Publishing Ltd, Birmingham.

Berk, Richard A. 2006. "An Introduction to Ensemble Methods for Data Analysis." *Sociological Methods and Research* 34 (3): 263–295.

Breiman, Leo. 2001. "Random Forests." *Machine Learning* 45 (1): 5–32.

Cantú, Francisco, and Sebastián M. Saiegh. 2011. "Fraudulent Democracy? An Analysis of Argentina's Infamous Decade Using Supervised Machine Learning." *Political Analysis* 19 (4): 409–433.

Chen, Chao, Andy Liaw, and Leo Breiman. 2004. *Using Random Forest to Learn Imbalanced Data.* Berkeley: University of California.

Conway, Drew, and John White. 2012. *Machine Learning for Hackers.* O'Reilly Media, Inc., Sebastopol

Ergül, Özgür. 2013. *Guide to Programming and Algorithms Using R.* Springer, New York.

Frohwein, Hendrik I., and James H. Lambert. 2000. "Risk of Extreme Events in Multiobjective Decision Trees Part 1. Severe Events." *Risk Analysis* 20 (1): 113–124.

Giles, Jim. 2012. "Making the Links." *Nature* 488 (7412): 448–450.

Grabau, Martina, and Simon Hegelich. 2016. "The Gas Game: Simulating Decision-Making in the European Union's External Natural Gas Policy." *Swiss Political Science Review*. doi: 10.1111/spsr.12202.

Grimmer, Justin, and Brandon M. Stewart.

2013. "Text as Sata: The Promise and Pitfalls of Automatic Content Analysis Methods for Political Rexts." *Political Analysis* 21 (3): 267–297.

Hainmueller, Jens, and Chad Hazlett. 2014. "Kernel Regularized Least Squares: Reducing Misspecification Bias with a Flexible and Interpretable Machine Learning Approach." *Political Analysis* 22 (2):143–168.

Hastie, Trevor, Robert Tibshirani, and Jerome Friedman. 2009. *The Elements of Statistical Learning.* 2 vol. New York: Springer.

Hegelich, Simon, Cornelia Fraune, and David Knollmann. 2015. "Point Predictions and the Punctuated Equilibrium Theory: A Data Mining Approach—US Nuclear Policy as Proof of Concept." *Policy Studies Journal* 43 (2): 228–256.

Hill, Daniel W., and Zachary M. Jones. 2014. "An Empirical Evaluation of Explanations for State Repression." *American Political Science Review* 108 (03): 661–687.

Hopkins, Daniel J., and Gary King. 2010. "A Method of Automated Nonparametric Content Analysis for Social Science." *American Journal of Political Science* 54 (1): 229–247.

Jacoby, William G., and David A. Armstrong. 2014. "Bootstrap Confidence Regions for Multidimensional Scaling Solutions." *American Journal of Political Science* 58 (1): 264–278.

James, Gareth, Daniela Witten, Trevor Hastie, and Robert Tibshirani. 2013. *An Introduction to Statistical Learning.* Springer, New York.

Lazer, David, Alex Sandy Pentland, Lada Adamic, Sinan Aral, Albert Laszlo Barabasi, Devon Brewer, Nicholas Christakis, Noshir Contractor, James Fowler, and Myron Gutmann. 2009. "Life in the Network: The Coming age of Computational Social Science." *Science* (New York, NY) 323 (5915): 721.

Mayer-Schönberger, Viktor, and Kenneth Cukier. 2013. *Big Data: A Revolution that will Transform how We Live*, Work, and Think. Houghton Mifflin Harcourt, London.

Mitchell, Tom M. 1997. *Machine Learning.* 1997. Burr Ridge, IL: McGraw-Hill, 45.

Montgomery, Jacob M., Florian M. Hollenbach, and Michael D. Ward. 2012. "Improving Predictions using Ensemble Bayesian Model Averaging." *Political Analysis* 20 (3): 271–291.

Mooney, Christopher Z. 1996. "Bootstrap Statistical Inference: Examples and Evaluations for Political Science." *American Journal of Political Science* 40(2)570–602.

Shikano, Susumu. 2006. "Bootstrap und Jackknife." in: Behnke, Joachim/ Gwschend, Thomas/Schindler, Delia/ Schnapp, Kai-Uwe (Eds.) *Methoden der Politikwissenschaft. Neuere qualitative und quantitative Analyseverfahren.* Baden-Baden Nomos 69 –79.

Silver, Nate. 2012. The Signal and the Noise: *Why so Many Predictions Fail-But Some Don't.* New York: Penguin.

Siroky, David S. 2009. "Navigating Random Forests and Related Advances in Algorithmic Modeling." *Statistics Surveys* 3: 147–163.

Suzuki, Takafumi. 2009. "Extracting Speaker-Specific Functional Expressions from Political Speeches Using Random Forests in Order to Investigate Speakers' Political Styles." *Journal of the American Society for Information Science and Technology* 60 (8): 1596–1606.

True, James L. 2009. "Historical budget records converted to the present functional categorization with actual results for FY 1947-2008." *Policy Agendas Project.*

European Policy Analysis - Volume 2, Number 1 - Spring 2016

The Role of Theories in Policy Studies and Policy Work: Selective Affinities between Representation and Performation?

Robert Hoppe[A] & Hal Colebatch[B]

In this article, we intend to take a few steps to mending the disconnect between the academic study of policy processes and the many practices of professional and not-so-professional policy work. We argue, first, that the "toolkit" of academically warranted approaches to the policy process used in the representative mode may be ordered in a family tree with three major branches: policy as reasoned authoritative choice, policy as association in policy networks, and policy as problematization and joint meaning making. But, and this is our second argument, such approaches are not just representations to reflect and understand "reality". They are also mental maps and discursive vehicles for shaping and sometimes changing policy practices. In other words, they also serve performative functions. The purpose of this article is to contribute to policy theorists' and policy workers' awareness of these often tacit and "underground" selective affinities between the representative and performative roles of policy process theorizing.

Keywords: governing, policy, policymaking process, policy analysis, policy work, representation, performation

"Policy" in the Analysis and Accomplishment of Governing

In the second half of the twentieth century, "policy" came to assume a much more prominent position in the analysis of the process of governing, but it is not clear how much this has made the analysis sharper (rather than simply broader). In spite of six decades of "policy sciences," scholars have not agreed on a shared definition of "policy."

This is not to say that they have no clue, of course. Rather than one definition, there is a cluster of different but related meanings or connotations to roughly indicate what "a policy" is. The concept sometimes refers to the (sustained, structured) activities of a collective actor such as a government or governmental body and sometimes to the results of these activities; in all cases a "policy" is designed. All these meanings somehow express the intention to normatively

[A] University of Twente
[B] University of New South Wales

doi: 10.18278/epa.2.1.8

frame the activity of governing in a way that highlights a certain set of values. Some simple definitions fall back on conventional state theory which locates sovereign decision making and authority in the state apparatus; so "policy" becomes anything a government chooses to do or not to do (Dye 1985, 1).

This conceptual fuzziness has left us with a number of problems in the analytical use of the term policy. First, it is not clear precisely what the term means and how it relates to other concepts in the analysis of governing. It rests on a distinction in English between "policy" and "politics" which has no equivalent in most other languages (Dutch being the main exception), and while Dye could confidently assert that "public policy is whatever governments decide to do or not to do", Lindblom saw "policymaking" as "the complex set of forces that together produces effects called "policies" … an extremely complex *analytical and political* process to which there is no beginning and no end and the boundaries of which are most uncertain" (Lindblom 1968, 4; Lindblom and Woodhouse 1993). Some recent handbooks (Fischer, Miller, and Sidney 2007; Moran, Rein, and Goodin 2006) take "policy process" and "policymaking process" as self-evident concepts not in need of definition.

Second, this leads to a similar vagueness about the activity which produces policy—the "policy process" or "process of policymaking". There is an (often tacit) assumption that the central element in the activity is a "decision", and Parsons (1996, 82) broadly describes policymaking as "focusing on *the relationship between the "pre-decisional" dimensions of policymaking and its decisional or post-decisional contexts.*" Or

the focus may be on the policy as problem-solving design, with the gaze tracked backward in time, seeing the policy process as *a selection of events, (collective or individual) actors, and actions over time, defined by reference to a particular "policy", that captures (or explains) the (time sequence and/or spatial distribution of) major events that, jointly, make up the "becoming", "adoption", and the "destiny" of that policy* (Van de Graaf and Hoppe 1996, 95). This recognizes that policy is seen as both *ex ante* intention and *ex post* results (performance outputs and outcomes). But it also raises a question: if policymaking is the construction of an intermediate "product" like a "decision", plan or announcement of collective action, why is it framed as a sustained or continuous flow, and not as a staged production process? Why do policy scholars leave it in the dark where exactly a policy process begins or ends, how to draw temporal and spatial or actorial boundaries around it; why do these questions remain highly contested in policy studies?

Third, there is the puzzling relationship between the different sorts of account of policy in governing—the abstract analytic accounts by academics and researchers, the accounts that participants give of their work, and the accounts derived from empirical observation of policy practice. Practitioners may say (for instance) that "the [stages] model is really about theory, not practice" (Howard 2005, 10); yet see it as important to present the outcome as a "decision" of the appropriate authority (another of the stages). Empirical accounts of policy practice often find it difficult to relate it to the stages of the abstract model but conclude that, the process is "messy"—that is, the failure of practice to conform to the model is a weakness in the practice, not in the model.

Fourth, there is the question of the extent to which the term embodies normative approval. For example, historical etymology for the Netherlands (Van de Graaf and Hoppe 1989, 15–18) shows that "policy" emerged and gained popularity in political discourse because in everyday parlance it was endowed with all desirable qualities that set it apart from the negative connotations of "politics" and "politicking". Hence, scholarly definitions of "policy" frequently intimate qualities like guidance and direction, leadership, coherence, conscious and conscientious deliberation, if not sagacity, wisdom; and order, transparency, strategic focus, and instrumentality in solving public problems.

Now, policy scholars have some good excuses to eschew all too precise definitions of key concepts like "policy" and "policymaking". The world of policy and policymaking hardly lends itself to controlled experimentation and theory testing. Although some scholars would adhere to the Popperian standard that a "theory" should be precise enough to be proven wrong, the field of policy process "theories" falls inevitably short of this standard. The vastly differentiated field is beset by ever newly emerging key concepts, differently interpreted and differently connected in new "theories" or "frameworks of analysis", and studied by very different research methods: from ethnography and history or process tracing of single cases, to standard large-N methods to discover correlations or causal mechanisms between "variables", small-N comparative studies using fuzzy set logic, and many, many more.

We fully agree with Sabatier who in *Theories of the Policy Process* (1999; 2007) stresses the "staggering complexity of the policy process" and discusses "theories" essentially as *simplifications* to make sense of them.

This article is therefore addressed to some particular problems in the theorizing of governing. It examines the place of "policy" in the giving of accounts of governing, and the ways in which different perspectives characterize the nature of "policy", and argues that these accounts are part of the reality that they describe—that is, they are performative as well as representational.

Representation and Performation

In Dvora Yanow's study of an Israeli community corporation, *How Does a Policy Mean*, she notes that at the public annual meeting of the corporation, the executive director would ask, "What are our goals and objectives?" She asks why this should be necessary, given the extent to which this is addressed in other settings, but goes on to point out that the corporation was in fact expanding its activities, and asking this question gave scope for the goals to be defined in a way which encompassed the activities being undertaken, and in doing so, justified the corporation's image as a modern, rational, goal-seeking organization. That is to say, the statement was not so much representing the goals as performing them (Yanow 1996, 199–202). In the representative idiom, scholars manage to project their inductively and/or deductively produced models onto the world, and warrant them as more or less "true", that is, as fairly good representations of a knowable reality, "out there". In the performative idiom, scholars and their theories are not judged by degree of "truth", but pragmatically by degree of effectiveness, performance, or worldly success.

In this article, we want to address the representational and performative roles of theories of the policy process in policy studies (see Figure 1). In *Working for Policy*, we addressed the same theme but with a different purpose in mind. There, we primarily showed the discrepancy between the *experiential* accounts of the policy process told by practitioners engrossed in their own policy work, and the *researched and theorized* accounts of that same process by academics (cf. Turnbull 2013). The question of how academics and practitioners speak to each other and with what impact on each others' work was addressed only superficially (Colebatch, Hoppe, and Noordegraaf 2010, 193ff). Here we explore the same theme, but from the angle of policy practices influenced—sometimes leavened and sometimes biased—by policy studies or science.

"Policy" is a particular way of framing the activity of "governing", seeing it as harnessing state authority to getting to more or less coordinated and deliberated collective, public action (Hoppe 2010, 2); a framing that purports to present both "policy" and the "policy process" as somehow logically coherent, authoritative, and appropriate. This framing happens, usually tacitly, in the reflection on and during practices of policy workers; but it also underlies the framing of policy in much academic work. In this article, we take as a starting point the policy scholars' efforts to describe, articulate, codify, and explain, as accurately as possible, what is, supposedly, "really" going on in practice.

This academic effort produces a fairly large number of formal accounts of the policy process, as propositions or warrantable assertions about such processes. As codified and abstract statements they "travel" easily, that is, they become widely socially distributed in the peer community of policy scholars and nonpeers with an interest in such theories. Thus, starting from "theory" (a rather immodest label, we will show) as representing practices of policy work (upward curved arrow in Figure 1) we move to performation in practices (downward curved arrow). In policy work practices, the formal accounts do influence the framing of practices, but now in nongeneral, narrativized form; and thus less or uncodified, very concrete, contextually specific and constrained by time and place, and limited in social distribution.

The question we ask is: are there selective affinities between academic policy process theories and narratives of policy practice—do policy process theories not merely perform substantive discourse on "observed truth" codified as warrantable assertions in systems of propositional knowledge (or "logos", as Gottweis 2012; Turnbull 2014 would say), but also as practical effort to negotiate social relations ("ethos") and feelings ("pathos") in policy process practices?

The next section deals with academic accounts of policymaking in the representative idiom. We show that, by and large, there are three big "families" of theoretical accounts; each with lots of branches and twigs, and quite some parasitic connections between the three major branches. The third section looks at these academic accounts, reframing them into a performative idiom, as expressive of or prescriptive for policy work practices.

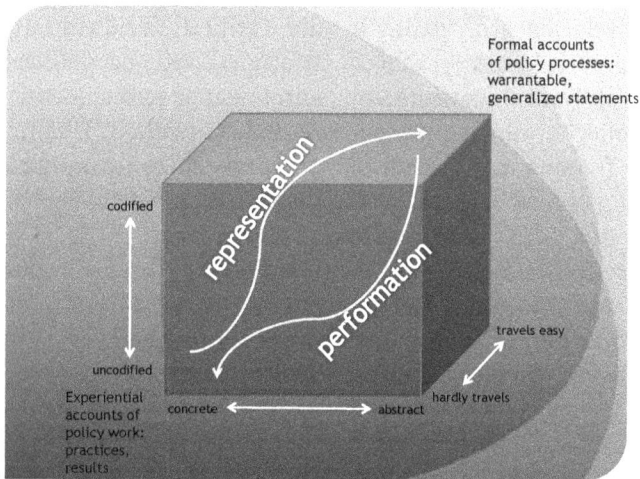

Figure 1. Representation policy science and performation in policy practice

Policy Process Accounts in the Representative Idiom

Three "Families" of Policy Process Framings

It is common for accounts of the policy process to refer to its "complexity"; it is less common to explain the source of the complexity or to discuss how the analysis should be framed so as to deal with this complexity. Our analysis starts from the proposition that "policy" is a particular way of making sense of governing, distinct from other concepts in use such as "politics", "professional judgment", "strategy", or "public management". These concepts attribute particular values to the action, and different constructs relate to different values, and these may complement one another, or compete for attention, or simply run in parallel, or even undermine each other. Even within the concept of "policy", there are multiple values, and we argue that the three key values are *authority*, *association*, and *problematization*. In this section, we will show how these values inform the sorts of accounts that analysts construct, and how both analysts and practitioners deal with the multiplicity of accounts in use.

One prominent account constructs policy as a process that leads to *reasoned and authoritative choice* about the goals and means of collective action. In this frame, the focus is on what Easton has called the "authoritative decision makers," that is, leading politicians in government or parliament, top-management of big (multinational) corporations, leaders of inter- and transnational global organizations, and top-level civil servants. The account sees policy as invoking joint political and scientific authority or expertise in tackling collective action problems. It posits actors as representatives of "governments" who have clear preferences and develop goals which will achieve these preferences.

It generates an instrumental account of the policy process as the pursuit of clear, authoritatively chosen goals. It underlies the survey volumes on "the x (name of political leader) government and public policy", which present governing as the framing and pursuit of the objectives of political leaders, who delegate instrumental problem solving to bureaucrats and scientists-as-advisers.

The second major account highlights the production of coordinated collective action as the result of inclusion or exclusion of policy actors, engaged in *strategic associations* that generate a continuous flow of negotiations and other types of transactions in order to influence the direction, resources, and results of collective action. Attention is drawn to different degrees and modes of structured interaction or ongoing *interactive involvement* in policy-related networks by "proximate policymakers", mid-level and street-level bureaucrats, and all kinds of interest groups and other relevant players with at least some "standing at the policy table". Policymaking practices tend to be stabilized through mutual familiarity, trust, and a commitment to managing. The focus is largely on policy activities as problem solving through organizational formation of habits or standard operating procedures, routinization, institutionalization, or standardization. But, distinct from both alternative accounts, the more agonistic aspects of policymaking also come into view as power struggles, hard bargaining, and other forms of public strife between networks of allies and antagonists.

A third account of policy and policymaking zooms in on analytical-cum-political processes of contested *problematization and joint meaning-* *making* around problematic situations, norms, and practices. Major concerns are critical deliberation, persuasion strategies, and the political struggle for enrolment of actors in competing policy-related networks. Different from the other two, there are no stable focal actors; policymaking is a "dance" of plurivocality and pluralism between all previously mentioned actors, plus ordinary but activist citizens, (transnational) nongovernmental organizations, civil society associations, faith-based organizations, think tanks, academics, specialized journalists and social media, and so on—all those who as collective or individual somehow substantively influence the mentalities, frames, discourses, narratives, and identities that inform policies from which governing practices and regimes emerge. The focus of this set of accounts is on policy as a continuing sociopolitical construction by people managing the problematic in an alternating and oscillating process of puzzling, powering, and shifting participation (Hoppe 2010).

In the next subsections, we will briefly elaborate on each of the three "branches" of this "family tree" of accounts of policy and policymaking.

Policy(making) as Authoritative Choice Shored up by Expertise

Since the Enlightenment and the French and American revolutions, most states appeal to doctrines of legitimacy, that is, state power recognized as legitimate and justified by both ruler and ruled. Usually this has taken the shape of rational legal authority, in which both democratically agreed laws and rational expertise certified by science are the major sources to justify state conduct. The rationality part of this development can be traced to the cameralistics, the "Polizeywisschaften" or "Staatswissenschaften", to other modes of governmentality knowledge, to the history of the social sciences in the late nineteenth and early twentieth centuries in Europe, and of the Progressives and public administration in the United States itself. This movement from mere "politicking" to expert-supported policymaking and government was continued in the United States in the 1950s through Lasswell's (1956) grounding of the field or "discipline" of the policy sciences. Since it was Lasswell's concern to find the policy sciences on the idea of inserting rationality into practices of government and administration, he departed from a broadly defined idea of how rational thinking and acting—that is, thought controls speech; speech controls action; action results feed back into thought— would become empirically traceable in a policy setting (good examples in Parsons 1996, 78–79). Since Lasswell, therefore, Policy Science 1.01 courses almost all begin with teaching students the notion of a policy cycle: a policy problem should, first, become an issue for public debate and acquire agenda status; then follows the stage of policy design or formulation, ending in adoption (or rejection); followed by implementation and, after some more time has elapsed, evaluation of results. If the policy is not terminated after evaluation, a next cycle starts—and so on, and so forth.

This stages approach to policy process analysis has acquired a paradoxical academic status. It has drawn a lot of criticism because of lack of empirical evidence and causal mechanisms driving the process from one stage to the next in the predicted, teleological, and rational sequence. All too often researchers were found guilty of imposing a reverse teleological interpretation on a merely contingent set of events. Yet, it has also informed, at least subliminally, most of the other approaches. One of the enduring legacies of the stages approach is the development of partial process theories along the policy preparation and formulation, and policy implementation "divide" (Hill and Hupe 2014). Another one is the development of evaluation studies as separate specialization (Furubo, Rist, and Speer 2013).

Policy design or formulation (sub)processes were basically specifying the thought styles or design logics or rules in use by policymakers. In doing so, they either refrained from positing any sequence, like Simon's satisficing (Simon 1957) or Lindblom's incrementalism (Lindblom 1968); or they developed rather sophisticated, contingent sequences, like in the empirical elaboration of mixed scanning (Etzioni 1968). In this sense, the stages heuristic was relativized from within, so to speak. Most recently, this relativization is even highly visible in theories about the practice of real-time policy evaluation (Furubo, Rist, and Speer 2013), sometimes jointly with stakeholders (Loeber 2010).

Finally, the stages account led to serious questions about the research strategies for studying policymaking. One of the major theoretical conundrums in all policy process research emerged in implementation studies: the problem of "too many variables" and "too few cases" (Goggin 1986). This problem had profound implications for the new kind of theorizing that followed the stages heuristic—causality-based versus narrativist explanation in nonteleological temporal modalities. It also affected empirical research in the field—single case studies, small-N comparative studies through mixed methods, or large-N quantitative research and standard causal analysis.

Another problem inherent in all stages accounts was that researchers needed *"caesuras"* to distinguish subprocesses from each other. This frequently meant focusing on artifacts indicative of "decisions" marking the transformation of one stage into another—especially different types of policy documents or texts, like party programs, hearings, statutes, terms-of-reference for policy advice, bills, decrees, and evaluation studies. This led to methodological questions about how precisely to study such intermediary policymaking "products"—for example, through argumentative analysis, goals—means analysis, discourse analysis, and so on—and how to assess their meaning in the larger policy landscape. These kinds of issues, originating in the discursive aspects of the stages heuristic, played a role in the transition to what is now known as "the argumentative turn in policy analysis and planning" (Fischer and Forester 1993).

In all this theorizing about "the authorities" and their expert-advisers, the "elephant in the room" was the fact of conflict. For some participants, the task could be seen as policymaking; for others, it was policy resistance. And resistance to one policy initiative may be in order to advance another. "The government" is less an actor than an arena, where struggles over claims are less likely to lead to conclusive determinations than to a temporary pause in a continuing campaign. How the experience of partisan contest could be reconciled with the image of authoritative choice was one important theme in the second "family" of approaches to the study of public policy.

Policy(making) as Association and Interactive Involvement

The second "family" of policy process approaches starts from the idea that policymaking is all about structured interaction and interactive involvement of associations of crucial policy actors. On the one hand, there are theories that focus on the logic of appropriateness embedded in roles and institutions that guide policymaking behavior to the reproduction of ordered practices; and bind policy actors together in ties of familiarity, trust, resources, organization, and commitment to management. In terms of powering (Allen 1998), such theories try to explain how people can act in concert by organizing and stabilizing *power-with*, and, with a view to achieve some collective purpose, *power-to*.

The development and significance of relationships between powerful associations of policy actors has been analyzed at different levels. At one level, it was shown how participants, linked functionally and strategically by a shared interest or resource interdependencies in problem processing on a particular policy domain, might also develop an increasingly shared sense of identity. Richardson and Jordan (1979) identified specialized "policy communities" in the United Kingdom. Some argued that such stable actor associations resembled "subgovernments" subject to the gaze of "attentive publics" (Atkinson and

Coleman 1992). More skeptical of seeing such associations as durable groupings, Heclo (1978), in an American context, thought that they were more like open and flexible "issue networks" where participants could opt in or out as they saw fit. On a second level, typical actor associations were theorized as characteristic for entire patterns of governing. Schmitter and Lehmbruch (1979), in a European context, labeled stable configurations of policy actors from government, business, and trade unions as "corporatism"; though in the United States it was more likely to be an interest in "urban regimes" (Dowding 2001). Others saw the emergence of a new paradigm for the "architecture of complexity" in the gradual erosion of "government" by authoritative direction and rise of "governance" by negotiation between self-organizing networks (Rhodes 1997).

A third level of theorizing the policy process as stabilizing association and practice through functional linkage is the application of institutional theories. Asking *how institutions and rules matter for policymaking*, these frameworks see interactions between policy actors as becoming stabilized through routines, habitual behavior, mutual recognition, labeling, and becoming "infused with value"(Selznick 1957, 17)—in other words, becoming institutionalized. Generally, institutional theories are said to explain long-term stability well, but not change. Three "new institutionalisms" are identified in the literature—historical (Streeck and Thelen 2005), economic (Ostrom 2009), and sociological (March and Olsen 1989)—each tending to generalize from favorite examples and paradigms of explanation within their

own originating disciplines—respectively, the logic of historical paths, the economic logic of interest-based calculation, and the social logic of appropriate behavior— and recently "discursive institutionalism" was added to the list (Schmidt 2008).

All institutionalists except for those who strongly advocate macroviews of modernization, prefer nonteleological ways of thinking. They either use the inductive methods of historical narrative in an eventful temporality in which policymaking processes are considered contingent, open-ended, and noncontinuous by definition. Occasionally, particular events, with the benefit of hindsight, can be assigned the status of origins of significant or pervasive changes in policymaking structures like networks or entire styles of policymaking. Alternatively, positivistically inclined institutionalists search for law-like sequences or causal mechanisms in policymaking processes by resorting to comparative explanation, in an experimental temporality where a small number of supposedly independent and equivalent cases is used to discover or test hypotheses inspired by (middle-range) social science theories (Sewell 2005, 81–123).

On the other hand, there are theories that see collective policy action arising through a more Hobbesian or Schmittian view of "Realpolitik", or a Mouffian view of inevitable agonistic competition and rivalry in politics (Mouffe 2000), that posit a logic of pure power domination or a Gramscian political strategy for hegemony (Gramsci 1971) as the big drivers behind public policy processes. Such theories argue that acting in concert requires *power-over* as instrumental to power-to and power-with (Haugaard 2014). The temporal and/or social inclusion or exclusion from the puzzling and powering that together make up policymaking determines the success or failure of actors' political bid for cognitive and organizational power. Not institutions as enabling or restraining parameters, but the intentions, frames, strategies, resources and modes of power acquisition and maintenance, or coercion, domination and hegemony, and cooperation and conflict are the key. Theories of hard bargaining in bureaucratic politics (Allison 1971), of political opportunity structures for social movements (Kriesi et al. 1995) and operational modes of cadre bureaucracies (e.g., Rothstein 2015) exemplify these agonistic policy process theories.

Policy(making) as Managing the Problematic

The third core value of policy that we identified was *problematization*, and much of the theorizing about policy, particularly in the last few decades, has focused on the concept of problem. It was not part of traditional theorizing about governing, which focused on order and how it was achieved and in what circumstances it could be considered legitimate to use coercion to achieve order. The development, between roughly the eighteenth to the mid-twentieth century, of cameralistics, "Polizeywisschaften" or "Staatswissenschaften", other modes of governmentality knowledge, the history of the social sciences in the late nineteenth and early twentieth centuries in Europe, and of the Progressives and public administration in the United States itself, culminated in Lasswell's call for the mobilization of academic social science in

the process of governing to create a "policy science" which was problem-focused, interdisciplinary, and explicitly normative, leading to the development in (mainly United States) universities (though it emerged from defense contracting and the RAND Corporation) of a technology of systematic choice grounded in microeconomics (Radin 2000; 2013). The function of policy analysis was to clarify the problem, predict the outcome of competing options, and evaluate the action taken; this was "speaking truth to power" (Wildavsky 1979).

Much of this "policy analysis" was done, though how much it was used in the policy process, and for what purpose, was questioned (Lindblom 1990), and it became clear that the nature of "the problem" was not self-evident, but emerged from intellectual clashes and political power play of different and partial perspectives. Majone (1989) argued that the work of the policy analyst was more like that of a courtroom lawyer, crafting a persuasive argument, than a laboratory scientist, and attention was directed to the processes of "problematisation": how situations were seen as normal or deviant, when deviant situations were seen as "problems", when "problems" demanded collective action, who should initiate such action, what actions were appropriate, how the utility of these actions could be assessed, and so on. The emerging "argumentative turn" in policy analysis strongly focused attention on this process (e.g., Fischer and Forester 1993; Hajer and Wagenaar 2003; Hoppe 2010; Yanow 1996).

In this perspective, the central question is: How and why do ideas, beliefs, images, ideologies, worldviews, paradigms, or other mental constructs impact on policy processes? Why do some ideas become the policies, programs, and policy philosophies that dominate politics and political decision making, while others become sidelined, marginalized, or neglected? We can distinguish here between ideas-based accounts traceable to cognitive psychology and cognitive science, and approaches embedded in a social-constructivist, meaning-based ontology of social reality (e.g., Fligstein and McAdams 2012, 32ff).

In the former, ideas have primacy over and are tightly coupled to speech and action; and theorists and researchers stick to mainstream, often quantitative methods of researching the policy process. Sabatier's "advocacy coalition framework" (Sabatier and Jenkins-Smith 1988) sees the policy-oriented behavior of actors as dominated by their "worldview", made up of "deep core beliefs" and "policy core beliefs". Advocacy coalitions are formed between actors, both public and nonpublic, on the basis of congruency (not consensus) in their belief system and coordinated political strategizing. On the other hand, Kingdon's "multiple streams" approach (1995) sees the mind-set of the actors as being more related to their skill-set and occupational position (the two being closely related). He identifies some actors as focusing on the nature and source of the concern (the "problem stream"), others as focusing on what could be done about it (the "policy stream"), and a third cluster concerned with what (if anything) should be done about it (is this something with which government should be concerned?), and more particularly, what were opportune moments for government to intervene. Kingdon argued that the three streams operated largely independently of one another and that a critical question in

policy analysis was to identify the ways in which links were made between them (see Zahariadis 2003).

Both of these approaches tend to focus attention on the stability of policy settings, resting as they do on the knowledge and values of the actors. But Jones and Baumgartner (2005) focus on change as well as stability, and on the relationship between them. They argue that policy subsystems dominated by stabilized policy images can be punctuated by bursts of nonincremental change through disproportionate decision making. So long-term patterns of periods of stability and incremental change with short outbursts of nonincremental change, returning to a new equilibrium, give their theory of political information processing and attention allocation its most well-known name: punctuated equilibrium theory. Its proponents claim to have integrated incremental and nonincremental patterns of policy change in an overarching new theory (Howlett and Migone 2011).

Accounts of the social construction of meaning take a broader perspective, starting with the social process of meaning-making and asking: How and why do sociopolitically constructed meanings impact the policy process? Politics is conceptualized as a struggle to control and impose shared meaning that governs collective action projects or, in Foucault's words, become hegemonic governmentalities (Dean 1999/2010). Edelman (1988) and Alexander (2010, 276ff) view politics as an elite-staged spectacle of performances where "background representations, scripts, actors, means of symbolic production, *mise en scène*, social and interpretive power, and audiences" either "felicitously" fuse in truthful and real narratives believed by the public, or become rejected by them as fake and contrived. Following Yanow (1996), in policymaking the vital question becomes: "*how do policies mean?*" Policymaking is a never-ending series of communications and strategic action moves by which various policy actors in all kinds of forums of public deliberation and coupled arenas of policy subsystems construct intersubjective meanings that inform collective action; and the socially constructed outputs and outcomes of these collective actions feed back into policy speech and policy thought with a disciplining impact on the behavior of citizens. This social constructivism in policy process accounts gained particular popularity in policy design and agenda-setting contexts, although it is also to be found in implementation settings.

Ingram and Schneider's (1995) theory of policy design argues that "target populations" are sociopolitically constructed—for example, as contenders, as advantaged, as dependents, or as deviants—in and through policies. Policymakers' shifting perceptions and attitudes (or stereotypes) of target populations during policy design are the independent variable; the authoritative policy texts and subsequent implementation practices are intermediary variables; impacting on the quality of democracy as dependent variable—that is, citizen perceptions of the policy in question, the policy's impact on their group identities, their orientations toward government, and their willingness and resources for political mobilization and participation. This state-of-democracy effect in turn becomes part of the subsequent political environment in which policymakers search for policies

that reward their efforts (e.g., through re-election) or ward off risks (e.g., by inadvertently strengthening contenders). Although the role of policymaking in the social construction of groups is relative (to advertisements, popular culture, and social discrimination), it should be seen as an important political tool for social change in the distribution and redistribution of people's life chances in society (Schneider, Ingram, and deLeon 2014). Recently, the approach has been generalized from its focus on policymakers' stereotypes of target groups to a generic approach of "policy feedback theory" (Mettler and SoRelle 2014; but also Hoppe 2010).

This concludes our overview of the major known and popular policy process frameworks, presented as three "families of frameworks", each one with a clear root metaphor—authority, association, and problematization—but all sprouting from the same trunk: policy process. Policy scholars in academia will keep quarreling over the representational qualities or degrees of verisimilitude (in Popper's terminology) of these accounts. Or they will create narratives of learning, wherein teleological and authoritative accounts of choice are being replaced by contingent and open-ended accounts of association and problematization—or combinations of both (Schlager 1999; 2007). Or they may tell tales in which the complete set of accounts is viewed, eclectically and pragmatically, as a toolkit from which researchers choose and pick those concepts and frameworks, and multiple registers of temporality (Sewell 2005, 107–110) and research methodologies that make a case or multiple cases understandable and transparent, as the researchers sees fit (in this direction, Cairney and Heikkila

2014). This is not the path we want to follow in this article. Rather, we would like demonstrate the importance of the other function of academic accounts: as performative for and in practice.

The Three Basic Approaches in the Performative Mode

Studying the Performative Mode of Policy Sciences

In his well-known *How To Do Things With Words*, Austin (1962) coined the notion of the performativity of particular speech acts. These are utterances that say something and actually do what they express simultaneously. A wedding officer in an official wedding ceremony uttering the words: "Hereby I declare you husband and wife" to a designated couple, thereby simultaneously changes the legal-marital status of the man and the woman involved. From this linguistic category, Callon (2007, 311–357) derived the concept of "performation" to denote how economics as academic discipline is involved in (co-)"performing" the economy, for example, by creating new product markets in line with the idea of a perfect market, new ways to improve calculative agencies and calculated contracts as the quintessential economic transaction, or new ideas for econometric modeling to better predict the future value of a firm's investments or a nation's Gross Domestic Product, and so on.

How do the selective affinities between disciplinary knowledge and "real-world" practices come about? The performation of the discipline of economics in and on the world of markets and the economy is not a self-executing

process, but relentless and continuous hard work. It involves discursive struggles, self-fulfilling prophecies, expression of roles as performances in institutional designs, and prescription. Holm (2007, 235), describing the introduction of Individual Transferable Quotas in Norwegian fisheries, observes:

"In order for market actors to calculate the probable outcomes of their choices buyer and seller must be produced as fairly separate and autonomous agencies. The object to be traded must be constructed as reasonably stable and thing-like. A minimum agreement as to the nature of property rights and how they can change hands must be negotiated. *These things do not lie in wait…but need to be constructed, often with tremendous amounts of hard work* (italics by rh&hc). …The more institutionalized, naturalized, technological, and thing-like they become, the better they will work *in dis-embedding agents and objects from their social, cultural, and technological contexts* (italics by rh&hc), setting them free to realize—put into reality—the market model invented by the economist."

Thus, theory impacts on practice by "dis-embedding" agents and objects from their life worlds and action contexts. Practitioners are nudged to disregard their habits and tacit knowledge, and heed, and adapt to their situation, precepts inspired by the abstract and more widely distributed formal insights from economics. Even stronger, if actors are unwilling to do so, they are either seduced into compliance by means of new incentive systems or simply replaced by other actors who are more willing to be enrolled in the new network and its rules of the game. A complementary, more neo-pragmatist route to performativity, predicts convergence of theories and institutionalized, routinized practices through suppression of questions and autonomization of answers, and thereby shaping of—organizationally embedded—predispositions to act or habits. Both Turnbull (2013, 121) and Hoppe (2010, 4, 243–244) point to the question suppressing or problem-structuring qualities inherent in *both* theories and ordinary practices as the sources of performativity.

Whatever be the social mechanisms through which the selective affinities in (co-) performance come about, we could (and should) study the performance of policy studies/sciences— the downward arrow in Figure 1—as distinct "object" of research. For example, we could ask how public choice informed policy analysis (as in Weimer and Vining 1998) really works out in policy practice when applied to regulating the salmon fishery system in Canada, or auctioning radio spectrum licenses; and how this feeds back into the "theory and methods" courses and new research in academia. Or we could ask how the theory and methods of (regulatory) impact assessment are translated in bureaucratic standard operating procedures; and how this does or does not feed back into policymaking theory and methods of policy analysis (Dunlop, Maggetti, and Radaelli 2012; Hoppe 2009; Staroňová 2010;2013). In this way, we would lay the foundation of sociology or anthropology of innovations in governance. This would systematically interrogate the relationship between disciplinary policy scientific knowledge and policymaking practices as innovation and stabilization "journeys" of policy ideas and derived policy instruments. Such innovation pathways of performance

have been explored already for a number of policy instruments: carbon emission trading, disentangling railway infrastructure management and train transportation of passengers and goods in public/private participation schemes, and the idea of "transition management"(Voss 2007; 2014).

However, a first task, one that can be performed in this article, is an exploration of modes or types of policy work and their selective affinities with the three basic representational approaches to the policymaking process. In this analysis, for practical reasons, we focus on institutional requirements and organizational settings, but also on the person-level skills required if policy work is primarily framed according to one of the three basic approaches.

Performation of Authoritative Choice

One may hypothesize that the "stubborn" permanence of the stages account of policymaking is due to at least a number of important ideas infusing policymaking practice. First, the stages idea corresponds to a common-sense notion of rationality inherent in the notion of "policy" itself (as shown above). This idea fits the practice of citizens delegating decision-making powers in nested accountability forums to bureaucratic or scientific experts and elected politicians. Experts—either as skilled and experienced civil servants, or as well-trained and high-reputation scientists—are the "rational actors" who as decision support specialists, having mastered lots of scientific methods and techniques of policy analysis (Dunn 2011), help elected leaders make policy decisions. The rationality idea also serves as some kind of meta-level in order to judge the outcomes and the quality of the decision-making process itself.

A second reason for the permanent influence of the stages frame is that it corresponds to normative democratic theory and its translation into the major events, or decision moments, of normal practices of separation of power under conditions of representative democracy and rule of law. For a democratic separation of powers and division of labor to function well, and for the nested system of democratic accountability to be transparent and work, there ought to be politically predefined and visible decisions on issues on the parliamentary and governmental agenda, when a policy-as-design is formally adopted as legally in force; and subsequent decision moments on how adopted designs are translated into administrative decrees, routines, contracts, or actions by other collective and private actors in achieving the results somehow promised and announced in the formal policy decision (Jann and Wegrich 2007; Van de Graaf and Hoppe 1996, 90–92).

Joined together as an ideal of rational-cum-democratic government, taught and advised by policy scholars, and continuously mimicked and applied, in earnest or "tongue in cheek", by policy practitioners, we get *the stages heuristic as a sacred enacted story* told in justification of political and administrative power to citizens and journalists alike. In policy studies, we see a lot of research in the authoritative and instrument choice paradigm that supports the rational democracy sacred story of reforms in policy practice. We limit ourselves here to just two examples.

First, under the spur of the revival of evidence-based policymaking (e.g., Bogenschneider and Corbett 2010), policy scholars have rediscovered empirical research into how skillful "rational" civil servants in policymaking jobs actually are. Apart from the ability to think in terms of clear and distinct ideas, these "hard" skills require the conventional good writing skills, but these days information technology skills are also required. Since policy analysts work in "real-time" and time pressure is always present, to be able to work on-the-fly, crisply, quickly, and timely also is a required skill. Large-N surveys are used to establish to what extent and how sophisticated these civil servants are in applying the typical policy analytic textbook methods and techniques (good overview in Kohoutek 2013). The results of such research morph into reforms for improved human resource management, professional education, and ultimately, hopefully improved state competence and capacity. And here a third advantage of the stages heuristic kicks in: it has the benefit of being easily teachable as a kind of "prototype" or "reference design" (like in architecture) of how policy studies understand their own subject. Other approaches are taught essentially as (sometimes necessary) "deviations" from this prototype.

Second, and probably much more influential, there is a true outpouring of comparative studies that measure and standardize all (un)desirable qualities—like rule-of-law, corruption, crime rate, public health, sustainability, sustainable governance, and so on— of modern, (neo)liberal, democratic, capitalist, and innovative states. Using such measurements—all crude or more sophisticated translations of key concepts in the social and political sciences in large indicator and "big" data sets—social science scholars in academia, think tanks, and advisory bodies use these data sets for comparative research to discover evidence-based causal pathways to better outcomes. For example, using the measurement of perceived corruption as pioneered by Transparency International and conventional, long-term measurement of growth in GDP by the IMF, WB or the OECD allow calculation of the statistical correlation between corruption and economic growth; interpreted causally, this delivers an estimate of how harmful corruption is to economic development. Using such novel "scientific" insights, states compete on "best practices", and transnational bodies like the World Bank and the International Monetary Fund or the OECD apportion not only praise and blame, but also allocate huge amounts of financial resources among the deserving nations. These practices of evidence-based comparative research and policy analysis cannot but lead to a lots of "govern like us" advice (Thomas 2015).

Obviously, the rational democracy and stages heuristic as sacred, front-stage and "on-the-table" story needs a profane, back-stage and "under-the-table" counter-narrative. Policy is less "public" than frequently assumed, and is not just the officially enunciated governmental plan it is often supposed to be; it is also, "what happens when neither the public nor elected policymakers have the ability to pay attention to what goes on in their name" (Cairney 2014). This is where other two policy process narratives come in.

Performation of Policy as Association

Radin (2000; 2013) observed two co-evolving trends in public policymaking in the United States: on the one hand, policy analysis as an academic profession had come of age and even reached mid-life; on the other hand, the now fully professionalized "policy analysts" more and more frequently experienced a "disconnect" between their training and skills required on the job, especially in nonfederal policy settings. Radin analyzes how policy analysis, originally created to counter bureaupolitics and politics as party-political and interest group conflict, was "gobbled up" by the structure and culture of American politics. And hence fragmented from one, clearly defined policy analytic unit in the top of federal government (agencies), to a "field of many voices, approaches, and interests." The most likely reason for Radin's observation was that professional-academic training, in terms of Gardner's theory of multiple intelligences (Gardner 1983), was biased toward linguistic and logical-mathematical skills. For example, even Dunn (2011, 1–2), who uses one of the broadest concepts of "rationality" to be found in the policy scientific literature defines policy analysis as the trained skills to use multiple *research methods* to create, critically evaluate, and communicate policy relevant *knowledge* (italics by rh&hc). Yet, policy practice, in addition, requires highly developed noncognitive, interpersonal, visual, and intrapersonal (motivational, emotional, and self-reflexive) modes of practical intelligence for successfully completing practical policy tasks.

In fact, a long time ago founding fathers of the policy science field with lots of practical experience like Dror (1967), Halperin (1974), and Meltsner (1976; 1979;1990) had already drawn attention to the non- and extra-rational dimensions, and the almost inevitable links between policy as analysis and policy as politics, communication, and face-to-face advice-giving in small groups. Drawing attention to the blurred demarcation between policy formulation/ adoption and implementation in policy process practices, Bardach (1977) pointed out that intimate knowledge of bureaucratic organizations and the "jungle" of implementation networks informed the practice of "fixers". Policy workers that "fix" the continuous translation of policy-as-decision into policy-as-standard-operating-procedures must be able to intervene effectively, know about the what, when, how, and who of operational routines, and make sense of the multiple flows of information about implementation games in one or more organizations—skills that are surely not entirely analytical.

In 1983, Kingdon (1984), harping on the theme of co-evolving demarcations between agenda setting (the "problem stream"), policy formulation (the "solution stream"), and the policy adoption (the "political stream"), pointed out the importance of policy entrepreneurs with the developed political sensibilities or intuition to "sniff out" political windows of opportunity for coupling policy ideas and solutions. In a later addition, Zahariadis (2003) stresses that, far from analytic skills, policy entrepreneurs "have a nose" for simplification, manipulation, and political opportunism or sheer serendipity. In the same line, it has been pointed out that in practical policymaking, the role of "spin doctors" and public-relations specialists in crafting policy frames and images is frequently more important than those of policy analysts and their expertise in crafting policy argumentation.

Thus, Radin's observation is not at all new, but somehow we did not openly include nonanalytic qualities and skills in the professional body of knowledge. Conceptually, Radin's disconnect is quickly repaired. Focusing on skills, Mintrom (2003) listed the importance of people skills for policy analysts, like networking and communication skills, team work, courtesy and likeability, and minimal emotional intelligence. Howlett and Ramesh (2014) now distinguish between analytical, managerial, and political capacities, also at the level of individual policy analysts. All this actually raised the issue of whether policy activity could be adequately conceived as "advice" followed by "choice". But, theoretically more important, Colebatch (2006) coined the concept of *policy work*. For him, "work" stood for any skilled, conscious, and directed activity requiring time commitment, located in a workplace, and usually remunerated. Linked to "policy", Colebatch performed the pragmatic turn, previously characteristic for the social studies of science and technology (cf. Sismondo 2004; 2011): no longer philosophy-of-science and epistemology-inspired textbook knowledge of "proper" methods of policy analysis and ways of (policy relevant) knowledge certification like "evidence-based policy" would be center stage; but observation and study of the entire spectrum of "what those professionally engaged in policy actually do, in other words, how policy is done and how policy practices evolve" is to be the core in empirical research and professional training. "Policy analysis" is a far too lofty, rationalistic, over-intellectualized label for the many kinds of hard and not-so-rational, down-to-earth "work" that makes policy. In other words, policy analytic professional training omitted important aspects of policy practice; precisely those aspects of association and interactive involvement that were highlighted in the second academic approach to policy process studies—that is, not just puzzling and cooperation for consensus formation, but patient institutionalization of (new) policy practices, and powering, competition, and political struggle for action in concert, frequently for continued domination or hegemony (Haugaard 2014). Briefly, the notion of "policy work" caught two birds with one stone: in performative studies of the policy process it brought back both the nonanalytic and the agonistic (de AlameidaFortis 2014; Mouffe 2000).

Empirically, these views were amply justified. Debunking the popular prejudice that only top-level civil servants and politicians in executive roles were actually making policy, Page and Jenkins (2005) were able to show that, actually, thousands of civil servant of middle ranks were deeply involved in policy design and the preparation of policy proposals for adoption in parliament. This confirmed insights from the Netherlands (e.g., Colebatch, Hoppe, and Noordegraaf 2010; Hoppe 1983; Hoppe, Van de Graaf, and Besseling1995; Hupe 1992; Woeltjes 2010). Reconstructing the policy formulation of some 20 policy white papers in the Netherlands, Mayer and his fellow researchers identified six styles of policy design and analysis, only three of which (rational, client advice, and argumentative styles) bore clear resemblances to traditional views of policy analysis; the other three, process management, interactive, and

participatory-democratic styles, were falling outside this purview (Mayer, Van Daalen, and Bots 2004). Echoing Radin's observation that process expertise had become one of trained policy analysts' most prominent practical assets, an entire "school" of public administration and policy analysis in the Netherlands turned to governance network theory (Kickert, Klijn, and Koppenjan 1997), placing process management and attendant skills as key in policymaking processes. Recently, Roe (2013) focused on the practical knowledge and skills in real time required of middle-management policy workers as "mess managers", who act as indispensable "facilitators" or "mediators" between grand-design policy visionaries at the apex of organizations and day-to-day practices of "street-level" bureaucrats at the bottom, in order to safeguard the reliable functioning of the huge socio-technical infrastructures of electricity generation, water provision, sewage processing, and internet services.

A similar story of relative neglect of certain skills in policy work can be told about the dimension of political strife and struggle, or the agonistic aspects of ordinary policymaking practices. This is in spite of the fact that Lindblom (1968) already stressed the dual nature of policymaking as "thinking out" and "fighting about" policy; and Wildavsky (1979) characterized policymaking as both cogitation and (competitive) interaction; and Heclo (1978) famously showed that policymaking entailed both intellectual puzzling and political powering between competing interests. These agonistic dimensions of policy work definitely give it the feel of being interactive, erratic, and relentlessly iterative, like many practitioners describe it. Contrary to policy entrepreneurs who, constructively, try to push issues on the governmental agenda, Cobb and Ross (1997) showed that there were also "policy saboteurs" who designed political strategies to deny or derail issues. Following up on Proctor and Schiebinger's (2008) book about "agnotology", that is, the cultural production and the deliberate mobilization and exploitation of political ignorance, Oreskes and Conway (2011) showed that there exists an entire policy analytic industry that exploits scientists' honest reporting of uncertainties in research, on, for example, smoking and climate change, to block or hinder those in favor of policy change on these issues. It might be argued that what Riker (1986) calls the art of heresthetics and political manipulation, or treatises on coalition building and consensus formation, and the art of negotiation (Fisher and Ury 1981/1991; Raiffa 1982) and contemporary power politics (BuenoDe Mesquita and Smith 2013), all pay sufficient attention to powering in policymaking. Yet, there are very few systematic efforts to describe and analyze the strategies and required skills of policy workers in this continuous struggle to support and oppose, raise or suppress issues, and foster or block political participation in collective (in)action for public policy change. One of the sparse efforts we are aware of is in Mahoney and Thelen (2010, 28–31). They argue that, depending on the goals of actors (abrupt or gradual policy change), characteristics in political contexts (strong or weak veto possibilities), and the institutional target (low or high levels of discretion in rule interpretation/enforcement), particular actor types and power strategies emerge (subversives, insurrectionaries, parasitic symbionts, and opportunists).

All in all, much less than in the frame of policy analytic skills, efforts in the performation of policy as association and structured interaction is a relatively neglected field of research. It is perhaps more difficult to study the power clustering and agonistic aspects of policymaking processes, but there is a clear need for this type of research effort in the study of public policy.

Performation of Policy as Problematization

The performative link (downward arrow in Figure 1) between theories of managing the problematic and policy work may be designated as the practice of reflective practitionership (Schön 1983), or prudence, or political wisdom (Hoppe 1983; Loeber 2004): the art and craft of selecting from "theory" those elements which, adapted and transformed in the light of a decision situation or policy practice, deliver a pragmatic way forward out of a problematic situation. It may be negatively described as rejection of well-known, "purified," or "essentialized" framings of policy work as (1) mere puzzling/analysis, following a logic of consequences or as (2) institutionalization/routinization, by applying the logic of appropriateness, or as (3) powering, using the logic of hegemony and domination (depicted as the horizontal upper line in Figure 2). Perhaps the best characterization of reflective practitionership in problematizing modes of policymaking is *mediation* between relevant stakeholders in such a way that problematic situations and events may gradually be turned into less or un-problematic routines and institutionalized practices (Depicted as the vertical middle line in Figure 2).

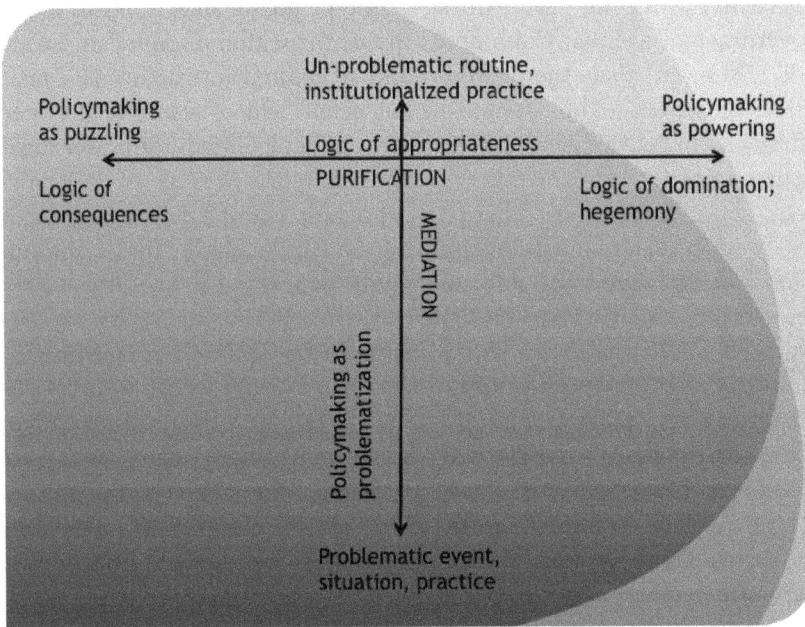

Figure 2. Problematizing policy work as mediation

More than other policy workers, "problematizers" are deeply convinced that policy problems are always claims of one group of citizens on another group (Hoppe 2010, 66–67); and, hence, that "policy issues spark a public into being" (Marres 2005). The inevitable implication is that in public policymaking puzzling, powering and institutionalizing are strongly intertwined and hence, in terms of policy workers' performance, equally important. Compared to other types of policy work, this demands an extraordinary amount of reflexive skills. It requires more than Schön's "double vision" of *ex post* reflection-*on*-action of the accomplished policy scholar who, as spectator, spots the exemplar or generative metaphor from his professional repertoire in a past problem situation; and the *ex durante* reflection-*in*-action of the accomplished practitioner who, as actor, conducts a reflective conversation with the current new problematic by respecting its uncertainty, instability, and uniqueness (Schön 1983). It actually, on top, requires a kind of "triple vision" of simultaneous awareness of puzzling, powering, and (de)institutionalizing, in full acknowledgement of the relational sometimes conflictual and agonistic character of these three activities. This makes the policy worker part of the chorus, not necessarily its conductor, engaged in the communicative performance of politics as making sense together (Forester 1989, 119–133; Hoppe 1999).

In terms of skills, policy workers as problematizers need excellent ethical awareness and sensitivity; skills in productively dealing with or boundary work between multi- and interdisciplinary dimensions of scientific contributions to policymaking (Hoppe 2014); and simultaneous possession of analytical acumen to judge the quality and/or the bias or distortion in policy arguments, and the rhetorical persuasiveness to bring crucial ethical, scientific, and instrumental messages across in a nonexpert like way to differently socialized and unequally educated audiences (Forester 1989). Leadership skills like emotion control, self-confidence, resilience, and patience are also desirable qualities in policymakers as problematizers and sense makers.

In terms of recognizable roles in actual policymaking, one could think of mediation specialists or consensus builders in public disputes (Forester 1989; 2013; Susskind 2006). What sets *mediators* apart from hard-bargaining negotiators (mentioned in the previous section) is that the former care deeply about the relationship, trust, and credibility with stakeholders or the broader public once disputes are settled. According to Landwehr (2014, 86–87) they not only guard rules of procedure and moderate the debate between stakeholder groups with vested interests, but summarize opinions and discussion results by highlighting areas of (dis)agreement and possible shared ground for solution. Other discernable roles for policy workers in problematizing practices deal with the initiation, management, and results of so-called deliberative mini-public policy exercises. Next to the already discussed role of a mediator, Landwehr (2014, 85–89) distinguishes between two more possible roles for policy workers. The *"moderator"* role is required in discussions where all listeners may also be speakers, and where the goal is establishing rational, justified premises for policymaking, and where passionate speaking or rhetoric is considered inappropriate. An even more demanding role is that of the *"facilitator"*, which is to help a deliberative group reach its own goals of achieving collective action through inclusive but plurivocal coordinated policy designs. No doubt, given the variety of forms and goals of deliberative policy exercises, more policy worker roles could be distinguished and will be discovered through systematic research into deliberative democratic practices.

In science–policy advisory interaction, too, problematizing and sense-making policy work is to be found, for example, the role of honest broker as depicted by Pielke (2007). Under the almost "new normal" conditions where policy disputes pivot around value disagreements that cannot be resolved by reduction of scientific uncertainties, policy advisors—whether scientists or not—are particularly hard-pressed to make sense of the problematic situation. In these conditions they have a choice to become an "issue advocate", who openly and publicly sides with a particular policy agenda or option proposed by one or a coalition of stakeholders. Together with the role of a "stealth advocate"—an issue advocate who cloaks himself in the role of a pure scientist—the "issue advocate" role fits the set of policy workers' roles under the previously discussed label of taking sides in the political struggle and strife. But, moving over to the problematizing and sense-making set of roles, the policy worker may alternatively opt for the role of an "*honest broker*", who clarifies the scientifically warrantable "facts", and, on that basis, elaborates on the existing range of policy options, sometimes identifying new options, and on the basis of strict goals–means and other forms of practical argumentation (Fischer 1980; 1995; Toulmin 1958) integrates stakeholder concerns with available scientific knowledge.

Policy work as analysis and bargaining easily fits the hegemonic political landscape of representative democracy, interest pluralism or neocorporatism, bureaucracy, and expert advice. Policy work as problematization and joint sense-making, however, institutionally draws on more participatory and deliberative modes of democracy. Even though the space for these modes of democracy seems to become larger, they sit uneasily in the prevailing political structures (Hoppe 2010). This means that there is another possible role for problematizing policy workers—the *institutional entrepreneur* (Garud, Hardy, and Maguire 2007; e.g., see cf. Sterrenberg 2010; Loeber 2010). When policy workers feel that most stakeholders are locked in permanent stalemates and no longer believe in the problem-solving capacities of existing organizational routines, governance networks, and decision-making procedures, they may start pondering the possibility of "creative institutional destruction", or "bricolage" or tinkering with different elements of the political infrastructure to cobble together a new governance network, with (partially) new actors, and thus new convictions and beliefs, willing to try new policy instruments and solutions. Using terminology from punctuated equilibrium theory, "policy entrepreneurs" become "institutional entrepreneurs" when they seriously try to push a policy subsystem out of its incremental dynamics of gradual change into the "punctuation" which

marks the transitional dynamics toward a very different type of equilibrium. Institutional entrepreneurs normally have their locus in the margins of or "above" well-institutionalized policy networks. Being familiar with more than one policy-framing and policy-political logic, they can think more innovatively and creatively than network "insiders". Having access to financial and communicative resources unavailable to routine players, they can start influencing the discourse, composition, modes, and rules of participation by actors, and introduce new rules of the game (Sørensen and Torfing 2005, 202–205).

Conclusion

When, in the aftermath of World War II, Lasswell reinvented the policy sciences for the United States, he distinguished between knowledge *of* and knowledge *in* policy. In the United States, but in European countries less so, this apparently logical practical division of academic labor led to a sharp demarcation between the academic-disciplinary study of public policymaking processes and a pragmatic-professional project to create through the establishment of schools of policy analysis a community of "policy analysts", and to insert them in the governmental structures of the United States (deLeon 1989). No doubt, this effort was successful. Policy "analysis" spread all over the institutions and levels of the different branches of US government; and much of the originally "expert" discourse on public policy entered everyday political, administrative, journalistic, and informed citizens' talk. But Radin's (2000; 2013) keen observation that nowadays many policy analysts feel a disconnect between their education and their daily professional practice means that the Lasswellian distinction had negative side effects and has run its course. It is high time to reconnect.

Therefore, in this article we have redubbed this distinction as the representative and performative modes of policy science; and, hopefully, we have shown that they exist sometimes as open and sometimes as hidden selective affinities. Hopefully, our exploratory breaking down the demarcation zone between knowledge of and knowledge in policy has brought to light linkages and convergences that indicate a more complex task field, a richer set of skills and broader set of analytic techniques than conventional accounts of policy analysis. Like in the sciences, these go beyond a linear connection from "pure" or "basic" to "applied" policy science (Nowotny, Scott, and Gibbons 2001; Ziman 2000). Rather, the idea of reconnection is to catalyze a permanent policy-reflective culture of listening and dialogue between the reflective and the performative modes of engaging with public policy. In such a way, practical accounts of policy workers will inspire policy scholars to reflect better; and academic accounts of policy processes will be used as a pragmatic-eclectic "toolkit" for re-thinking and creating possible practical trajectories.

References

Alexander, J.C. 2010. *The Performance of Politics*. Oxford: Oxford University Press.

Allen, A. 1998. "Rethinking Power." *Hypatia* 13 (1): 21–40.

Allison, G.T. 1971. (and P. Zelikow, 1999, Second Edition), *Essence of Decision: Explaining the Cuban Missile Crisis*. New York: Longman.

Atkinson, M.M. and W.D. Coleman. 1992. "Policy Communities, Policy Networks and the Problems of Governance." *Governance* 5: 154–180.

Austin, J.L. 1962. *How to do Things with Words*. Oxford: Oxford University Press.

Bardach, E. 1977. *The Implementation Game: What Happens After a Bill Becomes a Law*. Cambridge and London: MIT Press.

Bogenschneider, K. and T.J. Corbett. 2010. *Evidence-Based Policymaking. Insights from Policy-Minded Researchers and Research-Minded Policymakers*. London and New York: Routledge.

Bueno De Mesquita, B. and A. Smith. 2013. *The Dictator's Handbook. Why Bad Behavior Is Almost Always Good Politics*. New York: Public Affairs.

Cairney, P. 2014. "Defining Policy Shows how Messed up it Seems." (http://paulcairney. wordpress.com (accessed January 8, 2014).

Cairney, P. and T. Heikkila. 2014. "A Comparison of Theories of the Policy Process." *Sabatier and Weible* 363–390.

Callon, M. 2007. "What Does It Mean To Say the Economics is Performative?" In, eds. D. MacKenzie, F. Muniesa, and L. Siu. , 311–358.

Cobb, R.W. and M.H. Ross. 1997. *Cultural Strategies of Agenda Denial: Avoidance, Attack and Redefinition*. Lawrence, KS: Kansas University Press.

Colebatch, H.K. 2006. *The Work of Policy. An International Survey*. Lanham, MD: Lexington Books.

Colebatch, H.K., R. Hoppe, and M. Noordegraaf, eds. 2010. *Working for Policy.* Amsterdam: Amsterdam University Press.

deAlameida Fortis, M. 2014. "Bringing Politics and Administration Together: For An Agonistic Policy Model." PhD Thesis, Westminster University, London.

Dean, M. 1999 (2010, Second Edition). *Governmentality: Power and Rule in Modern Society.* London: Sage.

deLeon, P. 1989. *Advice and Consent: The Development of the Policy Sciences.* New York: Russell Sage Foundation.

Dowding, K. 2001. "Explaining Urban Regimes." *International Journal of Urban and Regional Research* 25 (1): 7–19.

Dror, Y. 1967. "Policy Analysts: A New Professional Role in Government Service." *Public Administration Review* 27 (3): 197–203.

Dunlop, C.A., M. Maggetti, and C. Radaelli. 2012. "The Many Uses of Regulatory Impact Assessment: A Meta-Analysis of EU and UK Cases." *Regulation and Governance* 6 (1): 23–45.

Dunn, W.N. 2011.*Public Policy Analysis: An Introduction*, Fifth Edition. Upper Saddle River, NJ: Pearson Prentice Hall.

Dye, T.R. 1985. *Understanding Public Policy*, Fifth Edition. Englewood Cliffs, NJ: Prentice Hall.

Edelman, M. 1988. *Constructing the Political Spectacle.* Chicago, IL: Chicago University Press.

Etzioni, A. 1968. *The Active Society: A Theory of Societal and Political Processes.* New York: Free Press.

Fischer, F. 1980. *Politics, Values and Public Policy: The Problem of Methodology.* Boulder, CO: Westview.

Fischer, F. and J. Forester, eds. 1993. *The Argumentative Turn in Policy Analysis and Planning.* Durham, NC: Duke University Press.

Fischer, F., G.J. Miller, and M.S. Sidney, eds. 2007. *Handbook of Public Policy Analysis: Theory, Politics, and Methods.* Boca Raton, FL: CRC Press.

Fisher, R. and W.L. Ury. 1981 (1991, Second Edition). *Getting to Yes: Negotiating Agreement Without Giving In.* Harmondsworth: Penguin

Fligstein, N. and D. McAdams. 2012. *A Theory of Fields.* Oxford: Oxford University Press.

Forester, J. 1989. *Planning in the Face of Power.* Berkeley: University of California Press.

Forester, J. 2013. *On the Theory and Practice of Critical Pragmatism: Deliberative Practice and Creative Negotiations.* London: Sage.

Furubo, J.E., R.C. Rist, and S. Speer, eds. 2013. *Evaluation and Turbulent Times. Reflections on a Discipline in Disarray.* New Brunswick/London: Transaction Publishers.

Gardner, H. 1983. *Frames of Mind* .New York: Basic Books.

Garud, R., C. Hardy, and S. Maguire. 2007. "Institutional Entrepreneurship as Embedded Agency: An Introduction to a

Special Issue." *Organization Studies* 28 (7): 957–969.

Goggin, M.L. 1986. "The Too Few Cases-Too Many Variables Problem in Implementation Research." *The Western Political Quarterly* 39 (2): 328–347.

Goldstone, J.A. 2014. *Revolutions: A Very Short Introduction.* Oxford: Oxford University Press.

Gottweis, H. 2012. "Political Rhetoric and Stem Cell Therapy in the United States: Embodiments, Scenographies, and Emotions." In *The Argumentative Turn Revisited: Public Policy as Communicative Practice*, eds. H. Gottweiss, and F. Fischer. Durham, NC: Duke University Press, 211–235.

Gramsci, A. 1971. *Prison Notebooks.* London: Lawrence and Wishart.

Hajer, M.A. and H. Wagenaar, eds. 2003. *Deliberative Policy Analysis: Understanding Governance in the Network Society.* Cambridge: Cambridge University Press.

Halperin, M.H. and P. Clapp. 1972 (2006, Second Edition). *Bureaucratic Politics and Foreign Policy.* Washington, DC: Brookings Institution.

Haugaard, M. 2014. "*Power Over* and Democracy: The Four Dimensions of Power as Conditions for the Possibility of Democracy." Paper presented at the IPSA, Montreal, July 2014.

Heclo, H. 1978. "Issue Networks and the Executive Establishment." In *The New American Political System*, ed. A. King. Washington, DC: American Enterprise Institute.

Hill, M. and P. Hupe. 2014.. *Implementing Public Policy. An Introduction to Operational Governance*, Third Edition. Los Angeles: Sage.

Holm, P. 2007. "Which Way is up on Callon." In *Do Economists make Markets? On the Performativity of Economics*, eds. D. MacKenzie et al. Princeton, NJ: Princeton University Press, 225–243.

Hoppe, R. 1983. *Economische Zaken schrijft een nota. Een onderzoek naar beleidsontwikkeling en besluitvorming bij nonincrementeel beleid*, (Economic Affairs Drafts a New Policy. A Study in Non-Incremental Policy Design and Decision-Making). Amsterdam: VU Uitgeverij.

Hoppe, R. 1999. "'Policy Analysis, Science, and Politics: From 'Speaking Truth to Power" to "Making Sense Together'." *Science and Public Policy* 26 (3): 201–210.

Hoppe, R. 2009. "Ex ante Evaluation of Legislation: Between Puzzling and Powering." In T*he Impact of Legislation.* A Critical Analysis of Ex ante Evaluation, MartinusNijhof, Leiden/Boston, 81–104

Hoppe, R. 2010. *The Governance of Problems. Puzzling, Powering, and Pariticpation.* Bristol: Policy Press.

Hoppe, R. 2011. "Institutional Constraints and Practical Problems in Deliberative and Participatory Policymaking." *Policy & Politics* 39 (2): 163–183.

Hoppe, R. 2014. "Patterns of Science/Policy Interaction in The Netherlands." In *Policy Analysis in the Netherlands*, eds. P. Scholten, and F. van Nispen. Bristol: Policy Press. ISBN: 9781447313335).

Hoppe, R., H. Van de Graaf, and E. Besseling. 1995. "Successful Policy Formulation Processes: Lessons from Fifteen Case Experiences in Five Dutch Departments." *Acta Politica* 2: 153–188.

Howard, C. 2005. "The Policy Cycle: A Model of Post-Machiavellian Policymaking?" *Australian Journal of Public Administration* 64 (3): 3–13.

Howlett, M. and A. Migone. 2011. "Charles Lindblom is Alive and Well and Living in Punctuated Equilibrium Land." *Policy and Society* 30 (1): 53–62.

Howlett, M. and M. Ramesh. 2014. "Three Orders of Governance Failures: Policy Capacity, Problem Context and Design Mismatches." Paper for the Panel on Governance, IPSA, Montreal, July 10, 2014.

Hupe, P. 1992. *Om de kwaliteit van de macht. Het Werkgelegenheidsplan van minister Den Uyl in vijfvoudbeschouwd.* Gouda: Quint (For the Quality of Power).

Ingram H. and A.L. Schneider. 1995. "Social Constructon (Continued): Response." *American Political Science Review* 89 (2): 441–446.

Jann, W. and K. Wegrich. 2007. "Theories of the Policy Cycle." In *Handbook of Public Policy Cycle*, eds. F. Fischer, G.J. Miller, and M.S. Sidney, CRC Press, 43–62.

Jones, B.D. and F.R. Baumgartner. 2005. *The Politics of Attention. How Government Prioritizes Problems.* Chicago, IL: University of Chicago Press.

Kickert, W., E.-H. Klijn, and J. Koppenjan, eds. 1997. *Managing Complex Networks: Strategies for the Public Sector.* London: Sage.

Kingdon, J.W. 1984 (1995, Second Edition). *Agendas, Alternatives and Public Policies.* Glenview and London: Scott Foresman and Comp.

Kohoutek, J., M. Nekola, and V. Novotny. 2013. "Conceptualising Policy Work as Activity and Field of Research." *Central European Journal of Public Policy* 7 (1): 28–58.

Landwehr, C. 2014. "Facilitating Deliberation: The Role of Impartial Intermediaries in Deliberative Mini-Publics." In *Deliberative Mini-Publics. Involving Citizens in the Democratic Process,* eds. K. Grönlund, A. Bächtiger, and M. Setälä. Colchester: ECPR Press, 77–92.

Lasswell, H.D. 1956. *The Decision Process: Seven Categories of Functional Analysis.* College Park. MD: University of Maryland Press.

Lindblom, C.E. 1968. *The Policy-making Process,* First Edition. Englewood Cliffs, NJ: Prentice Hall.

Lindblom, C.E. and E.J. Woodhouse. 1993. *The Policy-Making Process,* Third Edition. Englewood Cliffs, NJ: Prentice Hall.

Loeber, A. 2004. "Practical Wisdom in the Risk Society. Methods and Practice of Interpretive Analysis on Questions of Sustainable Development." PhD Thesis, University of Amsterdam, Amsterdam.

Loeber, A. 2010. "Evaluation as Policy Work: Puzzling and Powering in a Dutch Program for Sustainable Development." In eds. H. Colebatch, R. Hoppe, and M. Noordegraaf, 131–158.

MacKenzie, D.A., F. Muniesa, and L. Siu, eds. 2007. *Do Economists make Markets? On the Performativity of Economics.* Princeton and Oxford: Princeton University Press.

Mahoney, J. and K. Thelen, eds. 2010. *Explaining Institutional Change. Ambiguity, Agency, and Power.* Cambridge; Cambridge University Press.

March, J. and J.P. Olsen. 1989. *Rediscovering Institutions: The Organizational Basis of Politics.* New York: Free Press.

Marres, N. 2005. "Issues Spark a Public into being: A Key but Often Forgotten Point of the Lippman-Dewey Debate." In *Making things Public: Atmospheres of Democracy*, eds. B. Latour and P. Weibel. Karlsruhe/ Cambridge: ZKM/MIT Press, 208–217.

Mayer, I.S., C.E. Van Daalen, and P.W.G. Bots. "Perspectives on Policy Analysis: A Framework for Understanding and Design." *International Journal of Technology Policy and Design* 4 (2): 169–191.

Meltsner, A.J. 1976. *Policy Analysts in the Bureaucracy.* Berkeley: University of California Press.

Meltsner, A.J. 1979. "Don't Slight Communication: Some Problems of Analytical Practice." *Policy Analysis* 5 (3): 367–392.

Meltsner, A.J. 1990. *Rules for Rulers: The Politics of Advice.* Philadelphia: Temple University Press.

Mettler, S. and M. SoRelle. 2014. "Policy Feedback Theory." In *Theories of Policy Process*, eds. P.A. Sabatier, and C.M. Weible, Boulder, CO: Westview Press, 151–182.

Mintrom, M. 2003. *People Skills for Policy Analysts.* Washington, DC: Georgetown University Press.

Moran, M., M. Rein, and R.E. Goodin, eds. 2006. *The Oxford Handbook of Public Policy.* Oxford: Oxford University Press.

Mouffe, C. 2000. *Deliberative Democracy of Agonistic Pluralism, Political Science Series* 72. Vienna: Institute for Advanced Studies (December 2000) (ISSN: 1605-8003).

Nowotny, H., P. Scott, and M. Gibbons. 2001. *Re-Thinking Science. Knowledge and the Public in an Age of Uncertainty.* Cambridge: Polity.

Oreskes, N. and E.M. Conway. 2011. *Merchants of Doubt: How a Handful of Scientists Obscured the Truth on Issues from Tobacco Smoke to Global Warming.* New York: Bloomsbury Press.

Ostrom, E. 2009. "Beyond Markets and States: Polycentric Governance of Complex Economic Systems." *The American Economic Review* 100 (3): 641–672.

Page, C. and B. Jenkins. 2005. *Policy Bureaucracy. Government with a Cast of Thousands.* Oxford: Oxford University Press.

Parsons, W. 1996. *Public Policy: An Introduction to the Theory and Practice of Policy Analysis.* Aldershot and Brookfield: Edward Elgar.

Pielke, R.A. 2007. *The Honest Broker: Making Sense of Science in Policy and Politics.* Cambridge: Cambridge University Press.

Proctor, R.N. and L. Schiebinger, eds. 2008. *Agnotology: The Making and Unmaking of*

Ignorance. Stanford, CA: Stanford University Press.

Radin, B.A. 2000. *Beyond Machiavelli: Policy Analysis Comes of Age*. Washington, DC: Georgetown University Press.

Radin, B.A. 2013. *Beyond Machiavelli: Policy Analysis Reaches Midlife*, Second Edition. Washington, DC: Georgetown University.

Raiffa, H. 1982. *The Art and Science of Negotiation. How to Resolve Conflicts and Get the Best out of Bargaining*. Cambridge and London: Harvard University Press.

Rhodes, R.A.W. 1997. *Understanding Governance: Policy Networks, Governance, Reflexivity and Accountability*. Buckingham, Philadelphia, PA: Open University.

Richardson, J.J. and A.G. Jordan. 1979. *Governing under Pressure*. Oxford: Martin Robertson.

Riker, W.H. 1986. *The Art of Political Manipulation*. New Haven and London: Yale University Press.

Roe, E. 2013. *Making the Most of Mess. Reliability and Policy in Today's Management Challenges*. Durham, NC: Duke University Press.

Rothstein, B. 2015. "The Chinese Paradox of High Growth and Low Quality of Government: The Cadre Organization Meets Max Weber." *Governance* 28 (4): 533–548.

Sabatier, P.A., ed. 1999, 2007. *Theories of the Policy Process*. Boulder, CO: Westview.

Sabatier, P.A. and H. Jenkins-Smith. 1988. "Symposium Issue, 'Policy Change and Policy-Oriented Learning: Exploring an Advocacy Coalition Framework.'" *Policy Sciences* 21: 123–272.

Sabatier, P.A. and C.M. Weible, eds. 2014. *Theories of the Policy Process*, Third Edition. Boulder, CO: Westview.

Schlager, E. 1999, 2007. "A Comparison of Frameworks, Theories and Models of the Policy Process." In ed. P.A. Sabatier, 293–320.

Schmidt, V. 2008. "Discursive Institutionalism: The Explanatory Power of Discourse and Ideas." *Annual Review of Political Science* 11: 303–326.

Schmitter, P.C. and G. Lehmbruch. 1979. *Trends toward Corporatist Intermediation*. Beverly Hills: Sage.

Schneider, A.L., H. Ingram, and P. de Leon. 2014. "Democratic Policy Design: Social Construction of Target Populations." In eds. P.A. Sabatier, and C.M. Weible, 105–150.

Schön, D.A. 1983. *The Reflective Practitioner. How Professionals Think in Action*. New York: Basic Books.

Selznick, P. 1957. *Leadership in Administration: A Sociological Interpretation*. New York: Harper & Row.

Sewell, W.H. 2005. *Logics of History. Social Theory and Social Transformation*. Chicago and London: University of Chicago Press.

Simon, H.A. 1957. *Models of Man: Social and Rational*. New York: Wiley.

Sismondo, S. 2004 (2011, Second Edition). *An Introduction to Science and Technology Studies*. Chichester: Wiley-Blackwell.

Sørensen, E. and J. Torfing. 2005. "The Democratic Anchorage of Governance Networks." *Scandinavian Political Studies* 28 (3): 195–218.

Staroňová, K. 2010. "Regulatory Impact Assessment: Formal Institutionalization and Practice." *Journal of Public Policy* 30 (1): 117–136.

Sterrenberg, L. 2010. "Managing the Problematic in Policy Work." In, eds. H. Colebatch, R. Hoppe, and M. Noordegraaf., 115–130.

Streeck, W. and K. Thelen. 2005. *Beyond Continuity: Institutional Change in Advanced Political Economies*. Oxford: Oxford University Press.

Susskind, L. 2006. "Arguing, Bargaining, and Getting Agreement." In, eds. M. Moran et al., 269–295.

Thomas, M.A. 2015. *Govern Like Us: US Expectations of Poor Countries*. New York: Columbia University Press.

Toulmin, S.E. 1958. *The Uses of Argument*. Cambridge: Cambridge University Press.

Turnbull, N. 2013. "The Questioning Theory of Policy Practice: Outline of an Integrated Analytical Framework." *Critical Policy Studies* 7 (2): 115–131.

Turnbull, N. 2014. *Michael Meyer's Problematology: Questioning and Society*. London: Bloomsbury.

Van de Graaf, H. and R. Hoppe. 1996. *Beleid en Politiek* (Policy and Politics), Third Edition. Muiderberg: Coutinho.

Voss, J.P. 2007. "Designs on Governance: Development of policy instruments and dynamics in governance." Dissertation University of Twente, Enschede.

Voss, J.P. 2014. "Instrument Constituencies and the Supply Side of Policy Innovation: The Social Life of Emissions Trading." *Environmental Politics* 23 (5): 735–754.

Weimer, D.L. and A.R. Vining. 1998. *Policy Analysis. Concepts and Practice*, Third Edition. Upper Saddle River, NJ: Prentice Hall.

Wildavsky, A. 1979. *The Art and Craft of Policy Analysis*. London and Basingstoke: Macmillan.

Woeltjes, T.F.M. 2010. "Teamwork in het beleidsdepartement. Om de kwaliteit van beleidsontwikkeling in eengroep." PhD Thesis, University of Twente, Enschede (Teamwork in the Ministerial Department: The Quality of Policy Design by Groups).

Yanow, D. 1996. *How Does a Policy Mean?: Interpreting Policy and Organizational Actions*. Washington, DC: Georgetown University Press.

Zahariadis, N. 2003. *Ambiguity and Choice in Public Policy. Political Decision Making in Modern Democracies*. Washington, DC: Georgetown University Press.

Ziman, J. 2000. *Real Science. What It Is, and What It Means*. Cambridge: Cambridge University Press.

European Policy Analysis - Volume 2, Number 1 - Spring 2016

Knowing the Future: Theories of Time in Policy Analysis

Holger Strassheim[A]

The article gives a comparative and critical overview on theories of time in policy analysis. It is based on two central assumptions: First, the various ways time is conceptualized in policy analysis are closely related to underlying understandings of politics and political action. Theories of time are also always political theories. Debating time is thus not only of analytic value. It also has large implications on how power, rationality, and collectivity are related to each other. Secondly, theories of time as political theories can be highly influential in practice. When they find their way into policymaking, they may realign the time horizons and temporal orders of political action.

Keywords*: policy analysis, time, temporal order, rationality, evidence-based policy*

1. Introduction

How can we know the future? In his seminal article "Tiresias, or our knowledge of future events" Schütz (1959) introduces us to the intricacies of this question. Tiresias, the blind prophet of Thebes, is able to predict the things to come with great certainty. Being unable to either make them happen or to prevent them, however, he remains "an impotent onlooker of the future" (71). Like many prophets he is hesitant about sharing his wisdom and cryptic when finally revealing it. In advising Odysseus that his journey would be successful if, and only if, he and his men refrained from eating the cattle of Helios on Thrinacia, Tiresias remains silent about the final outcome of events.[1] Schütz wonders

---

[A] Department of Social Sciences, Humboldt University Berlin

[1] Forced to stay on the island by unfavorably winds, Odysseus' men slaughter the cattle and are subsequently all killed by a thunderstorm sent by Zeus. Odysseus himself is punished when Calypso on Ogygia keeps him from returning to Ithaca for seven more years.

doi: 10.18278/epa.2.1.9

whether Tiresias' knowledge about the future is in fact fragmentary and selective. How does this "mechanism of selection" work? Does the seer experience the future as an ongoing stream of events with an open horizon? Does that mean that the prophecy is always also a kind of prognosis anticipating what follows beyond this horizon? Or is Tiresias capable of selecting and seeing certain events as if they had already happened? "Neither assumption however explains what motivates Tiresias to select this and that particular moment […] Moreover, neither assumption explains why Tiresias" knowledge of the future, as in the case of his forecast of Odysseus' homecoming, is either fragmentary of heterogeneous…' (1959, 75). In taking the mythical figure of Tiresias as a starting point, Schütz applies these questions to the mortals of the lifeworld (1959, 77). How do we form anticipations of future events? Why are they relevant to us? In which ways do they determine our plans, projects, and motives? Answers to these questions are of fundamental importance. They provide insights into the problems and dilemmas of predicting the future. As Schütz, in criticizing Weber, had already made clear, anticipating a future in which one's own acts are already accomplished is the very moment that defines action and distinguishes it from mere behavior (Schütz 1974).

This article focuses on theories of time in policy analysis. It is being argued that existing concepts can be compared in terms of how they answer (implicitly or explicitly) Schütz' questions on knowing the future. Firstly, approaches analyzing policymaking in terms of cycles, sequences, or temporalities emphasize the influence of a "preorganized" stock of knowledge and norms (1959, 77, 76) as constraint and resource of political action. Secondly, conceptions of policy as a stream of events are concerned with the relevance structures and temporal selections of policymaking as it is confronted with ambiguity in every moment of action. A third group of theories analyzes the cultural and communicative construction of time in policy processes and inquires on how, in turn, these collectively validated understandings realign the time horizons of past, present, and future.

In giving a critical overview on these various theories and concepts, the article is based on two central assumptions: The various ways time is conceptualized are closely related to underlying understandings of politics and political action. Theories of time are also always political theories. Debating time is thus not only of analytic value but it also has large implications on how power, rationality, and collectivity are related to each other. Moreover and probably less obvious, theories of time as political theories can be highly influential in practice. When they find their way into policymaking and become what Helga Nowotny has once called "chronotechnologies", they may realign the time horizons of political action. Just like Tiresias in his answer to Odysseus, they reveal only a fragment of how we can know the future and, as a consequence, may therefore determine the actual experience of and the decisions upon future events. Thus, theories of time are not only political theories but also a form of political practice. Tiresias, it turns out, is all but an "impotent onlooker". This communicative dimension of knowing the future is something Schütz might have underestimated.

The article is structured as follows: Section 2 gives a brief overview on concepts of time in policy analysis and, more specifically, the concept of "political time" as a common denominator in current debates. Each of Sections, 3, 4, and 5, focuses on a specific group of theories: Policymaking as it is both embedded in and structured by cycles, sequences, and temporal rules (Section 3: Policymaking in Time), policymaking as contingent, selective, and manipulative action upon political events (Section 4: Policymaking by Time) and time as historically changing and context-depended cultural construction that is structuring and being restructured by policymaking (Section 5: Times of Policymaking). Section 6 argues that theorizing time is of practical relevance. Especially theories of policymaking *in time* have become most influential. In order to rationalize policymaking multiple chronotechnologies have been established ("synchronizing the past", "extending the present", and "colonizing the future"). The consequences are highly problematic. Section 7 summarizes the results and ends with a plea for a (self-) critical reflection on the "proper times" of politics—and a more creative exploration of the multiple ways of knowing the future in both theory and practice.

2. Political Time in Policy Analysis

Lamenting the lack of studies on time in policy analysis and political science has become a regular topos in research literature. Over the past two decades, however, the picture has changed (Howlett and Goetz 2014; Schedler and Santiso 1998; Straßheim and Ulbricht 2015). Time has entered a prominent place on the research agenda:

This is especially true for research on time and democracy. Since Juan Linz' dictum that "time and timing are [...] the essence of the democratic process" (Linz 1998, 34), studies have multiplied. Presidential and parliamentary systems can be systematically distinguished by their temporal structure, that is, "the timetables of democratic politics, its time budgets, its point of initiation and termination, its pace, its sequences, and its cycles" (Schedler and Santiso 1998, 8). Mandates, terms, tenures and time budgets of government, the rhythms of legislations, the role of filibusters and the time horizons embedded in decision-making procedures, the procedural pulse of parliamentary speeches, and the time investments of parliamentarians— all these temporal factors seem to significantly determine the character of democratic government (Palonen 2014; Riescher 1994; Scheuerman 2001; Skowronek 2008). Autocracies, in contrast, tend to operate in a mode of timelessness (Lechner 1995; Wright 2008).

In policy analysis, the insight that "policymakers are heirs before they are choosers" (Rose 1990, 263) has been fruitful for numerous studies on the legacy of institutional structures and on path dependency (Pierson 2004). Beyond the linear concepts of stochastic analysis, models on multiple streams, historical narratives, or punctuated equilibriums have furthered the understanding of different modes of change (Howlett and Rayner 2006; Zahariadis 2003). Public management studies are highlighting the role of administrative memory (or loss thereof), the cyclical dynamics of fashions of modernization, and the analytical value of "timeships" that navigate the past by floating on combinations of approaches (Aucoin 1990; Pollitt 2008; Thomson and Perry 2006). Especially in the context of studies on the European Union, temporal qualities such as timing, sequencing, speed, and duration are conceptualized as resources and restraints of political action, leading to important insights about problems of synchronization and desynchronization in multilevel systems (Goetz 2012; Goetz and Mayer-Sahling 2009). In diverse fields such as science, technology, and society studies (STS) or comparative public policy, the notion of "timescapes" has been introduced to analyze the "political role time plays in debates and justifications of technoscientific and societal choices, in the proclamation of urgent problems but also in requests for citizens" compliance with certain decisions—always in the name of a specific future that has to be achieved (Felt et al. 2014, 5; Straßheim 2015; Tucker 2014).

Finally, in a broader effort to temporally redefine the modernization process, several authors have begun to analyze forces of acceleration and deceleration (Rosa 2015; Scheuerman 2001). Following their assumptions, acceleration in terms of technology, social change and pace of life constitute a basic principle of modernity (Rosa 2015, 23). Very much in line with some of the research on democratic temporalities cited above these authors diagnose a fundamental dilemma of democratic systems associated with the acceleration-induced dynamics of society: "The aggregation and articulation of collective interests and their implementation in democratic decision making has been and remains time intensive. For this reason democratic politics is very much exposed to the danger of desynchronization in the face of more acceleratable social and economic developments" (Rosa 2015, 254). While there are good reasons to argue that the proponents of the paradigm of acceleration might underestimate the learning capacity of democracies (Merkel and Schäfer 2015), the transformation of time structures under the conditions of a post-national constellation seems to pose serious problems for policymaking. More than 50 years ago, Schütz has already pointed to the economic, social, and political dynamics that seem to be more relevant to us than ever while, at the same time, being less and less in our control (Schütz 1976 [1959]). It is thus for good reasons that the problems and dilemmas of time are currently at the center of policy debates.

If we were to define the common vantage point of these various approaches and concepts, it most certainly is the focus on "political time", that is, "the very diverse range of rules, norms, conventions, and understandings that serve as a resource and constraint for political institutions and actors regardless of their spatio-temporal location and affect many aspects of political and policymaking behavior, such as the timing of decision making and the processes of attempting to make public policies" (Howlett and Goetz 2014, 478; Skowronek 2008). Recent theories of time in policy analysis more or less systematically distinguish between a proto-sociological view on time in policymaking and the distinctive characteristics of *political time* as a variable in its own right. While political action like every social action has a temporal dimension, the analysis of political time refers to a more specific aspect: In this perspective, time is analyzed as medium, motive, and momentum of actions related to collectively binding decisions.

Analyzing political time thus focuses on the various norms, conventions, and meanings determining the rhythms and cycles of governing, forming a resource by opening up opportunity windows or setting deadlines, thereby influencing both the "space of experience" and the "horizon of expectations" (Koselleck 1979) in political action. While only few authors would explicitly agree, theorizing time is not only an analytical endeavor but also always a political act in itself. The lack of "utopian impetus" and the focus on a "merely formal chronos which is neutral to meaning" in a majority of concepts could lead to the paradoxical situation that we know more and more about time while knowing less and less about the future (Graeber 2015; Nassehi 1994).

The following three sections are ordering the complex landscape of research on time according to the underlying concepts of political action. It turns out that different groups of theories can be distinguished by how they are answering the questions posed by Schütz.

3. Policymaking in Time

A first group of theories is mainly concerned with *policymaking in time*, focusing on the multiple ways of policy preferences and actions, their preconditions, and outcomes structured by cycles, sequences, or rules of temporality. In Schütz' words, our knowledge of events to come is preorganized by typifications (1959, 80),

standard assumptions derived from the past and applied to the future, determining what seems to be relevant and worth of attention in order to reach our goals. Albeit differing greatly in respect to how types are conceptualized and what exactly the mechanisms of determination are, theories of this group basically converge in this working consensus.

Of course, one of the most influential standard assumptions in *both* policy analysis and policymaking has always been the policy cycle. This concept seems to have virtually been around forever (Fischer et al. 2015; Howard 2005; Howlett and Ramesh 1995; May and Wildavsky 1978). The idea of a circular nature of things is the symbol of the cycle as representation of the eternal rhythm of human and nonhuman nature makes it the prototypical typification of temporal relations (Elias 1984). Accordingly, for its proponents it is less a prescription of a predetermined number of steps or a strict set of procedures but an idea structuring our attention (or, as Schütz would have said: our "system of relevances") by drawing it to "beginnings, middles, and endings that may lead to new beginnings" (May and Wildavsky 1978, 10). All different versions of the policy cycle incorporate this idea by proposing that policymaking proceeds in stages; that it involves some kind of rational problem solving; that the stages differ from each other in terms of actors, processes, and institutions; and that one policy subsequently leads by some sort of feedback to another policy (Howard 2005, 6). Despite the fierce criticism of the "phase heuristic" and its unrealistically rational or even technocratic approach, its lack of causal theory, its inaccuracy given the multilevel character of policymaking, and its top-down bias proponents do not easily let go of "a useful friend" (Sabatier and Weible 2014). Regardless of all efforts to capture the temporal complexities of the policy process, the very thought of a stage based, cyclical mechanism which informs and rationalizes policymaking, strengthens its "evidence-base" and enhances its "policy analytical capacity" cannot be underestimated in its influence on both policy analysis and policymaking up to this day (Howard 2005; Howlett 2009; Straßheim and Kettunen 2014). We are returning to this subject in Section 6.

A further set of theories in this group emphasizes the embeddedness of policymaking in some sort of structured sequencing (Howlett and Goetz 2014; Howlett and Rayner 2006). Theories of path dependency draw on institutional mechanisms that lead to a "lock-in" of policymaking on a specific trajectory that cannot be easily left without high costs, loss of legitimacy, or deviating from the ordering force of narratives (Abbott 1992). Although the beginning of the trajectory may be contingent or even random and its results may be suboptimal, following the path—even if it is a "crooked path" meandering between different constellations of actors, ideas, and interests—is a rational strategy until a "turning point" or "critical juncture" is reached (Djelic and Quack 2005; Mahoney 2000; Pierson 2004). These moments of contingency have been highlighted in process models, identifying causal mechanisms such as "bandwagon effects" or "social cascades" that can explain why at some tipping point temporal dynamics go in a completely different direction (Baumgartner and Jones 2002; Gersick 1991). While these models do not deny the contingency of social processes, they

are based on the assumption that even the most revolutionary punctuations of former trajectories follow a certain causal logic. Proponents emphasize the superiority of this model in comparison to path dependency or other sequential approaches as it shows that "continuities across temporal cases can be traced in part to enduring problems, while more or less contingent solutions to those problems are seen as reflecting and regenerating the historical individuality of each period" (Haydu 1998, 354).

How do we know our future? Theories of *policymaking in time* answer this question by arguing that political action is embedded in institutions or structures of meaning, following suboptimal trajectories or quickly changing at certain turning points depending on the context or period of time. Still, political action is both driven by and capable of rational problem solving. Thus, in order to know the future it needs to be anticipated based on evidence and information.

4. Policymaking by Time

A second group of theories conceptualizes politics as "organized anarchy" (Cohen, March, and Olsen 1972; Kingdon 1984; Zahariadis 2003; Zohlnhöfer, Herweg, and Rüb 2015). Rational problem solving is seen as the exception, not as a norm. Policymaking is characterized by unstable participation in decision making, high turnovers of political or administrative actors, and a considerable influence of nongovernmental organizations such as unions or civil society groups. Preferences and problems are not well articulated, not least because of often-opaque decision-making procedures. Instead of problem solving, the best actors can do is using trial-and-error procedures. Choice is made not on a rational basis but as spontaneous selection from a fluid and incalculable stream of events. Sometimes, this strategy of "temporal sorting" means searching a problem for an already available solution. Time is scarce and so is attention.

In contrast to the first group of theories, rationality is bounded because of limited cognitive and organizational resources (Kahneman 2011; Simon 1982). More importantly, problems, solutions, and politics flow more or less independently of each other like streams of events, regardless of the policy agenda or the strategies of actors. Sometimes, an opportunity window opens up and can be used to couple problems, solutions, and/ or politics. It all comes down the right timing. The capability of political action depends on different zones of attentions, much like Schütz has described them: "There is a relatively small kernel that is clear, distinct and consistent in itself. This kernel is surrounded by zones of various gradations of vagueness, obscurity, and ambiguity. There follow zones of things just taken for granted, blind beliefs, bare suppositions, mere guesswork [...]. And finally, there are regions of our complete ignorance" (1959, 78). Ambiguity and ignorance are high.

Under these circumstances, the main mode of political action is temporal manipulation (Zahariadis 2003, 14–16; 2015). The presentations of problems as being urgent, the use of symbols such as a burning flag to raise awareness, "salami tactics" to enable sequential decision making, or the acceleration of procedures help to focus debates and move them into a desired direction. In

his analysis of deadlines, Zahariadis has shown that delimiting time horizons tends to dramatically change the temporal rhythm of the policy process. Deadlines are not politically neutral. Instead, they are "political devices" changing the long-term orientation of policymakers while accelerating decision making. By inducing an artificial termination, they reduce political conflicts, facilitate a more innovative and uninhibited policy style—but may also lead to a decrease in participation and to less democratic dynamics of exclusion (Zahariadis 2015).

For all these reasons, theories of *policymaking by time* tend to be skeptical about knowing the future. Under conditions of ambiguity, knowledge about the future may change at every moment. Policymakers carry on in an incremental fashion, aiming at taking their opportunities for both attention and action as the policy stream goes on.

5. Times of Policymaking

A third group of theories of time is inspired by pragmatist interpretations of time and the sociology of knowledge and culture (Berger and Luckmann 1967; Elias 1984; Nowotny 1994). It builds on William James' (1890) distinction between "knowledge about" and "knowledge of acquaintance", a basic difference also for Schütz who makes use of it in his constitutional theory of social reality (1959, 78). In modern societies, much knowledge is derived not from immediate observation but through highly objectified, shared systems of sense-making imposed on us by others in societal interactions (Schütz 1976; Srubar 1988).

Time, it turns out, has itself become such an institutionalized "ordering force" (Adam 2004; Felt et al. 2014): Time frames work as social "filters" and "lenses". Produced and reproduced in political, economic, or scientific interactions, they allow us to order certain events, to describe causalities by distinguishing between causes and effects, to experience surprises against a background of routines and regularities, and to develop complex descriptions of the past and the future. These time frames transcend the calculative measurements derived from clock time or astronomical events. They manifest themselves in culturally variable understandings of societies as cyclical or linear, as determined by a certain "telos", by critical moments or turning points. The resulting temporal arrangements composed of multiple time frames, temporal rules, and procedures have been described as temporal orders or "timescapes" (Adam 2004; Howlett and Goetz 2014). Analyzing policy in terms of temporal orders or timescapes requires investigating how multiple frames of experiencing and enacting time are embedded into discursive and institutional structures, leading to specific temporal features that determine the relevance and meaning of past, present, and future and thus define the scope of collective action. Temporal orders vary depending on the level and context of policies (Goetz 2012; Meyer-Sahling and Goetz 2009; Tucker 2014).

The result of such complex temporal orders is not one historical time but, as Koselleck has already pointed out following the German philosopher Herder, "many forms of time superimposed one upon the other" (Koselleck 2004, 2). Research following this line of inquiry asks for the multiple ways these temporal orders are constituted, maintained, and changed. Politics and time are mutually intertwined: "This also highlights the political role time plays in debates and justifications of technoscientific and societal choices, in the proclamation of urgent problems but also in requests for citizens" compliance with certain decisions—always in the name of a specific future that has to be achieved' (Felt et al. 2014, 5).

Studies analyzing the multiple times of policymaking have shown that imposing "knowledge of acquaintance" on the policy process actually has the potential to change time frames and temporal orders. In their research on obesity as a social phenomenon, Felt and colleagues demonstrate how the use of specific statistical agglomerates has helped to render linear trajectories of worldwide obesity dynamics as objective, constituting a health phenomenon that makes certain political measures appear more acceptable in public (Felt et al. 2014). The ever-growing complexity of modeling techniques and the sensitivity of computer-based simulations for irregularities and unexpected dynamics on different levels of societies in a long-term perspective have changed the conditions of both policy formulation and decision making in the present. Paradoxically and for reasons still subject to current research, the enhancement of simulation techniques and other foresight methods, however, does not seem to result in an increase in capacities for action. On the contrary, policymakers and citizens alike are experiencing a so far unknown change in the tempo of modern life, an acceleration of political and socio-technical dynamics, making policies—and the conduct of modern life in general—even more problematic (Adam 2003; Nowotny 1994; Rosa 2015).

Research on the multiple times of policymaking thus shows that political action, torn between contingent and potentially colliding orders of time, is strongly influenced by science-based temporal discourses in order to frame certain trajectories as fixed and inevitable. An alternative way, however, would be to "question the taken-for-granted assumptions about time and to consider ways of addressing the temporal issue of contemporary societies" (Felt et al. 2014, 17).

6. Theorizing Time in Practice: Past, Present, and Future

Especially the last two groups of theories point to the possibility that communicating the future has actually the potential to alter it. Theorizing time might change the time horizons of policymakers and have long-term consequences by providing justifications and imposing relevances. So far, one of the most influential theories of time in political practice has been the policy cycle (Howard 2005). It basically promises that policymaking as a rational process of problem solving will be improved if information is inserted at the right time and the policy cycle comes to its full loop. Evidence-based policymaking has been the most prominent expression of this theory (Nutley and Webb 2000; Office 1999; Straßheim and Kettunen 2014). Proponents have suggested strengthening the "policy analytic capacities" by adopting certain informational solutions at every stage of the process (Howlett

2009). Analyzing the past and forecasting the future is done by specific "chrono-technologies" (Nowotny 1994) such as benchmarking, experiments, and scenario techniques. Based on selected studies on the role of evidence in policymaking, it can be shown that these instruments change the collective experience of time by (a) synchronizing the past, (b) extending the present, and (c) colonizing the future. Based on very specific theories of time, science, and expertise help to both establish and affirm seemingly unquestionable temporal orders.

A. Synchronizing the past

In the last two decades, benchmarking, rankings, scorecards, and monitoring devices have become standard tools of policymaking (Hood 2007; Papaioannou, Rush, and Bessant 2006). Based on comparisons of selected performance indicators, these instruments transform the sequentiality of individual trial-and-error into the synchronicity of standardized observations. They are already common practice on the local, national, and transnational level. Evidence-based comparisons establish and reproduce "classification situations", that is, counting, ranking, measuring, and scoring "on various metrics of varying degrees of sophistication, automation, and opacity" (Fourcade and Healy 2013). Benchmarking tends to obscure the specific contexts and conditions that influence decisions in the present in order to find new ways of optimization in the future. "Thus this technique [...] may in practice become a way of absorbing or assuming away critical contextual differences which are crucial to understanding why a particular program or activity works reasonably well at one place or time but not at the other. It aggregates results but not rationales" (Pollitt 2008, 12). In their study on obesity, Felt and colleagues show that the "obesity epidemic" has become an international issue in politics as soon as comparative indicators suggested that developments observed in countries such as the United States form an epidemiological trajectory that could in principle be transposed into other national contexts, "and thus reveal how obesity will rise and spread" (Felt et al. 2014, 8). More importantly, based on biomedical models these epidemiological trajectories have also been downscaled to the level of individual life cycles: Being overweight in childhood is framed as an indicator of future health problems and, in turn, an issue of responsibility toward the collective. In the case of obesity, synchronizing the past of both collectives and individuals is done by imposing "a specific version of obesity that is mainly performed through numbers. [...] But a closer analysis of our two sets of materials has revealed how beneath the seeming consensus of what obesity is lies a complex multiplicity of different stories and accounts that constitutes multiple versions of this seemingly singular object" (Felt et al. 2014, 15). Downscaling evidence-based comparisons has consequences: With the spread of health measurements, credit classifications, or other techniques of analyzing behavior based on big data, the temporal order of synchronized pasts has become both a universal and highly individualized phenomenon (Fourcade and Healy 2013; Pasquale 2015).

B. Extending the present

A combination of complex problems and evidence-based policies has caused what Helga Nowotny describes as the "extended present" (Nowotny 1994; Pollitt 2008, 61). For decades, societal progress seemed to promise an open horizon, fuelling social expectations and aspirations with ideas of continuous growth, technological advancement, and social wellbeing. While it may never have been uncontroversial, this time frame of an open-ended and, in principle, better future has finally lost its appeal. Confronted with problems such as global warming, food insecurities, toxic waste, or financial risks, the future has become a dark place, characterized by discontinuities, unexpected events, and large-scale effects disturbing whatever kind of equilibrium may have existed before. It is, however, not alone this dystopian vision but the more recent refinement and invention of "chronotechnologies" that is putting enormous pressure on the present. Calculative and computational methods of modeling the unexpected have gained in relevance. While former models were based on linear extrapolations, new simulative evidence points to future large-scale irregularities and deviations resulting from the synthetic interaction of small events (Gramelsberger 2010; Nowotny 1989, 63). With the potential to predict future catastrophes, the pressure to develop solutions in the present increases. Solutions need to be found now: "The future has become more realistic, not least because the horizon of planning has been extended. [...] The invocation of the future in the name of which political action was justified for a long time had to be reduced and at least partly transferred to the present"(Nowotny 1994, 50). The temporal order of an extended present has large consequences for policymaking, resulting in a constant renewal, evaluation, and redesign of policy processes. Policy cycles are multiplied, repeated, paralleled (Nowotny 1989, 56). A direct expression of this cyclical character of the extended present is the new randomized controlled trials (RCT) movement (Munro 2014; Pearce and Raman 2014). RCTs and experimental designs are seen as the "gold standard" of an evidence-based policy. With the multiplication of randomized experiments at institutes such as the Abdul LatifJameel Poverty Action Lab (J-PAL) at MIT, multiple policy interventions can be tested and retested at the same time all over the world, providing policymakers with direct information on causal relations that can be used as "rule of thumb" in the further development of behavior changing policies (Berndt 2015; Straßheim and Korinek 2016). The extended present can therefore also be characterized by a dynamic that only seemingly creates a contradiction, namely the shrinking of time horizons "that is, by the breaking down of series of actions and experiences into ever smaller sequences with shrinking windows of attention" (Rosa 2015, 124). Extending and shrinking of time—it all happens in the name of better evidence and a better future.

C. Colonizing the future

The idea that the future is open to "exploration and exploitation, calculation, and control" forms the core of a third temporal order (Adam and Groves 2007, 2). It is both a counteraction to and a consequence of an extended present. With the shrinking of time horizons and the increasing pressure to provide solutions for problems yet to come, policymakers and experts alike seek to "colonize the future" (Giddens 1995, 5). The rise of scenario techniques and forecasts of foresight exercises and integrated assessments of possible futures can be interpreted differently. While some see it as new possibility to explore alternatives and new trajectories of action, others criticize it as a political quest to occupy temporal territory with the help of experts by defining "global trends" and determining the debates about the future (Andersson and Rindzeviciute 2015; Schulz 2016). Indeed, the analysis of the German debate on the energy transformation ("Energiewende") makes it clear that forecasts of the future are closely tied to the political, social, and economic constellations in the present. Scenarios represent the deep normative and cultural values as they are embedded in foresight practices and modeling techniques (Aykut 2015, 129). Evidence on future developments has become part of a political struggle on how to realign the collective "space of experience" with the "horizon of expectations" under the conditions of an extended present (Koselleck 2004). This struggle is not yet decided. In the case of the German energy transformation, it changed the discourse on the future in an unexpected way: "What some regretted as a progressive 'scientization' of the ecological movement through increasing reliance on expert knowledge has indeed led to an opening up of energy futures the West German energy debate. The future became political in the sense that social movements used the instrument of scenarios to engage in energy controversies. Alongside the occupation of construction sites, mass demonstrations, and the blocking of nuclear transports, scenarios emerged as a part of the contentious repertoire used by the antinuclear movement to make its voice heard and influence German energy policy" (Aykut 2015, 120). Other studies are more skeptical, arguing that their findings show that instruments such as integrated assessment modeling (IAM) in climate policy are still dominated by a closed circle of "expert arbiters". To be able to politically and ethically explore scenarios without refraining to some sort of scientifically proven rationale, the authors suggest to find ways of "deliberating beyond evidence": "The challenge is to produce ideas on possible futures without relying on a validating scientific counterfactual and, instead, to take up a position of deliberation without evidence (as opposed to justification through evidence)" (Vecchione 2012, 18). Indeed, deliberation beyond evidence might present one of the greatest challenges for policymaking if it is to explore the political and ethical dimensions of different trajectories into the future without colonizing it.

7. Outlook

This article has focused on theories of time in policy analysis. Existing concepts were compared in terms of how they answer Schütz' questions on knowing the future. Table 1 gives an overview of the results.

It could be shown that the various ways time is conceptualized are closely related to underlying understandings of politics and political action. Theories of time are also always political theories with

practical implications. When they become chrono-technologies, they may change or reaffirm existing temporal orders. Today, one of the most influential theories is that of rational and evidence-based problem solving. In their science-based fiction "The collapse of Western Civilization", Oreskes and Conway "imagine a future historian looking back on the past that is our present and (possible) future" (Oreskes and Conway 2014, ix). What their protagonist describes in his fictitious account of how things were before the "fall" are the fatal consequences of a highly rationalized and "reductionist" epistemic culture that dominated Western science. This culture was built on the premise "that it was worse to fool oneself into believing in something that did not exist than not to believe in something that did" (2014, 17). Indeed, it is a well-known insight that in striving for rationality and objectivity, political actions can have highly irrational consequences (Elster 2015). When listening to the prophet, it is well advised to keep in mind that he will always only provide fragments of the future. In a similar vein, Schütz reminds us that scientific prediction can provide not much more than a certainty taken for granted "until further notice" (1959, 83). Every action, however, has the potential to question these certainties "by way of fantasying. It is, to use Dewey's pregnant description of deliberation, *a dramatic rehearsal in imagination*" (1959, 84). It seems that both policymakers and (social) scientists alike need to choose between two alternative knowledge-ways by either aiming at foreseeing the future based on seemingly certain evidence or by continuously re-imagining it in search for new options.

Table 1: Theories of Time

Theories of time	Basic concepts	Political action as...	How do we know the future?
Policymaking in time	Cycles, sequences, and temporal structures	Rational problem solving	We anticipate it based on evidence and past knowledge
Policymaking by time	Ambiguity, opportunity, and policy streams	Temporal sorting and manipulation	We don't, but we carry on anyway
Times of policymaking	Time frames, temporal orders, and timescapes	Deliberation and discursive powering	We collectively rehearse and re-imagine it

References

Abbott, A. 1992. "From Causes to Events: Notes on Narrative Positivism." *Sociological Methods and Research* 20 (4): 428–455.

Adam, B. 2003. "Reflexive Modernization Temporalized." *Theory, Culture & Society* 20 (2): 59–78.

Adam, B. 2004. *Time*. Cambridge/Malden: Policy Press.

Adam, B. and C. Groves. 2007. *Future Matters: Action, Knowledge, Ethics*. Leiden: Brill.

Andersson, J. and E. Rindzeviciute, eds. 2015. *The Struggle for the Long Term in Transnational Science and Politics: Forging the Future*. New York/London: Routledge.

Aucoin, P. 1990. "Administrative Reform in Public Management: Principles, Paradigms, Paradoxes and Pendulums." *Governance* 3 (2): 115–137.

Aykut, S.C. 2015. "Energy Futures from the Social Market Economy to the Energiewende: The Politicization of West German Energy Debates, 1950–1990." In *The Struggle for the Long Term in Transnational Science and Politics: Forging the Future*, eds. J. Andersson and E. Rindzeviciute. New York/London: Routledge, 93–144.

Baumgartner, F.R. and Jones, B.D., eds. 2002. *Policy Dynamics*. Chicago, IL: University of Chicago Press.

Berger, P. and T. Luckmann. 1967. *The Social Construction of Reality: A Treatise in the Sociology of Knowledge*. New York: Anchor Books.

Berndt, C. 2015. "Behavioural Economics, Experimentalism and the Marketization of Development." *Economy and Society* 44 (4): 567–591.

Cohen, M.D.J.G. March, and J.G. Olsen. 1972. "A Garbage Can Model of Organisational Choice." *Administration Science*, Quarterly 17: 1–25.

Djelic, M.-L. and S. Quack. 2005. "Rethinking Path Dependency: The Crooked Path of Institutional Change in Post-War Germany." In *Changing Capitalism? Internationalization, Institutional Change, and Systems of Economic Organization*, eds. G. Morgan and R. Whitley. Oxford: Oxford University Press, 137–166.

Elias, N. 1984. *Über die Zeit*. Frankfurt a.M.: Suhrkamp.

Elster, J. 2015. *Explaining Social Behaviour. More Nuts and Bolts for the Social Sciences (revised edition)*. Cambridge: Cambridge University Press.

Felt, U., K. Felder, T. Öhler, and M. Penkler. 2014. "Timescapes of Obesity: Coming to Terms with a Complex Socio-Medical Phenomenon." *Health* 18 (6): 646–664.

Fischer, F., D. Torgerson, A. Durnová, and M. Orsini. eds. 2015. *Handbook of Critical Policy Studies*. Cheltenham, UK/ Northampton, MA: Edward Elgar.

Fourcade, M. and K. Healy. 2013.

"Classification Situations: Life-Chances in the Neoliberal Era." *Accounting, Organizations and Society* 38: 559–572.

Gersick, C.J.G. 1991. "Revolutionary Change Theories: A Multilevel Exploration of the Punctuated Equilibrium Paradigm." *Academy of Management Review* 16 (1): 10–36.

Giddens, A. 1995. *Affluence, Poverty and the Idea of a Post-Scarcity Society (UNRISD Discussion Paper* 63). Genf: United Nations Research Institute for Social Development.

Goetz, K.H. 2012. *Time and Political Power in the EU*. Oxford: Oxford University Press.

Goetz, K.H. and J.-H. Mayer-Sahling. 2009. "Political Time in the EU: Dimensions, Perspectives. Theories." *Journal of European Public Policy* 16 (2): 180–201.

Graeber, D. 2015. *The Utopia of Rules: On Technology, Stupidity, and the Secret Joys of Bureaucracy*. New York/London: Melville House.

Gramelsberger, G. ed. 2010. *From Science to Computational Sciences. Studies in the History of Computing and its Influence on Today's Sciences*. Zürich: diaphanes.

Haydu, J. 1998. "Making use of the Past: Time Periods as Cases to Compare and as Sequences of Problem Solving." *American Journal of Sociology* 104 (2): 339–371.

Hood, C. 2007. "Public Service Management by Numbers: Why does it Vary? Where Has it Come From? What Are the Gaps and the Puzzles?" *Public Money & Management* 27 (2): 95–102.

Howard, C. 2005. "The Policy Cycle: A Model of Post-Machiavellian Policy Making?" *Australian Journal of Public Administration* 64 (3): 3–13.

Howlett, M. 2009. "Policy Analytical Capacity and Evidence-Based Policy-Making: Lessons from Canada." *Canadian Public Administration* 52 (2): 153–175.

Howlett, M. and K.H. Goetz. 2014. "Introduction: Time, Temporality and Timescapes in Administration and Policy." *International Review of Administrative Sciences* 80 (3): 477–492.

Howlett, M. and M. Ramesh. 1995. *Studying Public Policy—Policy Cycles and Policy Subsystems*. Oxford: Oxford University Press.

Howlett, M. and J. Rayner. 2006. "Understanding the Historical Turn in the Policy Sciences: A Critique of Stochastic, Narrative, Path Dependency and Process-Sequencing Models of Policy-Making over Time." *Policy Sciences* 39: 1–18.

James, W. 1890. *Principles of Psychology: Vol. 1*. New York: Henry Holt.

Kahneman, D. 2011. *Thinking, Fast and Slow*. London: Penguin Books.

Kingdon, J.W. 1984. *Agendas, Alternatives, and Public Policies*. Boston, MA: Little Brown and Company.

Koselleck, R. 1979. *Vergangene Zukunft. Zur Semantik geschichtlicher Zeiten*. Frankfurt a.M.: Suhrkamp.

Koselleck, R. 2004. *Futures Past: On the Semantics of Historical Time*. Cambridge:

MIT Press.

Lechner, N. 1995. "El (maltido) Factor tiempo." *Espacios* 5: 66–72.

Linz, J.J. 1998. "Democracies Time Constraints." *International Political Science Review* 19: 19–37.

Mahoney, J. 2000. Path Dependence in Historical Sociology." *Theory and Society* 29 (4): 507–548.

May, J.V. and A. Wildavsky. 1978. *The Policy Cycle*. London: Sage.

Merkel, W. and A. Schäfer. 2015. "Zeit und Demokratie: Ist demokratische Politik zu langsam?" In *Die Zeit der Politik. Demokratisches Regieren in einer beschleunigten Welt (Leviathan Sonderband 30)*, eds. H. Straßheim, and T. Ulbricht. Baden-Baden: Nomos, 218–238.

Meyer-Sahling, J.-H., and K.H. Goetz. 2009. "The EU Timescape: From Notion to Research Agenda." *Journal of European Public Policy* 16 (2): 325–336.

Munro, E. 2014. "Evidence-Based Policy." In *Philosophy of Social Sciences*, eds. N. Cartwright, and E. Montuschi. Oxford: Oxford University Press, 48–67.

Nassehi, A. 1994. "No Time for Utopia. The Absence of Utopian Contents in Modern Concepts of Time." *Time & Society* 3 (1): 47–78.

Nowotny, H. 1989. *Eigenzeit. Entstehung und Strukturierung eines Zeitgefühls*. Frankfurt a.M.: Suhrkamp.

Nowotny, H. 1994. Time: *The Modern and Postmodern Experience*. Cambridge/Malden: Polity Press.

Nutley, S.M. and J. Webb. 2000. "Evidence and the Policy Process." In *What Works? Evidence-Based Policy and Practice in Public Services*, eds. H.T.O. Davies, S.M. Nutley, and P.C. Smith. Bristol: The Policy Press, 13–41.

Office, C. 1999. *Professional Policy making for the Twenty First Century. Report by Strategic Policy Making Team*. London: Cabinet Office.

Oreskes, N. and E. Conway. 2014. *The Collapse of Western Civilization. A View From the Future*. New York: Columbia University Press.

Palonen, K. 2014. *The Politics of Parliamentary Procedure. The Formation of the Westminster Procedure as a Parliamentary Ideal Type*. Opladen/London: Barbara Budrich Publications.

Papaioannou, T., H. Rush, and J. Bessant. 2006. "Benchmarking as a Policy-making Tool: From the Private to the Public Sector." *Science and Public Policy* 33 (2): 91–102.

Pasquale, F. 2015. *The Black Box Society. The Secret Algorithms That Control Money and Information*. Cambridge/London: Harvard University Press.

Pearce, W. and S. Raman. 2014. "The New Randomised Controlled Trials (RCT) Movement in Public Policy: Challenges of Epistemic Governance." *Policy Science* 47: 387–402.

Pierson, P. 2004. *Politics in Time: History, Institutions, and Social Analysis*. Princeton, NJ: Princeton University Press.

Pollitt, C. 2008. *Time, Policy, Management: Governing with the Past*. Oxford: Oxford University Press.

Riescher, G. 1994. *Zeit und Politik: Zur institutionellen Bedeutung von Zeitstrukturen in parlamentarischen und präsidentiellen Regierungssystemen*. Baden-Baden: Nomos.

Rosa, H. 2015. *Social Acceleration. A New Theory of Modernity*. New York: Columbia University Press.

Rose, R. 1990. "Inheritance Before Choice in Public Policy." *Journal of Theoretical Politics* 3: 263–291.

Sabatier, P. and C.M. Weible, eds. 2014. *Theories of the Policy Process*, Third Edition. Boulder, CO: Westview.

Schedler, A. and J. Santiso. 1998. "Democracy and Time: An Invitation." *International Political Science Review* 19 (1): 5–18.

Scheuerman, W.E. 2001. "Liberal Democracy and the Empire of Speed." *Polity* 34 (1): 41–67.

Schulz, M.S. 2016. "Debating Futures: Global Trends, Alternative visions, and Public Discourse." *International Sociology* 31 (1): 3–20.

Schütz, A. 1959. "Tiresias, Or Our Knowledge of Future Events." *Social Research* 26 (1): 71–89.

Schütz, A. 1974. *Der sinnhafte Aufbau der sozialen Welt. Eine Einleitung in die verstehende Soziologie.* Frankfurt a.M.: Suhrkamp.

Schütz, A. 1976. "The Stranger: An Essay in Social Psychology." In *Collected Papers II: Studies in Social Theory*, ed. A. Schütz. Den Haag: MartinusNijhoff, 91–105.

Schütz, A.1976 [1959]. "The Well-Informed Citizen. An Essay on the Social Distribution of Knowledge." In *Collected Papers II: Studies in Social Theory*, ed. A. Schütz. Den Haag: MartinusNijhoff, 120–134.

Simon, H.A. 1982. *Models of Bounded Rationality.* Cambridge, MA: MIT Press.

Skowronek, S. 2008. *Presidential Leadership in Political Time: Reprise and Reappraisal.* Lawrence, KS: University Press of Kansas.

Srubar, I. 1988. Kosmion. *Die Genese der pragmatischen Lebenswelttheorie von Alfred Schütz und ihr anthropologischer Hintergrund.* Frankfurt a.M.: Suhrkamp.

Straßheim, H. 2015. "Politics and Policy Expertise: Towards a Political Epistemology." In *Handbook of Critical Policy Studies*, eds. F. Fischer, D. Torgerson, A. Durnová, and M. Orsini. Cheltenham, UK/Northampton, MA: Edward Elgar, 319–340.

Straßheim, H. and P. Kettunen. 2014. "When does Evidence-Based Policy Turn into Policy-Based Evidence? Conficurations, Contexts and Mechanisms." *Evidence & Policy* 10 (2): 259–277.

Straßheim, H., and R.-L. Korinek. 2016. "Cultivating 'Nudge': Knowing Behavioural Governance." In *Knowing Governance (Palgrave Studies in Science, Knowledge and Policy)*, eds. R. Freeman, and J.-P. Voss. Houndmills: Palgrave (forthcoming).

Straßheim, H. and T. Ulbricht, eds. 2015. *Die Zeit der Politik. Demokratisches Regieren in einer beschleunigten Welt (Leviathan Sonderband 30).* Baden-Baden: Nomos.

Thomson, A.M. and J.L. Perry. 2006. "Collaboration Processes: Inside the Black Box." *Public Administration Review* 66 (s1): 20–32.

Tucker, H.J. 2014. "Visualizing Timescape Issues in the Comparative Study of the American States." *International Review of Administrative Sciences* 80 (3): 533–552.

Vecchione, E. 2012. *Deliberating beyond Evidence: Lessons from Integrated Assessment Modelling (IDDRI Working Papers N° 13/12).* IDDRI: Paris.

Wright, J. 2008. "To Invest or Insure?: How Authoritarian Time Horizons Impact Foreign Aid Effectiveness." *Comparative Political Studies* 41 (7): 971–1000.

Zahariadis, N. 2003. *Ambiguity and Choice in Public Policy: Political Decision Making in Modern Democracies (American Governance and Public Policy).* Washington, DC: Georgetown University Press.

Zahariadis, N. 2015. "Plato's Receptacle: Deadlines, Ambiguity, and Temporal Sorting in Public Policy." In *Die Zeit der Politik. Demokratisches Regieren in einer beschleunigten Welt (Leviathan Sonderband 30)*, eds. H. Straßheim, and T. Ulbricht. Baden-Baden: Nomos, 113–131.

Zohlnhöfer, R., N. Herweg, and F. Rüb. 2015. "Theoretically Refining the Multiple-Streams Framework: An Introduction." *European Journal of Political Research* 54 (3): 412–418.

European Policy Analysis - Volume 2, Number 1 - Spring 2016

Integrative Political Strategies—Conceptualizing and Analyzing a New Type of Policy Field[1]

Basil Bornemann[A]

Traditionally, policymaking has been described as taking place within the boundaries of differentiated and institutionalized policy fields. Regarding some newer issue areas, such as sustainability or climate change, this "sectoralized" pattern of policy development does not seem to be an adequate description anymore. Here, a different type of policymaking that practitioners regularly qualify as "integrative" and "strategic" can be observed: policymaking transgresses the boundaries of established policy fields and integrates differentiated policy areas by means of overall political strategies. How can scholars make sense of these supposedly new forms of policymaking in contemporary policy systems? On what conceptual grounds and with what kinds of tools can they analyze the respective policy practices? In this paper, I critically review the current literature on "integrative political strategies" (IPS) and argue that existing conceptualizations and studies of IPS are flawed since they rest on problematic functional presumptions and do not consider the analytical implications of "integration" and "strategy" as practical cornerstones of IPS. Aiming at more conceptual and analytical clarity, I propose interpreting IPS in terms of a new, "reflexive" type of policy field that emerges from countermovements to two dominant trends that have shaped contemporary policy systems—integration as a countermovement to the continuing differentiation of policies, on one hand, and strategy as a flexible form of boundary work that contrasts with the pattern of institutionalization, on the other hand. I outline an analytical repertoire for systematically on the basis of this, taking account of policy integration and political strategy in contemporary policymaking. I conclude with some implications of my propositions for future policy research.

Keywords: integrative political strategies, policy field, policy integration, political strategy

[1] I am grateful to two anonymous reviewers, whose comments helped to improve the paper. I am particularly indebted to Thomas Saretzki and Ralf Tils for the discussions that led to this paper.

[A] Department of Social Sciences, Sustainability Research, Bernoullistrasse 16, CH-4056 Basel, Switzerland

doi: 10.18278/epa.2.1.10

1. Introduction

When policymakers try to take up and resolve a certain societal problem, they are usually not only guided by the fundamental problem structure, the institutional framework of their respective political systems, and the broader societal context, but they also find themselves in differentiated and institutionalized policy fields that structure their actions and interactions with other policymakers. These include the "classic" fields of national government action, such as foreign policy, domestic policy, justice, finance, and economic and social policy, in which problems are processed as necessary for maintaining the capacity of the state itself. Also, more recent policy fields, such as research and technology policy, energy and environmental policy, or consumer protection, are based on processes of differentiation and institutionalization that create order, predictability, legitimacy, and relative autonomy by setting rules, assigning responsibilities and obligations, as well as defining procedures, which organize the interactions among policymakers in these fields.

Regarding more recent issue areas, such as climate change and sustainable development, political actors face overarching problem structures, which require no less than major societal and political transformations, at least over the long term (Elzen, Geels, and Green 2004; Haberl et al. 2011; Lange 2008; Markard, Raven, and Truffer 2012; Pelling 2011). Given the scope of the related problems, policymaking within institutionally demarcated, sectoral policy areas does not appear to be a promising path of problem solving (Adelle and Russel 2013). In fact, policy actors themselves have acknowledged the institutionalized boundaries of established policy fields as an obstacle to the effective governance of sustainability and climate problems (OECD 2004; Swanson et al. 2004; Swanson and Pintér 2007). Rather than establishing a new sectoral department or dissolving the boundaries of differentiated policy areas, policy actors have begun to launch "integrative" forms of problem solving, that is, initiatives of policymaking that cut across and relate various sectoral policy areas. These integrative approaches are frequently linked to a new understanding of politics that departs from conventional concepts of policies, programs, or plans, and instead revolves around the notion of "strategy."

From the perspective of a scientific observer, the emergence of these allegedly integrative and strategic forms of policymaking in practice raises several questions. How can these activities be conceptualized? How do they relate to and differ from other forms of policymaking? How can integrative and strategic practices in contemporary policy systems be analyzed in a differentiated manner? In this paper, I take these questions as the starting point for a conceptual inquiry into "integrative political strategies" (IPS), a class of policy phenomena that other authors have grouped under various other categories, such as "new pattern[s] of strategy formation in the public sector," (Steurer and Martinuzzi 2005) "integrated policy strategies," (Rayner and Howlett 2009b) "integrated strategies," (Casado-Asensio and Steurer 2014) or "multi-sectoral strategies" (Nordbeck and Steurer 2015). My goals are twofold: first, I want to add to the conceptual understanding of IPS and provide a sound basis for analyzing these phenomena in a differentiated manner. Second, in so doing, I strive to contribute to the understanding of policy fields as well as the constitution and dynamics of contemporary policy systems more generally.

I begin with a review of more recent perspectives and research on IPS (Section 2). On the basis of several critical points regarding the existing literature, I propose an alternative conceptualization of IPS as a new, "reflexive" type of policy field (Section 3). Subsequently, the analytical implications of this reconceptualization are developed, and the contours of an integration- and strategy-oriented policy-field analysis are outlined (Section 4). I conclude this paper with some remarks on the future perspectives of an integration- and strategy-oriented policy research (Section 5).

2. Integrative Political Strategies: A Critical Review of Recent Research

Over the last 20 years or so, IPS have become significant phenomena of contemporary policymaking (Casado-Asensio and Steurer 2014). Starting out from industrialized countries in the early 1990s, they are now present in many countries all over the world (see, e.g., Swanson et al. 2004). Most prominently, IPS have been developed at the national level, but there are also IPS at the subnational and supra-national levels (Gouldson and Roberts 2000; Kern 2008; Schreurs 2008). IPS cover multiple issue areas, mostly associated with the environmental domain, such as land management (Rayner and Howlett 2009b), natural resource management (Howlett and Rayner 2006), climate mitigation and adaptation (Bauer, Feichtinger, and Steurer 2012; Biesbroek et al. 2010; Mickwitz et al. 2009), or sustainable development (Brodhag and Talière 2006; Steurer 2008). However, other cases of IPS encompass nonenvironmental issue areas, such as poverty alleviation (Cejudo and Michel 2015; Gould 2005). Only recently studies have started to relate the different experiences from these various areas and reveal similar patterns of policymaking and governance (Casado-Asensio and Steurer 2014; Nordbeck and Steurer 2015).

The emergence of integrative strategies and their persistence are explained in various ways. Some observers view the development of IPS as triggered by international obligations and transnational diffusion processes (Busch and Jörgens 2005; Casado-Asensio and Steurer 2014), with the creation of IPS resulting from the pressure to fulfill international agreements. While this mechanism might be plausible for some IPS, it is insufficient for explaining other IPS cases where international obligations are absent (e.g., innovation and resource management) or not directly relevant (such as subnational IPS). Here, other factors related to internal dynamics in the policy system seem to be important. Some authors argue that the development of these strategies is a reaction to some form of dissatisfaction of political actors with the policy space where they operate. For example, from a series of case studies on integrative land-use strategies in Canada, Rayner and Howlett (2009a, 166) conclude that such strategies "are rarely adopted until there is widespread dissatisfaction with the disorganized character of the existing policy regime," which results from "long periods of incremental policy change characterized by processes of layering and drift." These processes of policy layering have in turn been promoted by an era of considerable policy innovations that were brought in by ever-diversifying forms of governance: "With new actors came new ideas, creating a rich mix of policy elements that, in a context of institutional ambiguity, proved hard to gather up into optimal policy designs" (Rayner and Howlett 2009b, 101). According to this interpretation, integrated strategies often represent conscious efforts to combine multiple policy elements in a more coherent way and overcome the disorganized character of the existing policy system (see also May et al. 2005; May, Sapotichne, and Workman 2006). In-depth case studies on the national sustainability strategy in Germany point to less ambitious goals of policymakers. Besides following international obligations, sustainability strategies are perceived by policymakers as opportunities to overcome existing institutional constrictions and gain action capacity within a highly institutionalized and fragmented policy system (Bornemann 2011; 2014; Tils 2005; 2007).

There are obviously many different empirical forms of IPS within and across different fields and policy levels (see, e.g., Swanson et al. 2004). However, in various reviews several recurring elements have been identified (Bornemann 2014; Casado-Asensio and Steurer 2014; 2008; Steurer and Martinuzzi 2007). First, at the core of an IPS, there is usually a (set of) programmatic document(s), such as a national sustainability strategy or a climate adaptation strategy, in which problems, goals, and means are defined. Second, these strategies emerge and are enacted in a certain organizational arrangement.

Typically, such an arrangement consists of some interdepartmental coordination structure that spans various administrative departments and includes elements that ensure consultations with scientific actors, as well as the broader public. Finally, IPS bear a procedural dimension as both the organizational arrangement and the strategy documents are subject to regular revisions and adaptations over time.

Despite these general empirical commonalities regarding the form of IPS, the academic literature has not offered an unambiguous understanding of what IPS are, how they can be distinguished from other forms of policymaking, and how they ought to be analyzed to capture their peculiarities. In fact, there are several conceptual propositions and analytical perspectives on IPS. These are based on various heterogeneous sources, ranging from political agreements and guidelines for practitioners prescribing what administrators can and should do to formulate and implement IPS (Dalal-Clayton and Bass 2002) to empirically informed theoretical reflections (Meadowcroft 2007; Steurer 2007; 2010; Tils 2007). These various perspectives focus on different aspects of politics and are based on diverse presumptions regarding the functions of IPS, as well as the forms they are supposed to take in order to fulfill these functions.

Early investigations have examined and analyzed IPS as a new form of policymaking and steering that cuts across various sectors but aims at solving complex policy problems by setting long-term goals and defining measures (Jänicke 2000; Nordbeck 2001; Wurster 2013). Following this policy perspective, IPS are all about defining and solving problems in a comprehensive and rational manner.

More recently, policy-oriented observers have come to regard IPS as representing more than "just" policy instruments. For example, Rayner and Howlett highlight two functions. Aside from setting and pursuing "substantive policy objectives," they regard IPS as means of policy design, that is, "attempt[s] to create or reconstruct a policy domain with coherent policy goals and a consistent set of policy instruments that support each other in the achievement of the goals" (Howlett and Rayner 2007; Rayner and Howlett 2009b).

A second perspective that has dominated empirical research on IPS falls under the category of "strategic management" (Steurer 2007; Steurer and Martinuzzi 2005). Drawing on models from management studies and the literature on new public management, the management perspective broadens the policy view in a process-oriented direction (see Tils 2007). It focuses on management cycles and highlights functions, such as the monitoring, controlling, and revision of governmental activities. Following the strategic management perspective, IPS are an expression of strategic public management and, thus, pave the middle way between failed policy-planning approaches and incrementalism (Steurer 2007).

Following a different interpretation, IPS can be regarded as manifestations of reflexive governance (Meadowcroft 2007). This interpretation emphasizes the democratic and participatory dimension of IPS, specifically the inclusion of stakeholders and citizens in governmental policymaking. According to his view, IPS are expected to facilitate learning processes directed at reflecting on and transforming established governance routines.

Most recently, Casado-Asensio and Steurer (2014) seem to combine various perspectives when they emphasize three basic functions of IPS. First, their policy function consists of setting goals and defining measures to address complex problems. Second, their management and governance function refers to improving governing processes by enhancing vertical and horizontal policy integration, as well as learning through a cyclical governing process that involves monitoring and reporting. Finally, their communication or capacity function relates to raising public and media awareness of the issues addressed in these strategies. Taken together, these functions render IPS as meta-governance activities, in other words, "comprehensive governing processes" that "aim to achieve policy objectives more effectively by providing direction, structure, and control with regard to governance modes (e.g., hierarchy, networks, market), policy instruments and actors" (Casado-Asensio and Steurer 2014, 441).

Concerning these ideal–typical functions, the empirical performance of IPS is regularly assessed as weak or almost nonexistent. Integrative strategies do not meet the functional expectations regarding policy, governance, and capacity building (Casado-Asensio and Steurer 2014; Nordbeck and Steurer 2015) or other sets of success criteria (Meadowcroft 2007; Steurer and Martinuzzi 2005). Overall, "[they] have proved to be comparatively weak administrative routines (or informational policy instruments) and preoccupied with low-key communication rather than high-profile policy coordination. Consequently, they are usually not capable of implementing the policies necessary to meet the targets they specify" (Casado-Asensio and Steurer 2014, 459).

Based on these rather pessimistic assessments of the past performance of integrative strategies, various options of how to deal with them in the future are discussed (see Casado-Asensio and Steurer 2014; Meadowcroft 2007; Nordbeck and Steurer 2015). First, the optimistic view is to improve them so that they can meet the standards. Second, on the other end of the spectrum, critics suggest abandoning these strategies altogether. Since they have proven to be unsuccessful for a long time, there is no reason to expect better performance in the future. Other authors suggest retailoring integrative strategies. Rather than trying to set up comprehensive and all-encompassing strategies, policy designers should focus on sectoral strategies, which are less complex and, therefore, can serve as "real" leverages for policy change. While this choice implies abandoning the idea of integration, a different suggestion is to revise integrative strategies in such a way as to strengthen their core function of communication.

Overall, previous research on IPS has contributed rich and detailed empirical knowledge, mostly involving country case studies, about the many forms IPS can take and their performance with regard to several functions. Some conceptual accounts also attempt to theorize about IPS or at least offer a more general understanding of the phenomena. Some more recent stock-taking articles have promoted rather skeptical views on IPS and argue that these have by and large failed in practice. Based on my own in-depth analysis of national sustainability strategies in Germany (Bornemann 2011; 2014), I agree on much of the skepticism regarding the IPS performance in solving pressing policy problems and making the policy system coherent. However, I also claim that it might be too early to sing the farewell song on IPS since parts of the empirical skepticism might result from the way IPS are conceptualized and analyzed. My concerns about much of the research related to IPS are twofold.

First, current approaches for analyzing IPS are based on a rather confined conceptual basis. Despite an increasing number of conceptual propositions and some attempts to embed IPS in policy theory (Rayner and Howlett 2009a; 2009b), there is limited theorizing on what IPS are and how their particular form and functioning can be analyzed in relation to other forms of policymaking. In fact, prevalent conceptualizations are structured by normative presumptions, which are based on certain idealized models of policymaking (originating from management studies and policy design, etc.). Accordingly, IPS are understood as means to fulfill particular expected (and taken-for-granted) goals for the policy system which are associated with "strategy" (i.e., solving long-term problems) and "integration" (i.e., creating some form of policy coherence in a disordered policy system).

Second, as a consequence of the first point, empirical analyses tend to focus on the performance of IPS with regard to the assumed functions. This entails evaluations of the policy and governance performance of IPS, as well as explanations for deviations from an optimal policy design, that is, the coherence between overall and specific policy goals, as well as the consistency between goals and targets. Moreover, these function-oriented analyses are based on rather decontextualized and hermetic project views focusing on the strategy documents, the organizational arrangements, and the procedures that are directly related to IPS. Thereby, scholars barely gain a deeper understanding of how IPS actually work in relation to other ways of nonintegrative and nonstrategic policymaking. And they miss taking into account the broader and long-term implications of IPS on the policy system, more generally.

Overall, there is no clear direction in how one should understand and analyze IPS. Drawing on functional conceptualizations of their objects, current analyses disregard a differentiated picture of what real-world actors might do for what reasons and to what effects when opting for IPS. By narrowing down the analytical perspective to certain functions, such a functional perspective might miss parts of the story to be told about IPS— and come up with misleading "evidence-based" recommendations to abandon this presumably failed form of steering, management, or governance.

Against the backdrop of these critical concerns, I suggest stepping back to reconsider how IPS are conceptually understood and analytically examined. This approach shall provide the grounds for a picture of IPS that is free from implicit functional presumptions (and, therefore, can serve as a more adequate basis for subsequent functional assessments and prescriptions). For this purpose, I combine a practical orientation with a conceptual-critical stance. Practical orientation means that I follow the policy actors in their declared ambition to pursue new ways of policymaking. Therefore, I organize the conceptualization around the notions that are relevant for the policy actors themselves in their practical efforts, namely, integration and strategy. However, a conceptual–critical approach implies

that I do not simply adopt practitioners' concepts for scientific analysis. Rather, I systematically elaborate on the "conceptual space" within which their orientations and practical aspirations might evolve. I do so by developing an analytical repertoire for critically assessing understandings and practices of integrative and strategic policymaking.

Consequently, I proceed in two steps. First, I highlight a conceptual understanding of IPS in terms of a newly emerging type of policy field, reflecting the practical attempts of policy actors toward an integrative and strategic policymaking (Section 3). Second, to fully comprehend the form and functioning of this type of policy field, I propose shifting the focus to the two cornerstones of these newly emerging "reflexive" policy fields— integration and strategy—and sketch the contours of an integration- and strategy-oriented policy analysis (Section 4).

3. Conceptualizing Integrative Political Strategies as a New Type of Policy Field

In searching for an alternative perspective with the potential to look at IPS in a less instrumental, yet more comprehensive, embedded, and differentiated way, the "policy-field" concept appears to be a good starting point. The notion of "field" does not only refrain from a priori presumed normative functions and, thus, indicates a shift from prescription to analysis (Martin 2003), but it also opens the view to more encompassing configurations of elements (Fligstein and McAdam 2012). Moreover, the field concept comes with of being well established in policy analysis while remaining open to different interpretations. In fact, the notion of policy field has played a role in policy analysis for some time, but debates on its meaning continue to evolve (Blätte 2015; Blum and Schubert 2011; Döhler 2015; Loer, Reiter, and Töller 2015; Massey and Huitema 2013).

Generally, policy fields can be regarded as relevant spheres for organizing and analyzing public policymaking (Döhler 2015). Policy fields are assumed to make a difference: political problem solving is not only the result of political, institutional, social, or cultural conditions, but it is also subject to a specific policy-field effect (Heinelt 2009; Rehder, Winter, and Willems 2009). Conceiving the policy system of a certain political community (such as a nation state, a region, or a local municipality) as representing the entirety of its public problem-solving activities, a policy field denotes a specific structured partition of this comprehensive policy system that has developed around a certain issue area and is endowed with relative autonomy in functioning vis-à-vis neighboring policy fields (Döhler 2015). A policy field is different from a mere political program (a policy in the strict sense). Whereas a political program is the concrete result of a certain problem-solving activity, a policy field represents a structured and relatively stable problem-solving arrangement (Windhoff-Héritier 1987)—a meeting and interaction space for different actors who deal with a certain type of issue (such as environmental, social, or family issues). A policy field may form around a particular policy, but not every policy serves as a crystallization seed of a policy field (Kay 2006).

There have been several attempts to define the fundamental dimensions or elements that constitute a policy field. Loer, Reiter, and Töller (2015), for example, define policy fields in terms of specific enduring constellations of problems, actors, institutions, and instruments. Other authors refer to similar sets of elements (Döhler 2015; Howlett, Ramesh, and Perl 2009). Drawing on general field theory, some authors highlight the socially constructed nature of policy fields (Stecker 2015). Following this view, one can only meaningfully speak of a policy field when actors themselves regard it as an important condition for their actions (Fligstein and McAdam 2012; Martin 2003). A "policy field" is, therefore, bound to its action-guiding effects. It is a sphere of public action that multiple policy actors regard as relevant for their own actions and the collective regulation of certain issues; therefore, it organizes their thinking and doing of policy.

Against the backdrop of these conceptual reflections, can IPS be considered policy fields? My answer is yes—but with additional qualifications. On the one hand, IPS can be clearly subsumed under the general definition of a policy field as they refer to problems, involve actors, build on some organizational structure, and deploy instruments. Moreover, they come with some enduring time frame, and they seem to be of relevance for policy actors themselves. On the other hand, IPS seem to somehow overstretch the definitional boundaries of established policy-field concepts since they refer to rather complex problems constellations that cut across the boundaries of other established policy fields; they involve policy actors who are also engaged in other policy fields; they build on organizational structures that link the institutional infrastructures of various existing policy fields; and they deploy a particular class of instruments that address activities in already established policy fields; finally, with regard to their substance matter, IPS seem to be rather flexible and transitory. Overall, the general concept of a policy field seems to fit, but it might at the same time dilute some of the peculiarities of IPS, that is, their cross-cutting and dynamic nature.

To capture these distinct features, I opt for conceptual differentiation and suggest understanding IPS in terms of a new, "reflexive" type of policy field that differs from an old, "modernist" type.[2] The differences among these types lie in the pattern of field formation, which plays out in two dimensions (see Figure 1).[3] The first *dimension* refers to the genesis of the area that constitutes a policy field. A policy field can emerge by means of differentiation, that is, by breaking off from an existing policy field and forming a specialized area of problem solving, or it can be constituted by means of integration, that is, by combining various existing policies into a new policy field. The second dimension describes the

mode of boundary *delineation*, that is, how a policy field attains and ensures autonomy vis-à-vis other policy fields. The multiple forms of boundary delineation that are theoretically conceivable can be boiled down to two ideal modes. On the one hand, policy boundaries can come in an institutionally fixed form, that is, demarcations that build on relatively stable and commonly accepted norms, which come to bear in some form of action-guiding and taken-for-granted organizational structure. On the other hand, the boundaries can be fluid and flexible—subject to constant struggles and strategic attempts to be (re-) adjusted or (re-)moved.

Based on these two dimensions of policy-field formation,[4] the old "modernist" type of policy fields reflects the dominant view of policy fields as the result of continuing differentiation and institutionalization in the policy system (Blätte 2015; Döhler 2015). These policy fields arise in response to novel problem constellations by decoupling from existing policy fields and forming a more specialized problem-solving arena. The

---

[2] To be clear, these qualifications are not meant to come with normative implications. Rather, they reflect a certain historical and, at the same time, logical sequence. The historical sequence implies that the new/reflexive type of policy field succeeds the old/modernist type. However, this succession does not take the form of a historical progression from old to new (with the new replacing the old). Rather, the logical sequence implies that new/reflexive policy fields cannot exist without old/modernist ones since the former emerge on grounds of the latter.

[3] My focus on formation is descriptive only and does not attempt to explain why policy fields emerge. For explanatory perspectives on the formation of policy fields, see Haunss and Hofmann (2015) and Stecker (2015).

[4] Only recently, Blätte (2015) has suggested a distinction of types of policy fields that is based on degrees of centralization/decentralization. He distinguishes among the "normal" case of concentrated policy fields on the one hand, and decentered fields on the other (i.e., cross-cutting action fields). In the middle between these two extremes, he locates partially concentrated policy fields, that is, policy fields that are organized around an institutional center, but spread out to various areas. Blätte's proposition is a highly valuable contribution to the long overdue typological discussion on policy fields. However, according to my reading, his conceptualization cannot sufficiently take account of "integrative strategic

	Genesis	Delineation
Old "modernist" type	Differentiation	Institutional logic
New "reflexive" type	Integration	Strategic logic

Figure 1: Types of policy fields

boundaries around these types of fields are institutionally drawn and stabilized. This means that a commonly accepted organizational infrastructure (consisting of a defined set of rules and procedures, budgets and staff allocations) serves to delineate, stabilize, and order the differentiated problem-processing areas (Döhler and Manow 1997; Janning 2011).

In contrast, IPS can be regarded to approximate a new, "reflexive" type of policy field that emerges from two movements that counter the predominant patterns of differentiation and institutionalization in policy systems. Rather than following the logic of differentiation, IPS are based on a pattern of "integration," that is, the combination of policies to form more encompassing and integrated policy arrangements. This means that these new policy fields do not break off from existing policies, but result from their assembling. Dispersed policies (or parts of policies) are tied together and merge into complex policy constellations.

Historically, this turn from a pattern of policy differentiation to a pattern of integration is not unprecedented. Rather it can be regarded as a recurring movement in the policy system following periods of increased sectoralization and specialization (Bornemann 2014; Christensen and Lægreid 2007; Hood 2005).

The second countermovement in the policy system propelling the emergence of IPS is a shift in the logic of policy-field delineation. Rather than through the normative power of relatively stable institutions, IPS are demarcated from their policy environment by flexible strategic arrangements and practices. This means that the boundaries of these fields are subject to a constant jockeying with actors trying to define what is inside and outside a policy field. Drawing on actor orientations, this turn from institutions to strategy can be interpreted as a shift from an (institutional) logic of appropriateness to a (strategic) logic of consequences

---

policy fields," which are constituted by the relating of existing policy areas and demarcated by strategies. Upon closer examination, Blätte seems to mix up two dimensions in his conceptualization: one the degree of centralization/decentralization and other some degree of institutionalization. Keeping these dimensions apart would point in the direction of the conceptual proposition I make in the following, and, therefore, allow for taking account of "integrative policy fields." Based on an adapted two-dimensional space, integrative policy fields could be described as concentrated and not institutionalized (but strategic) policy fields.

(March and Olson 1989). Historically, it can be related to a more fundamental transformation (and reflexivization) of the modernist institutional political order (see Beck 2002; Hajer 2003). Following Hajer's diagnosis of policymaking increasingly taking place in an institutional void, the turn to "strategy" reflects the emergence of "new political spaces," that is, "ensemble[s] of mostly unstable practices [...] to address problems that the established institutions are for a variety of reasons, unable to resolve in a manner that is perceived to be both legitimate and effective" (Hajer 2003, 176).

Together both countermovements give rise to a new type of policy field that can be called "reflexive" for three reasons. One, these policy fields emerge from the existing policy system in terms of an additional layer of policymaking. This means that they represent second-order or meta-policy fields that refer back to, and, thereby, reflect other established first-order policies and policy fields. Two, as elaborated earlier, the emergence of these fields can be interpreted as reaction to two dominant movements in the policy system. More specifically, in line with propositions of "reflexive modernization"

(Beck et al. 2003), they come with a problematization of the modernist patterns of differentiation and institutionalization. Three, both integration and strategy are not solely descriptions by external policy analysts to refer to "objective" developments, but are also used by policy actors to reflect on their own orientations. Policy actors themselves claim that they organize policymaking in integrative and strategic ways. Accordingly, "integration" and "strategy" represent practical orientations for real-world policymakers' thinking and doing (see Bornemann 2014; Tils 2005). Therefore, these concepts can be interpreted as commonly shared but contestable meanings of what this new type of field is all about, that is, the "field force" that organizes the form and functioning of integrative–strategic policy fields.[5]

What follows from this conceptual understanding of IPS as a new type of policy field? First, conceptualizing IPS in terms of a policy field serves to overcome the functional presumptions of given perspectives on IPS. It implies examining IPS in a more analytical, de-normativized way. Rather than inquiring about what IPS are supposed to be (i.e., a certain

---

[5] Integration and strategy also play a role in other conceptualizations of (policy) fields. In fact, some scholars use "integrative" to define policy fields per se (May, Sapotichne, and Workman 2006). However, they use the term to refer to the inner cohesion of policy fields, rather than a pattern of field emergence, as I suggest. Similarly, by using the qualifier "strategic" in their general theory of social fields, Fligsten and McAdam (2012) imply that strategy, that is, the capacity of actors to "vie for advantage" by taking account of other actors in a field, is a definitional component of a social field as such. In contrast to this understanding, I refer to strategy as a specific pattern of field delineation that replaces an "institutional logic." This comes with the more general theoretical proposition that "institutional logics" are not to be regarded as (conceptual) alternative to social fields as Fligstein and McAdam (2012, 10) seem to suggest. Rather, I suggest conceiving of institutional and strategic logics as two different logics of field delineation corresponding with March and Olson's (1989) distinction between "logic of consequences" (strategy) and "logic of appropriateness" (institution).

prescribed function, such as steering), a field perspective draws attention to their actual forming and functioning. From a field perspective, IPS are not necessarily means for governing the policy system toward certain ends, but venues for interactions, which have to be described before they are assessed with regard to their functional implications.

Second, in line with general field theoretical accounts (Fligstein and McAdam 2012), a policy-field perspective highlights the socially constructed nature of IPS, that is, what IPS mean to policymakers and how this meaning affects policymaking. Therefore, a field-theoretical perspective reorients the view from objectively measurable effects of policy programs to the subjectively relevant action-guiding effects of IPS: the construction of a shared but not necessarily consensual understanding of IPS's purposes, and how this understanding structures the thinking and doing of policy actors, that is, the "field effect." Considering both their theoretical significance for capturing the formation of policy fields and their actual practical relevance for orienting policymaker, "integration" and "strategy" can be regarded as cornerstones around which the construction of IPS and, therefore, the field effect emerges.

Third, considering IPS in terms of a new type of policy field (rather than a policy program, a way of steering, problem solving, or the like) broadens the analytical view in several respects. A field perspective does not only open up to more dynamic inquiries about what happens over time around and within IPS, that is, their changing configurations and boundaries, but it also implies that IPS are part of a larger and evolving policy landscape, a "complex web of strategic action fields" (Fligstein and McAdam 2012, 8) with which they are connected in multiple ways, and, therefore, expands the analysis toward their nestedness in a broader environment of policy fields.

Overall, I argue that IPS should be regarded not only as instrumental means to solve complex problems and govern the policy machinery toward certain long-term goals, but they also signify a new type of policy field emerging from two broader movements in the policy system—the integration of increasingly differentiated areas of policymaking, on the one hand, and the rise of strategy, on the other hand. IPS are manifestations of these types of policy fields. Rather than following the logic of differentiation, IPS are based on a rationale of integration; and instead of drawing on stable institutionalized boundaries, IPS build on the logic of strategy which is geared toward flexible boundary work. This concept of IPS as manifestations of new types of policy fields has major implications for how IPS are to be analyzed. These are further elaborated in the following section.

4. Toward an Integration- and Strategy-Oriented Policy Analysis

Following the proposition that integration and strategy signify the emergence of a new type of policy field and serve as important practical orientations for policymakers—how can policy analysis systematically take account of these cornerstones of integrative–strategic policy fields? In the following two subsections, I outline an integration- and strategy-oriented policy analysis that is supposed to deploy a finer-grained picture of integrative-strategic policy fields. I do so by developing a generic analytical repertoire for critically assessing understandings and practices of integrative and strategic policymaking. While policy integration as an analytical focus draws attention to a certain pattern of policy-field genesis (i.e., the combining of policies to form integrated policy arrangements), the political strategy perspective is meant to reveal patterns of strategic boundary work that serve the delineation of policy fields. Together, integration and strategy form an analytics that can be used for empirically reconstructing understandings and practices of policymaking that charac-terize the form and functioning of integrative-strategic policy fields.

4.1. Policy Integration as Analytical Focus

Policy integration is not a new concept in policy analysis. Belonging to a broader class of analytical perspectives that address policy interdependencies and overlapping subsystems (see Lang and Tosun 2014; May and Jochim 2013), policy integration refers to activities of coordinating policymaking in such a way that external effects are minimized and complex problems can be solved in a coherent manner (Briassoulis 2005; Meijers 2004). Most prominently, policy integration has been implemented and analyzed as a principle of environmental politics (Jordan and Lenschow 2008; Lenschow 2002). Despite the constantly growing conceptual and empirical literature, considerable conceptual confusion and contestations remain. It is far from clear what policy integration is all about and based on which criteria empirical phenomena of policy

integration are to be analyzed. Moreover, the concept has problematic a priori political and normative implications, focusing on either the promotion of some goals vis-à-vis other ones (Lafferty and Hovden 2003) or a coherent and rational policy design (Underdal 1980). This blurs an analytical view on policy integration, that is, a differentiated understanding of the multiple forms of policy integration, which might have shaped and emerged around IPS and, thus, form the "substance" of integrative-strategic policy fields.

To grasp the plurality of possible understandings and real-world phenomena of policy integration, I propose a generic understanding of policy integration in terms of an analytical perspective (PI perspective). The PI perspective is a selective way of observing the policy world that complements the dominant "sectoral" view (Bönker 2008). It consists of a differentiated "universe" of conceptually conceivable forms of policy integration. This range of conceptual meanings is based on two fundamental questions referring to the "what" and "how" of policy integration (see Bornemann 2014).

The first question (*What* is integrated?) refers to the objects of policy integration and involves a clarification of "policy." Taking into consideration multiple theoretical and methodological perspectives, public policy is a term given to a multilayered constellation that is meant (and created with the idea) to address issues of public concern (Colebatch 2002; Howlett, Ramesh, and Perl 2009; Scharpf 1997). Such a general understanding can be further specified along four basic dimensions, each comprising several more specific elements. These dimensions can serve as references for defining the identity of one policy versus another, hence delineating the boundaries of policies.

First and most fundamentally, a policy can be described as a certain ensemble of substantive problems, goals, and means. Problems, conceived of as perceived difference between a given and a desired state of the world, mark the starting point of a certain policy and policy actions (Dery 1984; Hoppe 2011). Policy goals specify an envisioned end state of policymaking; and a policy tool (as the means) comprises a set of interventions that is expected to transform a policy problem into a policy solution. These substantial policy elements span two mutually constitutive layers, which can be considered policy-related excerpts of the subjective and objective worlds (Majone 1980). Policies are usually written in some form of (symbolic) policy text (such as a bill, a law, a regulation, or a manifesto). These policy texts are interpreted and enacted in some form of (material) policy action "on the ground" (such as the allocation of resources to build an infrastructure and so forth).

Second, the social dimension of a policy reflects the assumption that "public policy is a matter of human agency" (Schneider and Ingram 1997, 1). Following this, the policy substance (problems, solutions, and means) cannot be meaningfully understood in isolation from the actors who make and interpret a policy. These actions take place in some form of policy arena (Ostrom 1999), which includes various kinds of actors who are part of specific, more complex actor constellations, and engage with one another in various spheres that are characterized by either "opening" (debates) or "closing" (decisions) forms

of interactions (Scharpf 1997; Stirling 2008).

Third, the temporal dimension reflects the widespread assumption that a policy is not a singularity or a static entity. Rather than a "still," a policy is understood as a "movie" (Kay 2006), implying that its substantial elements and social arena evolve over time as a sequence of different temporal states. Most prominently, this notion has been expressed in models such as the policy cycle (Jann and Wegrich 2007) or other temporal ideas highlighting the chaotic and contingent character of policy developments (Kingdon 2014; Zahariadis 2007). These different policy temporalities can be captured according to more general, time-related criteria (Pierson 2004; Prittwitz 2007), such as duration, dynamics, or velocity.

Similar to time, the spatial dimension of a policy is fundamental as it underlies the other dimensions. Most prominently, the notion of policy space is reflected in concepts, such as multilevel policymaking, suggesting that a policy may extend over several functional or jurisdictional levels of governance (Piattoni 2010). The many ways of thinking about and conceptualizing policy space can be reduced to two: a vertical subdimension covering various policymaking levels that are related in some form of hierarchical order (from the local to the international) and a horizontal one referring to various policy areas at a certain level, which are demarcated by jurisdictional borders.

The second question (*How are policies integrated?*) relates to the modes of policy integration and can be approached by more closely looking at the meaning of "integration." Following a generic understanding, "integration" is about relating at least two dispersed parts (integrands) to each other in such a way that they constitute an integral whole (a third) (Bornemann 2014). Furthermore, the literature presents three understandings of integration; each can be associated with a certain qualifier—as a process (integrating), a structure (integrated), or a function (integrative). A procedural perspective highlights relating the parts and forming the integral whole. A structural perspective offers a static understanding of integration as a stable arrangement of related parts and an integral whole. The functional perspective emphasizes integration as the potential or the capacity to relate parts such that they form an integral whole (Bornemann 2014, 85f.). These understandings come with more specific "modes of integration," meaning the interpretations of *how* (and with what effects) elements are related and form an integral whole. Out of the many integration modes that can be distinguished (Bornemann 2014, 87ff.), the following three will illustrate what these are all about and how they imply a variety of interpretations and forms of policy integration.

First, the structural criterion, integration directionality, refers to the kinds of ties established among the integrated parts, a factor that carries implications for the appearance of the integral whole. This criterion involves the question of whether the parts are related in a one-directional or a reciprocal manner. A mode of unidirectional integration implies that the relating of parts proceeds as a one-sided hegemonic penetration in which one or more parts unilaterally constrain the autonomy of another part or other parts, causing the integral whole to adopt a shape that mainly reflects the

dominant parts. In contrast, reciprocal integration is characterized by the establishment of mutual relations between the parts and a mutual agreement on the limits placed on their autonomy. Within the current discourse and practice of PI, unidirectional integration is represented in many concepts of environmental policy integration, which envisions injecting environmental concerns or goals into other nonenvironmental policy processes. However, there are also some concepts of reciprocal PI that highlight mutual relations between policies (Briassoulis 2005; Collier 1994).

Second, as a functional criterion, integration productivity captures the net effects of changes in the autonomy of the integrated parts and the integral whole. According to a rather common understanding, integration, in general, and PI, in particular, yield positive net effects. This assumption of positive policy integration is observed in synergistic ideas, such as the whole being more than the sum of its elements, or with reference to "positive-sum games" or "win-win solutions" (Collier 1994). However, from a critical perspective, it becomes clear that this optimistic description is merely one possible interpretation of the productive function of PI. There could be other interpretations according to which integration brings with it a net loss of autonomy, in which the whole becomes less than the sum of its parts (Luhmann 2009, 188)—a mode of negative integration that has also been described as over-integration (Lange and Schimank 2004). Regarding policy, these dysfunctional forms of integration are rarely explored but are both logically and empirically relevant. In some instances, an integrated policy arrangement (e.g., a central planning unit) may be less capable of solving certain problems than the prior, dispersed (i.e., nonintegrated) policy arenas.

Third, from a procedural perspective, integration duration refers to the length of the process. Given the inherent temporality of policies (as previously explained), their integration can be restricted to a certain point in policy time, referring to a particular stage such as agenda setting or implementation (punctual integration), or it can extend over a longer policy period, covering multiple stages (enduring integration). Such a differentiation between punctual and enduring modes of PI (along with the acknowledgment of possible intermediate forms on the spectrum) critically implies that PI is not necessarily an all-encompassing phenomenon, but may end at some point in the course of policymaking.

In sum, the two concepts that define the conceptual space for thinking about and analyzing PI—policy and integration—are fairly complex and exhibit a diverse range of meanings. Together they constitute the "universe of policy integration"—the conceptual space of conceivable forms of PI constituting the analytical PI perspective. Thereby, the PI perspective emphasizes the multifaceted nature and potential complexity of policy integration, that is, the fact that different elements of policies can be integrated in different ways. This helps overcome the dominating narrow and politically biased understandings of policy integration and allows for a finer-grained empirical analysis of the multiple forms that policy integration can take on in practice. In fact, my own in-depth analysis of the German sustainability strategy has shown

that policy integration is realized in a much more differentiated and nuanced way than established approaches of PI would have been able to take into account (Bornemann 2014). The reconstruction of the policy arrangement that has emerged from the German sustainability strategy reveals a highly differentiated and multifaceted pattern of policy integration, which combines several policy objects in multiple modes, on the levels of both understandings and manifestations. Thus, the study reveals that policymakers follow very particular pathways of integrative policymaking and yield highly differentiated forms of policy integration, which in some respects match the normative integration requirements of the sustainability idea.

Overall, the PI perspective comes with a differentiated conceptual repertoire for analyzing the combination of policies within integrative–strategic policy fields. A systematic analysis of IPS from the perspective of policy integration opens the view for the multiple forms that integrative policy fields can take, that is, which (aspects of) policies are integrated and how this is done.

4.2. Political Strategy as Analytical Focus

Although strategy is an emerging concept in political and policy studies (Mulgan 2010), many studies of strategy in the public sphere disseminate models of strategic management. This might reflect "a widely shared consensus on contemporary strategising in the public sector that emerged from decades of strategic management research" (Casado-Asensio and Steurer 2014, 457; see also Steurer and Martinuzzi 2005). However, the adoption of models of strategic management presumes that policymakers act as if they were managers. Such a presumption is problematic since it narrows down the focus (and criteria) of analysis (and evaluations) to certain managerial orientations and practices of policymakers while blocking other forms of strategic orientations and practices that emerge from and within political contexts.

To shed light on the boundary work around integrative–strategic policy fields, I draw on conceptualizations of strategy that have been explicitly promoted for the analysis of strategic action in political contexts (Raschke 2002; Raschke and Tils 2013; Tils 2005; 2011). The corresponding political strategy approach can be qualified by three main principles. First, it is actor oriented, which implies that it puts strategic actors and their actions at the core of its interest. Second, it presumes a broad understanding of "the political", combining aspects of polity, politics, and policy, to understand how actors formulate and implement strategies. Third, it combines rational with interpretive paradigms in understanding the orientations of strategic actors. According to the political strategy perspective, actors attempt to intentionally optimize their action courses within certain subjectively perceived action spaces (Tils 2005, 69).

Within the scope of these basic principles, a political strategy is defined as an action construct that relies on situation-transgressing, success-oriented, and dynamic calculations, which refer to goals, means, and contexts (Tils 2005, 25). This definition suggests that actors act strategically when they attempt to achieve their goals by taking account of available means and their action contexts. More specifically, strategic action draws

on a certain orientation that combines goals, means, and contexts in such a way that the chances of success are increased. Based on this general understanding, a differentiated conceptual basis has been developed covering various dimensions, such as strategic capacity, strategy formulation, and strategic steering, as well as related subdimensions and elements (Raschke and Tils 2013; Tils 2011). This conceptual basis has been employed to analyze strategic capacities of political parties or strategic steering in party government (Nullmeier and Saretzki 2002; Raschke and Tils 2013; Tils 2011). These applications indicate that the political strategy perspective is neither confined to, nor was it developed for analyzing patterns of policy-field demarcation around IPS. However, given its generic ambitions, some of its basic categories shall be adapted to illuminate how integrative–strategic policy fields are demarcated. More specifically, assuming that the boundary drawing around integrative–strategic policy fields adheres to a strategic, rather than an institutional logic, strategic analysis shall shed light on these patterns of strategic boundary work.

Boundary work more generally refers to drawing a line between the inside and the outside (Gieryn 1983; Lamont and Molnár 2002). In relation to policy fields, boundary work is about defining the coverage and scope of a certain policy field vis-à-vis its policy and nonpolicy environments. The definition of a policy field's boundaries has major strategic implications. By defining what a policy field is all about, actors set the stage for political and policy processes in these fields—and for attaining their individual goals. Boundary work is of particular relevance in policy fields that emerge in an institutional void, that is, the absence of relatively stable institutionalized boundaries. Strategic boundary work with regard to these policy fields refers to all kinds of strategic moves and interactions that are designated to (re-)negotiate, (re-)define, (re-)move, and (de-)stabilize the boundaries of both existing and newly created policy fields (for generic types of boundary work, see also Gieryn 1999). Following the general understanding of political strategy outlined earlier, I suggest analyzing strategic boundary work with regard to the following basic categories: strategic actors, strategic orientations, strategic practices, and strategic interactions.

First, the political strategy perspective assigns strategic actors a central role in defining and redefining the boundaries of policy fields. The universe of strategic boundary workers includes two types of actors—those who already participate in the policy arenas that constitute an integrative-strategic policy field (see Section 4.1); and additional actors who have not been engaged in the policy arenas of integrated policies. Whereas the former comprise all kinds of political, administrative, and societal policy actors; the latter ones involve boundary workers with a specific integration task, such as governmental core executives (Bornemann 2011). Regardless of these contexts, the actors can adopt different roles in creating and maintaining an integrative policy field. They can play an active part in constructing or deconstructing field boundaries, mediate among conflicting actors, or assume more passive roles as external observers.

Second, these actors follow

specific strategic orientations that consist of success-oriented and dynamic goal–means–context calculations. Elaborating on insights about the differences between political and administrative logics of action (Hansen and Ejersbo 2002), a political strategy perspective draws attention to fundamentally different strategic orientations that are aligned with the particular action contexts of the actors. Considering the complexity of "the political" within modern policy systems (Tils 2005) the diverse orientations of multiple policy actors in creating and demarcating policies can be captured by referring to polity, politics, and policy. Administrative actors, for example, are oriented toward policy and polity aspects, such as resources, expertise, administrative practicability, and legality (Raschke and Tils 2013; Smeddinck and Tils 2002; Tils 2001). Therefore, they can be expected to engage in boundary-demarcation strategies with a focus on pushing through their expertise to enhance resources and competencies for their own administrative unit in relation to other (competing) units. Party elites in governmental positions follow a different orientation as they attempt to succeed in both policies and politics. They consider the demarcation of a policy field from the viewpoint of power and its profiling possibilities within the political context of party competition, coalition government, mass media, lobbying, and so on. They seek to cut a policy area to elicit a positive response from the public and the voters. In contrast, other actors, such as those in civic organizations, are primarily interested in substantial aspects of policy-field demarcation. They might want to tailor problem-solving processes and structures to arrive at the best possible solutions. Their strategies of field delimitation orient toward the problem characteristics and the requirements of adequate problem solving.

Third, to realize these basic orientations, strategic actors adopt various practices. These practices can be directed at either creating and developing new or dissolving established boundaries, rendering them permeable or even unstable. They can also be oriented toward moving boundaries (i.e., cutting out parts of a policy field and reframing them as elements of a new policy) or strengthening or defending established boundaries. The diverse strategic practices may refer to substantial, social, spatial, or temporal boundaries of policies (see Section 4.1). Substantial boundary work is about redefining or stabilizing the material and symbolic fundament of a policy (e.g., by means of resource distribution, reframing of problems, meaning, use of knowledge and expertise to (re-)configure the form and meaning of issues, etc.). Social boundary work involves creating or reshuffling actor constellations (by means of coalition building, mobilization, or demobilization, and opening or closing existing arenas to certain actors). Spatial boundary work deals with the spatial embedding of a policy and involves practices such as scaling an issue up or down within a multilevel system. Temporal boundary work entails defining and redefining the temporal parameters of policies by expanding or narrowing down the time horizon or the policy-specific temporal patterns.

Fourth, a strategic perspective focuses on the interplay of strategic actors with different orientations. This strategic interplay results from individual strategic practices that actors adopt when they follow their orientations. It consists of a temporarily stabilized pattern of boundary demarcations, representing a strategic equilibrium at a certain point in time. This can become manifest (as in the case of many IPS) in a formal strategy document or a certain organizational arrangement. However, following the perspective of political strategy, this equilibrium is subject to continued contestation. A pattern may break up and become fluid again. These dynamics of opening and closing lie at the heart of strategic analysis.

Overall, strategic analysis draws attention to the ways integrative–strategic policy fields are demarcated by means of strategic action. From the perspective of political strategy, the boundaries of integrative–strategic policy fields are not institutionally defined. Rather, they represent temporarily defined strategic equilibria resulting from the strategic interactions of multiple actors, who follow different strategic orientations and adopt various strategic practices of boundary work.

5. Conclusion and Outlook

I have started with the observation that policymakers are increasingly opting for ways of policymaking that fall under the IPS category. In asking how to understand and analyze these relatively new policy phenomena, I have aimed to contribute to the conceptual discussion about IPS and their analysis. To do so, I have reviewed the existing research on IPS and revealed several shortcomings in the current academic debate. I am especially concerned that there is no clear conceptual understanding of these new phenomena. In fact, IPS are conceptualized according to several functional expectations, which are in turn based on various (normative) models of policymaking. Second, resulting from this functional bias, empirical research tends to focus on assessing the performance of IPS rather than capturing what occurs in and around IPS. Based on overly ambitious standards that reflect the ascribed functions of IPS, several rather skeptical outlooks have emerged, certifying the overall failure of IPS.

Following the critical review, I have proposed an understanding of IPS as a new, "reflexive" type of policy field, emerging from two more recent movements in the policy system. These movements counter two trends that have dominated modern policy systems—the integration of policies as a countermovement to the continued differentiation of the policy system on the one hand, and the turn to strategy as a flexible form of policy boundary work that contrasts with the pattern of firm institutionalization on the other hand. To analyze the form and functioning of these new types of policy fields and grasp the peculiarities of integrative–strategic policymaking, I have suggested perceiving integration and strategy as the central terms of analysis and elaborated the analytical repertoires that come with both terms. I argue that the analytical complexity of these concepts should be taken seriously to acquire differentiated empirical understandings of IPS, which can serve as basis for further inquiries on the function and performance of IPS in contemporary policy systems.

The conceptual propositions I make in this paper contribute to the study of IPS and contemporary policymaking in three ways. First, understanding IPS in terms of a new type of policy field comes with a fresh perspective on these increasingly important phenomena of current policymaking. It opens the view for a more analytical (and less instrumental) understanding of IPS, and it paves the way for a more systematic, theoretical embedding of IPS in policy theory. Second, highlighting two fundamental dimensions of policy-field formation (i.e., genesis and delineation), adds to the conceptualization of policy fields as a relevant though neglected object of policy research in general. In particular, the distinction among ideal types of policy fields contributes to the typological discussion on the issue (Blätte 2015). Third, I have outlined a differentiated analytics to capture the conceptual cornerstones of the new type of policy field, namely policy integration and political strategy. The analytics of policy integration provides a basis for a more nuanced understanding of the constitution of complex policy arrangements that form IPS. It emphasizes and allows for a differentiated inquiry about both the "what" (elements) and the "how" (modes) of policy integration. The analytics of political strategy serves as a basis for improving the knowledge about the boundary work that is performed in and around IPS. Specifically, it enables an analysis of the political (polity, politics, and policy) conditions and orientations of policy actors working for or against the creation of (as well as within) IPS. Taken together, an integration- and strategy-oriented policy analysis provides the grounds for a finer-grained comprehension of IPS as policy fields and the underlying mechanisms that shape the emergence of these phenomena.

Viewing IPS in terms of a new type of integrative–strategic policy field has several implications for future theoretical and empirical work, as well as policy practice. First, the propositions might challenge established theoretical models of policy change. How can the dynamics within established integrative–strategic policy fields be explained? Furthermore, from the perspective of normative theory, the relationship between IPS and democratic principles, such as accountability, might arise. How do integrative–strategic policy fields challenge established practices of democratic policymaking? Second, the proposition to analyze integrative strategies in terms of new policy fields rather than operational policy programs implies an extension of current empirical research on IPS. Before assessing whether and to what extent IPS can fulfill certain functions, their integrative and strategic qualities are to be empirically described. What forms of integration and strategy can be identified around various IPS in different contexts? Such more differentiated analyses can provide new insights into the working of IPS and will serve as a basis for more reflected assessments of their impacts within the broader policy system. Further empirical research should also reveal the relationship between integration and strategy (including possible synergies and tensions). What kinds of strategy promote which forms of policy integration under which conditions and vice versa? What comes first in the orientation of policy actors—integration or strategy? Does the integration of policies result from strategic action, or is strategic action caused by integration efforts? Do strategy and integration always occur together or are there other types of differentiated strategic or integrative institutional policy fields? Finally, an improved analysis of IPS that considers integration and strategy in a more sophisticated way will

strengthen practical efforts of setting up and improving IPS toward *politically* defined goals. A strategy- and integration-oriented analysis that increases the understanding of the emergence of particular forms of policy integration and the strategic interactions behind them can provide insights to help policymakers develop "better," that is, more integrative and strategically reflected policy designs. Thus, it can increase the capacity of practice-oriented policy analysis to help fulfill the high expectations placed on IPS in solving today's complex societal problems (Rayner and Howlett 2009b).

References

Adelle, Camilla, and Duncan Russel. 2013. "Climate Policy Integration: a Case of Déjà Vu?" *Environmental Policy and Governance* 23 (1): 1–12. doi:10.1002/eet.1601.

Bauer, Anja, Judith Feichtinger, and Reinhard Steurer. 2012. "The Governance of Climate Change Adaptation in 10 OECD Countries: Challenges and Approaches." *Journal of Environmental Policy and Planning* 14 (3): 279–304.

Beck, Ulrich. 2002. *Macht und Gegenmacht im globalen Zeitalter: Neue Weltpolitische Ökonomie*, First Edition. *Edition zweite Moderne*. Frankurt am Main: Suhrkamp.

Beck, Ulrich, Wolfgang Bonss, and Christoph Lau. 2003. "The Theory of Reflexive Modernization: Problematic, Hypotheses and Research Programme." *Theory, Culture and Society* 20 (2): 1–33.

Biesbroek, G.R., Rob J. Swart, Timothy R. Carter, Caroline Cowan, Thomas Henrichs, Hanna Mela, Michael D. Morecroft, and Daniela Rey. 2010. "Europe Adapts to Climate Change: Comparing National Adaptation Strategies." *Global Environmental Change* 20 (3): 440–450.

Blätte, Andreas. 2015. "Grenzen und Konfigurationen Politischer Handlungsfelder: Skizze einer Typologischen Theorie." *dms—der moderne Staat* 8 (1): 91–112.

Blum, Sonja, and Klaus Schubert. 2011. *Politikfeldanalyse*, Second Edition. Wiesbaden: VS Verlag für Sozialwissenschaften.

Bönker, Frank. 2008. "Interdependenzen zwischen Politikfeldern—die vernachlässigte sektorale Dimension der Politikverflechtung." In *Die Zukunft der Policy-Forschung: Theorien, Methoden, Anwendungen*, eds. Frank Janning, and Katrin Toens. Wiesbaden: VS Verlag für Sozialwissenschaften, 315–330.

Bornemann, Basil. 2011. "Regierungszentralen und Policy-Integration: Die Bedeutung des Bundes-kanzleramts für ein integratives Policy-Making am Beispiel der nationalen Nachhaltigkeitsstrategie." In *Regierungskanzleien im Politischen Prozess*, eds. Stephan Bröchler, and Julia von Blumenthal. Wiesbaden: VS Verlag für Sozialwissenschaften, 153–177.

Bornemann, Basil. 2014. *Policy-Integration und Nachhaltigkeit: Integrative Politik in der Nachhaltigkeitsstrategie der deutschen Bundesregierung*, Second Edition. Wiesbaden: Springer VS.

Briassoulis, Helen. 2005. "Complex Environmental Problems and the Quest for Policy-Integration." In *Policy Integration for Complex Environmental Problems: The Example of Mediterranean Desertification*, ed. Helen Briassoulis. Burlington, Vt: Ashgate, 1–49.

Brodhag, Christian, and Sophie Talière. 2006. "Sustainable Development Strategies: Tools for Policy Coherence." *Natural Resources Forum* 30 (2): 136–145.

Busch, Per-Olof, and Helge Jörgens. 2005. "The International Sources of Policy Convergence: Explaining the Spread of Environmental Policy Innovations." *Journal of European Public Policy* 12 (5): 86084.

Casado-Asensio, Juan, and Reinhard-Steurer. 2014. "Integrated Strategies on Sustainable Development, Climate Change Mitigation and Adaptation in Western Europe: Communication Rather than Coordination." *Journal of Public Policy* 34 (3): 437–473.

Cejudo, Guillermo M., and Cynthia Michel. 2015. *Addressing Fragmented Government Action: Coordination, Coherence, and Integration: Paper Presented at the 2nd International Conference in Public Policy, Milan, July 2015*. http://www.icpublicpolicy.org/conference/file/repon se/1434668940.pdf.

Christensen, Tom, and Per Lægreid. 2007. "The Whole-of-Government Approach to Public Sector Reform." *Public Administration Review* 67 (6): 1059–1066. http://dx.doi.org/10.1111/j.1540-6210.20 07.00797.x.

Colebatch, Hal K. 2002. *Policy*, Second Edition. Buckingham/Philadelphia: Open University Press.

Collier, Ute. 1994. *Energy and Environment in the European Union. The Challenge of Integration*. Aldershot (u.a.): Ashgate.

Dalal-Clayton, Barry, and Stephen Bass. 2002. *Sustainable Development Strategies. A Resource Book*. Paris/New York: OECD (Organisation for Economic Co-operation and Development) / UNDP (United Nations Development Programme).

Dery, David. 1984. *Problem Definition in Policy Analysis*. Lawrence, KAN: University Press of Kansas.

Döhler, Marian. 2015. "Das Politikfeld als analytische Kategorie." *dms—der moderne staat* 8 (1): 51–69.

Döhler, Marian, and Philip Manow.1997. *Strukturbildung von Politikfeldern: Das Beispiel bundesdeutscher Gesundheitspolitik seit den fünfziger Jahren*. Opladen: Leske + Budrich.

Elzen, Boelie, Frank W. Geels, and Ken Green, eds. 2004. *System Innovation and the Transition to Sustainability. Theory, Evidence and Policy*. Cheltenham, UK/ Northampton, MA: Edward Elgar.

Fligstein, Neil, and Doug McAdam. 2012. *A Theory of Fields*. New York: Oxford University Press.

Gieryn, Thomas F. 1983. "Boundary-Work and the Demarcation of Science from Non-Science: Strains and Interests in Professional Ideologies of Scientists." *American Sociological Review* 48 (6): 781–795.

Gieryn, Thomas F. 1999. *Cultural Boundaries of Science: Credibility on the Line*. Chicago: University of Chicago Press.

Gould, Jeremy. 2005. *The New Conditionality: The Politics of Poverty Reduction Strategies*. London, New York: Zed Books.

Gouldson, Andrew, and Peter Roberts, eds. 2000. *Integrating Environment and Economy: Strategies for Local and Regional Government*. London: Routledge.

Haberl, Helmut, Marina Fischer-Kowalski, Fridolin Krausmann, Joan Martinez-Alier, and Verena Winiwarter. 2011. "A Socio-Metabolic Transition Towards Sustainability? Challenges for Another Great Transformation." *Sustainable Development* 19 (1): 1–14.

Hajer, Maarten. 2003. "Policy without Polity? Policy Analysis and the Institutional void." *Policy Sciences* 36 (2): 175–195.

Hansen, Kasper M., and Niels Ejersbo. 2002. "The Relationship between Politicians and Administrators—A Logic of Disharmony." *Public Administration* 80 (4): 733–750.

Haunss, Sebastian, and Jeanette Hofmann. 2015. "Entstehung von Politikfeldern— Bedingungen einer Anomalie." *dms—der moderne staat* 8 (1): 29–49.

Heinelt, Hubert. 2009. "Politikfelder: Machen Besonderheiten von Policies einen Unterschied?" In *Lehrbuch der Politikfeldanalyse 2.0*, eds. Klaus Schubert and Nils C. Bandelow. München: Oldenbourg, 115–130.

Hood, Christopher. 2005. "The Idea of Joined-Up Government: A Historical Perspective." In *Joined-Up Government*, ed. Vernon Bogdanor. Oxford: Oxford University Press for the British Academy, 19–42.

Hoppe, Robert A. 2011. *The Governance of Problems: Puzzling, Powering, Participation*. Bristol, England: Policy Press.

Howlett, Michael, M. Ramesh, and Anthony Perl. 2009. *Studying Public Policy: Policy Cycles and Policy Subsystems*, Third Edition. Ontario: Oxford University Press.

Howlett, Michael, and Jeremy Rayner. 2006. "Convergence and Divergence in 'New Governance' Arrangements: Evidence from European Integrated Natural Resource Strategies." *Journal of Public Policy* 26 (2): 167–189.

Howlett, Michael, and Jeremy Rayner. 2007. "Design Principles for Policy Mixes: Cohesion and Coherence in "New Governance Arrangements"." *Policy and Society* 26 (4): 1–18.

Jänicke, Martin. 2000. "Strategien der Nachhaltigkeit—Eine Einführung." In *Umweltplanung im internationalen Vergleich. Strategien der Nachhaltigkeit. Unter Mitarbeit von Kristina Hahn und Claudia Koll*, eds. Martin Jänicke and Helge Jörgens. Berlin: Springer, 1–12.

Jann, Werner, and Kai Wegrich. 2007. "Theories of the Policy Cycle." In *Handbook of Public Policy Analysis: Theory, Politics, and Methods*, eds. Frank Fischer, Gerald J. Miller, Mara S. Sidney and Gerald Miller.

Boca Raton: CRC Press, 43–62.

Janning, Frank. 2011. *Die Spätgeburt eines Politikfeldes: Die Institutionalisierung der Verbraucherschutzpolitik in Deutschland und im Internationalen Vergleich*, First Edition. Baden-Baden: Nomos.

Jordan, Andrew, and Andrea Lenschow, eds. 2008. *Innovation in Environmental Policy?: Integrating the Environment for Sustainability*. Cheltenham, UK/ Northampton, MA: Edward Elgar.

Kay, Adrian. 2006. *The Dynamics of Public Policy: Theory and Evidence. New Horizons in Public Policy*. Cheltenham, UK/Northampton, MA: Edward Elgar.

Kern, Kristine. 2008. "Sub-national Sustainable Development Initiatives in Federal States in Germany." In *In Pursuit of Sustainable Development: New Governance Practices at the Sub-National Level in Europe*, eds. Susan Baker and Katarina Eckerberg. London: Routledge, 122–144.

Kingdon, John W. 2014. *Agendas, Alternatives, and Public Policies: Update Edition, with an Epilogue on Health Care*, Second Edition. Harlow: Pearson Education Limited.

Lafferty, William M., and Eivind Hovden. 2003. "Environmental Policy Integration: Towards an Analytical Framework." *Environmental Politics* 12 (3): 1–22.

Lamont, Michèle, and Virág Molnár. 2002. "The Study of Boundaries in the Social Sciences." *Annual Review of Sociology* 28 (1): 167–195.

Lang, Achim, and Jale Tosun. 2014. "Policy Integration und verwandte Ansätze: Möglichkeiten der Theorieintegration." *Zeitschrift für Politikwissenschaft* 24 (3): 353–371.

Lange, Hellmuth, ed. 2008. *Nachhaltigkeit als radikaler Wandel: Die Quadratur des Kreises?*, First Edition. Wiesbaden: VS Verlag für Sozialwissenschaften.

Lange, Stefan, and Uwe Schimank. 2004. "Governance und gesellschaftliche Integration." In *Governance und gesellschaftliche Integration*, eds. Stefan Lange and Uwe Schimank. Wiesbaden: VS Verlag für Sozialwissenschaften, 9–44.

Lenschow, Andrea, ed. 2002. *Environmental Policy Integration: Greening Sectoral Policies in Europe.* London/Sterling, VA: Earthscan.

Loer, Kathrin, Renate Reiter, and Annette E. Töller. 2015. "Was ist ein Politikfeld und warum entsteht es?" *dms—der moderne staat* 8 (1): 7–28.

Luhmann, Niklas. 2009. "Gesellschaft." In *Soziologische Aufklärung 1: Aufsätze zur Theorie sozialer Systeme*, Eight Edition, ed. Niklas Luhmann. Wiesbaden: VS Verlag für Sozialwissenschaften, 173–193.

Majone, Giandomenico. 1980. "Policies as Theories." *Omega* 8 (2): 151–162.

March, James G., and Johan P. Olson. 1989. *Rediscovering Institutions: The Organizational Basis of Politics.* New York: The Free Press.

Markard, Jochen, Rob Raven, and Bernhard Truffer. 2012. "Sustainability Transitions: An Emerging Field of Research and its Prospects." *Special Section on Sustainability Transitions* 41 (6): 955–967.

Martin, John L. 2003. "What Is Field Theory?" *American Journal of Sociology* 109 (1): 1–49.

Massey, Eric, and Dave Huitema. 2013. "The Emergence of Climate Change Adaptation as a Policy Field: The Case of England." *Regional Environmental Change* 13 (2): 341–352. doi.org/10.1007/s10113-012-0341-2.

May, Peter J., Bryan D. Jones, Betsi E. Beem, Emily A. Neff-Sharum, and Melissa K. Poague. 2005. "Policy Coherence and Component-Driven Policymaking: Arctic Policy in Canada and the United States." *Policy Studies Journal* 33 (1): 37–63. doi:10.1111/j.1541-0072.2005.00091.x.

May, Peter J., and Ashley E. Jochim. 2013. "Policy Regime Perspectives: Policies, Politics, and Governing." *Policy Studies Journal* 41 (3): 426–452. doi.org/10.1111/psj.12024.

May, Peter J., Joshua Sapotichne, and Samuel Workman. 2006. "Policy Coherence and Policy Domains." *Policy Studies Journal* 34 (3): 381–403. doi:10.1111/j.1541-0072.2006.00178.x.

Meadowcroft, James. 2007. "National Sustainable Development Strategies: Features, Challenges and Reflexivity." *European Environment* 17 (3): 152–163.

Meijers, Evert. 2004. "Policy Integration: A literature review." In *Policy Integration in Practice: The Integration of Land Use Planning, Transport and Environmental*

Policy-Making in Denmark, England and Germany, eds. Dominic Stead, Harry Geerlings and Evert Meijers. Delft: DUP Science, 9–21.

Mickwitz, Per, Francisco Aix, Silke Beck, David Carss, Nils Ferrand, Christoph Görg, Anne Jensen, Paula Kivimaa, Christian Kuhlicke, Wiebren Kuindersma, Maria Máñez, Matti Melanen, Suvi Monni, Anders B. Pedersen, Hugo Reinert, and Séverine van Bommel. 2009. *Climate Policy Integration, Coherence and Governance*. Helsinki: PEER (Partnership for European Environmental Research). PEER Report, No. 2.

Mulgan, Geoff. 2010. *The Art of Public Strategy: Mobilizing Power and Knowledge for the Common Good*. Oxford: Oxford University Press.

Nordbeck, R., and R. Steurer. 2015. "Multi-Sectoral Strategies as Dead Ends of Policy Integration: Lessons to be Learned from Sustainable Development." *Environment and Planning C: Government and Policy* (online first, November 24, 2015). doi: 10.1177/0263774X15614696.

Nordbeck, Ralf. 2001. *Nachhaltigkeitsstrategien als politische Langfriststrategien: Innovationswirkungen und Restriktionen: FFU-Report 01-02*. Berlin: FFU (Forschungsstelle für Umweltpolitik, Freie Universität Berlin).

Nullmeier, Frank, and Thomas Saretzki, eds. 2002. Jenseits des Regierungsalltags: *Strategiefähigkeit politischer Parteien*. Frankfurt/Main, New York: Campus.

OECD. 2004. *Sustainable Development in OECD Countries. Getting the Policies Right*, prepared by Richard Herd, Boris Cournede and Douglas Sutherland. Paris: OECD (Organization for Economic Co-operation and Development).

Ostrom, Elinor. 1999. "Institutional Rational Choice: An Assessment of the Institutional Analysis and Development Framework." In *Theories of the Policy Process*, ed. Paul A. Sabatier. Boulder, CO: Westview Press, 35–71.

Pelling, Mark. 2011. *Adaptation to Climate Change: From Resilience to Transformation*. London, New York: Routledge.

Piattoni, Simona. 2010. *The Theory of Multi-Level Governance: Conceptual, Empirical, and Normative Challenges*. Oxford: Oxford University Press.

Pierson, Paul. 2004. *Politics in Time. History, Institutions, and Social Analysis*. Princeton/Oxford: Princeton University Press.

Prittwitz, Volker von. 2007. *Vergleichende Politikanalyse*. Stuttgart: Lucius & Lucius.

Raschke, Joachim. 2002. "Politische Strategie. Überlegungen zu einem politischen und politologischen Konzept." In *Jenseits des Regierungsalltags: Strategiefähigkeit politischer Parteien*, eds. Frank Nullmeier and Thomas Saretzki. Frankfurt/Main, New York: Campus, 207–241.

Raschke, Joachim, and Ralf Tils. 2013. *Politische Strategie. Eine Grundlegung*, Second Edition. Wiesbaden: Springer VS.

Rayner, Jeremy, and Michael Howlett. 2009a. "Conclusion: Governance Arrangements and Policy Capacity for Policy Integration." *Policy and Society* 28 (2): 165–172.

Rayner, Jeremy, and Michael Howlett. 2009b. "Introduction: Understanding Integrated

Policy Strategies and their Evolution." *Policy and Society* 28 (2): 99–109.

Rehder, Britta, Thomas v. Winter, and Ulrich Willems, eds. 2009. *Interessenvermittlung in Politikfeldern: Vergleichende Befunde der Policy- und Verbändeforschung*, First Edition. Wiesbaden: VS Verlag.

Scharpf, Fritz W. 1997. *Games Real Actors Play: Actor-Centered Institutionalism in Policy Research*. Boulder: Westview Press.

Schneider, Anne L., and Helen Ingram.1997. *Policy Design for Democracy*. Lawrence, KAN: University Press of Kansas.

Schreurs, Miranda A. 2008. "From the Bottom Up: Local and Subnational Climate Change Politics." *The Journal of Environment and Development* 17 (4): 343–355.

Smeddinck, Ulrich, and Ralf Tils. 2002. *Normgenese und Handlungslogiken in der Ministerialverwaltung: Die Entstehung des Bundes-Bodenschutzgesetzes: eine politik- und rechtswissenschaftliche Analyse*, First Edition. Baden-Baden: Nomos.

Stecker, Rebecca. 2015. "Zur Entstehung des neuen Politikfeldes Klimawandelanpassungspolitik in Deutschland." *dms—der moderne staat* 8 (1): 71-89.

Steurer, Reinhard. 2007. "From Government Strategies to Strategic Public Management: An Exploratory Outlook on the Pursuit of Cross-Sectoral Policy Integration." *European Environment* 17 (3): 201–214.

Steurer, Reinhard. 2008. "Sustainable Development Strategies." In *Innovation in Environmental Policy?: Integrating the Environment for Sustainability*, eds. Andrew Jordan and Andrea Lenschow. Cheltenham,

UK/Northampton, MA: Edward Elgar, 93–113.

Steurer, Reinhard. 2010. "Sustainable Development as a Governance Reform Agenda: Principles and Challenges." In *Nachhaltigkeit regieren: eine Bilanz zu Governance-Prinzipien und -Praktiken*, eds. Reinhard Steurer and Rita Trattnigg. München: Oekom Verlag, 33–52.

Steurer, Reinhard, and André Martinuzzi. 2005. "Towards a New Pattern of Strategy Formation in the Public Sector: First Experiences with National Strategies for Sustainable Development in Europe." *Environment and Planning C: Government and Policy* 23 (3): 455–472. doi:10.1068/ c0403j.

Steurer, Reinhard, and André Martinuzzi, ed. 2007. "Sustainable Development Strategies in Europe. Taking Stock 20 Years After the Brundtland Report." *European Environment*, Special Issue, 17 (3).

Stirling, Andy. 2008. ""Opening Up" and "Closing Down": Power, Participation, and Pluralism in the Social Appraisal of Technology." *Science, Technology and Human Values* 33 (2): 262–294.

Swanson, Darren, and László Pintér. 2007. "Governance Structures for National Sustainable Development Strategies." In *Institutionalising Sustainable Development*, ed. OECD. Paris: OECD (Organization for Economic Co-operation and Development), 33–65.

Swanson, Darren, László Pintér, François Bregha, Axel Volkery, and Klaus Jacob. 2004. *National Strategies for Sustainable Development. Challenges and Approaches and Innovations in Strategic and Co-*

ordinated Action. Based on a 19-country Analysis. Winnipeg, Manitoba/Eschborn: IISD (International Institute for Sustainable Development) / GTZ (= Deutsche GesellschaftfürTechnischeZusa-mmenarbeit).

Tils, Ralf. 2001. "Professionelle Koordination: Handlungslogiken in der Ministerialverwaltung." In *Gesetzesproduktion im Administrativen Binnenbereich*, eds. Edmund Brandt, Ulrich Smeddinck and Ralf Tils. Baden-Baden: Nomos, 31–66.

Tils, Ralf. 2005. *Politische Strategieanalyse. Konzeptionelle Grundlagen und Anwendung in der Umwelt- und Nachhaltigkeitspolitik.* Wiesbaden: VS Verlag für Sozialwissenschaften.

Tils, Ralf. 2007. "The German Sustainable Development Strategy: Facing Policy, Management and Political Strategy Assessments." *European Environment* 17 (3): 164–176.

Tils, Ralf. 2011. *Strategische Regierungssteuerung: Schröder und Blair im Vergleich*, First Edition. Wiesbaden: VS Verlag für Sozialwissenschaften.

Underdal, Arild. 1980. "Integrated Marine Policy: What? Why? How?" *Marine Policy* 4 (3): 159–169.

Windhoff-Héritier, Adrienne. 1987. *Policy-Analyse. Eine Einführung.* Frankfurt a.M./ New York: Campus Verlag.

Wurster, Stefan. 2013. "Staatstätigkeit II: neue Formen politischer Steuerung." In *Studienbuch Politikwissenschaft*, eds. Manfred G. Schmidt, Frieder Wolf and Stefan Wurster. Wiesbaden: Springer VS, 351–377.

Zahariadis, Nikolaos. 2007. "The Multiple Streams Framework: Structure, Limitations, Prospects." In *Theories of the Policy Process*, Second Edition, ed. Paul A. Sabatier. Boulder, CO: Westview Press, 65–92.

European Policy Analysis - Volume 2, Number 1 - Spring 2016

Juggling Multiple Networks in Multiple Streams

Evelyne de Leeuw,[A] Marjan Hoeijmakers[B] & Dorothee T.J.M. Peters[C]

This paper suggests a new conceptual gaze at theorizing the policy process. Alternating between practical, empirical, and theoretical perspectives, we describe how the hybridization of Multiple Streams, Policy Network, and Frame theories leads to a juggling metaphor to describe the process. From the initiation of this research program, we found that the information our research yielded was vastly more complex and dynamic than what is generally reported in similar research. In particular we discovered that dynamic interactions between actors in the different (policy, problem, and politics) streams, when appraised through a policy network lens, produce different network configurations in each stream. We also found that Kingdon's "Policy entrepreneurs" are likely to engage more in shaping the problem stream network configuration (through the process Kingdon labels "alternative specification"—which requires great perspicacity with words) than in the other streams. We therefore postulate that hybridization of policy network theory with Multiple Streams theory would create a more powerful conceptual toolbox. This toolbox can be enhanced further by insights from network management conceptualisations and frame theory. Finally, we have embraced the criticism that has been voiced of the stages heuristic and proposes that a more useful metaphor for policy processes is juggling: those processes may appear chaotic, but keen discipline, coordination, and acuity are required for policy students and operators to keep all balls in the air.

Keywords: *Networks, multiple streams, theory, policy process, health*

Introduction

In this paper, we propose the hybridization of different theoretical propositions from political science to appreciate and further engage in the development of health policy. We follow a theoretical narrative that unfolds through empirical discovery: having started with the rigorous application of

[A] Professor and Director, Centre for Health Equity Training, Research & Evaluation (CHETRE), Part of the UNSW Australia Research Centre for Primary Health Care & Equity, A Unit of Population Health, South Western Sydney Local Health District, NSW Health. A member of the Ingham Institute, Australia

[B] Director, Gezondheid in Beweging, The Netherlands

[C] D Academic Medical Center—University of Amsterdam, Department of Public Health, The Netherlands

doi: 10.18278/epa.2.1.13

Kingdon's Multiple Streams Framework we discovered—through our direct engagement with a range of policy actors—that we could understand events and couplings within and between policy, politics, and problem streams better by adopting a policy network theoretical gaze. We contend that further hybridization (adding even more conceptual gazes) may establish an even more fine-grained understanding of health policy processes. In particular, we would be interested in connecting and contrasting policy rhetoric (e.g., Stone 2002) and framing theory (Schön and Rein1995) with network mapping and alternative specification perspectives.

First, however, we need to establish the parameters for our particular health policy perspective (de Leeuw, Clavier, and Breton 2014). Health is created outside the healthcare sector. The healthcare sector aims to cure or mediate disease, and is ill equipped to deal with the "causes of the causes" of health and disease (i.e., the social, economic, and political determinants that create opportunities for people to make—healthy—choices; see, for instance, de Leeuw 2016a; 2016b). This assertion has been made and validated for over three decades now by scholars (e.g., Blum 1974; Laframboise 1973; Navarro 1986) and reputable national and global forums (Lalonde 1974; World Health Organization Commission on Social Determinants of Health 2009). A problem remains, though: if health is not created by the sick care sector, why should the sick care sector manage policy development for health? It would make much more sense if policy development for health is managed across those socio-economic realms where health is made.

Ideologically, the character of true "policies for health" has been established since the early 1980s. The Declaration of Alma-Ata on Primary HealthCare (International Conference on Primary Healthcare 1978) and the Ottawa Charter for Health Promotion (World Health Organization, Canadian Public Health Association, and Health Canada 1986) recognized that broad and integrated policies would support and sustain the conditions for good health across individuals, groups, communities, and populations. Rhetorically, however, this is a troubled area. Many concepts are proposed and peddled, for example, Healthy Public Policy, Health in All Policy, and intersectoral policy (Peters et al. 2014), with only nominal differences in flavor or perspective. We would prefer the simple designation "policy for health." Such policy consists of different subsets of sector or issue driven policies, jointly addressing the broad determinants of health. Yet—it is useful to describe the different flavors and perspectives, which we will do next.

The notion of Healthy Public Policy (thus, a subset of "policy for health") endeavors to explicitly introduce health considerations in each of the underlying policy sectors, building momentum for change of all these policies towards health development (Kickbusch 2010). Following Gusfield's notions that actors can own or disown social problems (Gusfield 1981; 1989), health agencies (ministries, public health services) have assumed ownership of health as a problem—and thus appropriating its policy solution. However, this may be true to a lesser extent for the much broader Healthy Public Policy. In very operational terms health agencies have been charged through traditional governance arrangements to develop two distinctive subsets of policies for health: public health policy, and health care policy. In their very nature these two are qualitatively different from each other, which becomes obvious when we look at the policy elements each is supposed to address. Traditionally, healthcare policy deals with operations, access to services, individual patients, and resource allocations. Public health policy, on the other hand, is driven by notions of risk, populations, settings (such as workplaces or schools), and particular risk areas. It seems that, because of the diverging nature of the policy elements, policy development parameters that are deployed in one may be ineffective in another subset. Making policy for health, therefore, is certainly not a case of "one size fits all"; it needs to take into account the unique conditions of each policy domain.

In this paper we invite you to follow our investigative journey and reflect on the theoretical political science propositions that we used. We will need to use a few empirical approaches and findings, but our intent is to relate the development of our conceptual toolbox. This will lead to an admittedly praxis-based set of theoretical suggestions.

Policy Entrepreneurs Opening a Window

One theoretical perspective popularly applied to policy development issues in the health arena is Kingdon's Multiple Streams Framework (1995) (Figure 1). In its simplest narrative, this theory claims that there exist three continuously evolving streams around issues in society. For a complete reflection and meta-review see Jones et al. (2016).

Some of these issues become problems, and the nature of these problems is constantly massaged on and off agendas of those participants who feel engaged with the issue. Some of these participants are "visible," that is, legitimate problem stream actors. They may include special interest groups, academics, and the media. Others are "invisible" and are called upon to provide (or they volunteer) their under-the-radar-services and capacities to contribute to problem framing. An invisible participant may be a lobbyist or a political staffer. Their "invisibility" relates not only to their legitimacy to act, but also to the formal role attributed to them. Visible and invisible participants similarly play roles in the other two streams, those of politics, and policies. An actor visible in one stream may well be invisible in another.

In the politics stream the essential phenomenon is the raw nature of politics as determined by Lasswell (1936): Who gets what, when and how? The dynamic nature of the politics stream is determined by a degree of seasonality (terms of Parliament, electoral cycles, etc.), the political preferences of those in power and those in opposition, and the shifting sands of *"what's hot and what's not."*

Finally, the policies stream is characterized by the evolution, existence and engagement of public policies in their social context. Some of these policies are only symbolic (as, for instance, most public health mass media campaigns), while some are truly redistributive in nature. (Perceived) incremental change to existing policy is often easier argued than radical policy shifts.

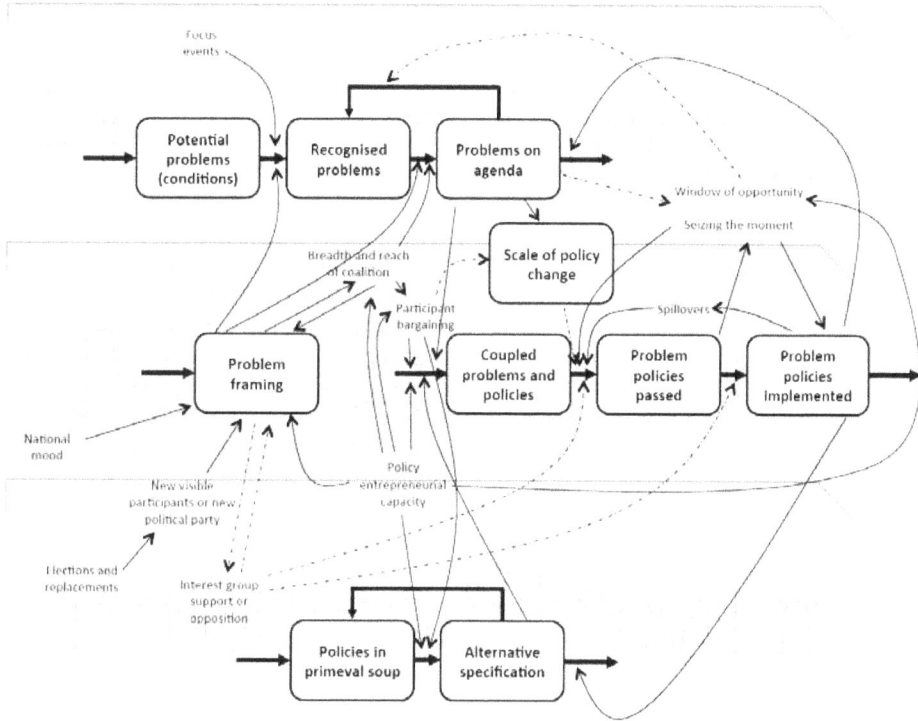

Figure 1: Events in the multiple streams (our interpretation of descriptions in Kingdon, 1995). Solid connections indicate a positive impact, dotted ones may also have negative impact

All the participants in each of these streams play their visible and invisible roles, either trying to maintain the status quo, or in trying to fuel arguments for change. Kingdon describes the players advancing policy change as "policy entrepreneurs," although Skok (1995, 326) has described these roles also as the "social entrepreneur," "issue initiator," "policy broker," "strategist," or "caretaker." Kingdon's work is heavily based on a multitude of empirical observations. From these, he asserts that policy entrepreneurs endeavor to link participants and issues across streams, through a process called "alternative specification," so as to open "windows of opportunities" for policy change. In Figure 1, we endeavor to map some of the events that can take place in and between the three streams. It is obvious that the creation of windows of opportunity, and resulting policy change, happens in a complex networked environment.

Empirical Gaze

In the first stages of our health policy development research (de Leeuw 1999; Hoeijmakers et al. 2007) we looked at the question whether social or policy entrepreneurs were present in the complex health environment, and if so, what they did in order to open windows of opportunity for local health policy development. Similar research in the health promotion domain has been published more recently (Harting et al. 2010). A key finding of this work was that the very nature of the health domain dictates a very dense network, and that effective entrepreneurs need to have the tools to engage in shaping nodes and connections in it. Laumann and Knoke in their seminal "The Organisational State" (1987) mapped healthcare and energy domains in the United States, finding that the most effective policy operators allocate substantive resources to monitor communicative actions of the other actors in the network. Similarly, from our work some initial lessons could be gleaned for the development of policy for health (and, perhaps, the entrepreneurship of those engaged in policy development and health promotion). First, stakeholders may be assisted in structuring and aiming their health promotion (policy making) actions by acquiring insight into their position in these networks relative to the positions of others. Second, stakeholders would be supported in their actions if these were tactically and strategically informed by appropriate knowledge of actions of others in the network.

Networking for Health, and Policy

Network Conceptualisations

Policy network theory is a rich, fast proliferating, yet developing field. Policy network theoreticians and analysts have been challenged to "deliver" and to show the—theoretical or practical—benefits of a network perspective to policy development. Börzel (1998) described two perspectives: an American/Anglo-Saxon one where networks are being mapped on particular policy issues (such as "health" or "energy"), and a German/North-European one where policy networks are used as theoretical models describing new forms of governance. Neither, Börzel claims, has the potential to demonstrate its relevance to "on the ground" policy-making. In other words, in 1998 she claimed (and a good body of the *current* literature sustains that view, for example, Lecy, Mergel, and Schmitz 2014) that the current state of play in both policy network perspectives yields explanatory yet no predictive power. Our findings challenge that view.

Further theoretical advances have been offered to generate policy-making relevance. Kenis and Raab (2003) proposed a course of action to develop a sound policy network theory. Howlett (2002) found that further theorizing on the nature of the policy problem and characteristics of network participants would yield demonstrable insight into the impact of network configurations on policy outcomes. Hill and Hupe (2006) argued that mapping interaction capabilities of actors across different types and levels of governance parameters would enhance policy implementation potential.

Empirical Application

Anticipating these new insights, we responded through a project which we carried out in a group of small municipalities in the southern province of Limburg, in The Netherlands

(Hoeijmakers et al. 2007). In this Dutch study, our aim was to examine Kingdon's streams in terms of the behavior of actors in those streams, the presence and activities of any policy entrepreneurs, a number of "context" factors, and—based on the partly participatory research approach—discover whether there was a difference in health policy development between two municipalities that at the start of the project had expressed an interest in health policy, and two matched ones that did not.

Making policy for health is a statutory requirement in The Netherlands. Under the Dutch Collective Prevention legislation, municipalities in The Netherlands must develop and implement local health policies. These were supposed to be policies for health, inspired by the national Dutch government's efforts in the 1980s through what was called "Nota 2000," a policy paradigm directly related to the European WHO Health for all by the Year 2000 strategies (de Leeuw and Polman 1995). In the first iteration of the legislation such a broad perspective was reaffirmed, and specified in its background documents and evaluations of its predecessors (Lemstra 1996; Ministerie van VWS 2000; Ministerie van VWS et al. 2001). Explicitly and expressly, these local health policies aim at the promotion of health across sectors, with a strong community involvement, and based on available epidemiological information. However, in the successive—amended—Public Health Law, the broad understanding of local health policy prescribed more precisely the particular (public health) policy elements. This may have traded off the opportunity to develop broad systemic health policy against the willingness of local governments to engage. Since the adoption of the legislation virtually every stakeholder in this policy community has been challenged in driving this process forward or even assuming appropriate ownership and responsibility (de Goede et al. 2010; Harting et al. 2011; Jansen et al. 2010). No one at the local level has assumed ownership of broadly-defined-health. Hoeijmakers et al. (2007), applied the social network theory (e.g., Wasserman and Faust 1994) and concluded the same in studying local health policy making. This is no surprise, as in the local discourse few actors advocate for *health*; rather, they advocate for *absence of disease* (e.g., the Public Health Service), *access to and efficiency of services* (healthcare and social work providers), or *patient interests* (QUANGOs such as local chapters of Cancer Council, or the Patient and Consumer Platform). Municipalities report a lack of operational knowledge and due to lack of sufficient resources, they are professionally unable to formulate comprehensive health policies (Jansen et al. 2010). In desperate quests for "health" advice they end up in the preventive care realm and focus on healthy lifestyle issues rather than systemic change. Besides, since the Public Health Law does not control and enforce whether policies are broadly defined, no explicit incentive (or sanctioning) mechanism is present in its legal framework.

This notion that "health" is an intangible, fluid and orphaned policy issue is mirrored by the findings of Putland, Baum, and Ziersch (2011) who investigated lay understandings of (the causes of) health inequity. The authors concluded that "... *the findings in this study are evocative of a kind of collective inertia within the public health field. The lack of congruence between explanations and public policy responses suggests that public health arguments directed at addressing the social determinants of health have not become absorbed into bodies of lay knowledge.*" No one owns health, and hence no one can be mobilized for its advocacy. We suggest that such a void of understanding necessarily leads to limited political expediency to address the issue. Also, the broad conceptualisation of (social determinants of) health is not a policy frame that resonates in the "lay" community. One of very few research efforts to consider what it would take to mobilize communities politically towards a more substantive social determinants policy effort has been undertaken by the Robert Wood Johnson Foundation, Carger, and Westen (2010). Over four years they systematically investigated frames and metaphors for health in the United States and found that there is a meaningful divide between language and rhetoric deployed by public health professionals and scholars on the one side, and what the US public (across the Democratic-Republican spectrum) feels on the other. Popular support for broad health policy seems absent, but can be framed meaningfully toward some degree of awareness and advocacy. The social determinants message needs to resonate at a deep metaphorical level. The framing of the "health is created outside the healthcare sector" issue appears difficult—at one level because the language that needs to be used generally eludes health practitioners and scholars (de Leeuw 2016a; 2016b).

Recognising that we were facing a stagnant policy environment with a multitude of actors, we started our inquiry with a stakeholder analysis.

Stakeholder analysis is popular in organizational analysis, policy analysis and programme development (Brugha and Varvasovszky 2000). Stakeholders may include individuals, organizations and different individuals within an organization, as well as networks of individuals and/or organizations. Stakeholder analysis is used as a tool to map the actors who have a stake in a policy, organization or programme and to describe the characteristics of these actors. For example, stakeholder analysis in policy-making is used to create support for policy decisions and commitment for the implementation of policy (Provan and Milward 1995).

Our investigation into Dutch local government policy for health looked at the following characteristics of identified stakeholders: their ideas about local health policy, interests, collaboration with other actors in public health, influence and the contribution they made towards policy development. These attributes formed the principal constituents of the annual interviews with stakeholders; they also structured our approach to participatory observation. Over 3 years, we monitored the change or stability of the characteristics of stakeholders. We were interested in knowing how these characteristics related to the policy development process and whether stakeholders engaged in entrepreneurial activities for policy change (Hoeijmakers 2005). With a very small initial sample, we used "snowball sampling" to reach a stable research population (Salganik and Heckathorn 2004) and subsequently one Delphi round to identify the most important stakeholders to the issue of "broadly-defined-health" policy making in the municipal cases under study.

Of interest is that we were eager to know if citizen groups, neighbourhood committees, resident associations, etc. would be included in the list. Even when communities are symbolically at the centre of the health argument, they may be absent from the policy game (e.g., de Leeuw and Clavier 2011; Löfgren, Leahy, and de Leeuw2011). Community groups were indeed included as stakeholders and from here we adopted a normative approach to explicitly monitor the participation of these groups in the policy making process and their position and connectedness in the policy networks. Ultimately, we found that their role and position were peripheral.

Conceptual Reflection

Whereas stakeholder analysis provides information on the set of actors who (should) have a stake in a certain issue, social network analysis provides information on the interactions between these actors. In other words, stakeholder analysis describes the actor differentiation; whereas network analysis describes the actor integration related to a certain issue. Network analysis is a tool to describe and analyse the interactions between a defined set of actors. Network analysis considers the presence and the absence of relations among actors (individuals, work units, or organizations) more powerful in explaining social phenomena than the attributes of these actors (see e.g. Brass et al. (2004) for an overview). Consequently, actors are embedded within a network of interconnected relationships that provide opportunities for and constraints on their organizational and political behavior. As stated above, the most central tenet of network mapping is that networks

exist around certain issues: the same set of actors involved in the implementation of vaccination programs may display an entirely different network configuration when mapped for their annual Mardi Gras participation. In the exploratory phase of our research, therefore, we reviewed whether "local policy for health" was in fact such a demarcated issue (Laumann, Marsden, and Prensky 1989). Stakeholders informed us that this was not the case, and that they felt that they interacted differently, and on different dimensions, with other local stakeholders in engagements that not necessarily were construed to be related to "health." From this feedback we decided to map three networks for all four municipalities: communication for health policy development, involvement in public health action, and strategic (or opportunistic) collaboration. These approaches to network mapping emerged from the participatory engagement with local policy for health processes, and were not initially operationally aligned with Kingdon's Multiple Streams work. The data on interaction between stakeholders in these domains were obtained from a structured questionnaire filled out during interviews. We calculated density, centralization and actor centrality of the abovementioned networks. The result of these calculations indicated that all networks described were relatively stagnant over the three year period that they were observed, without discernible policy entrepreneurial activity, with policy ownership attributed to (and possibly reluctantly accepted by) local government, and generally unaware of the potential and capacity there was for the development of local health policy.

Practical Consequences

Such findings have been found repeatedly in follow-up studies. Most of these have started from the premise that something is going wrong at the nexus between research, policy and practice (de Goede et al. 2010; Jansen et al. 2010). Such studies have, for instance, endeavored to develop and validate local health reports for policy making (Van Bon-Martens et al. 2011), similar to the Health Profiles that have been part of Healthy City efforts in Europe and elsewhere (Waddell 1995). Others have taken this idea a step further by exploring the utility of such reports as perceived by institutional actors (i.e., the public sector stakeholders formally mentioned in the relevant legislation) in the local health domain (de Goede, Putters, and van Oers 2012) and a third perspective has endeavored to map relationships between such actors and academia in already existing collaborative arrangements (Hoeijmakers, Raab, and Jansen 2012), similar to the program to reduce health inequities in Montreal (Bernier et al. 2006). Ultimately, policy action needs also be grounded and sustained by a social agenda for changed rooted in the community (de Leeuw 2016a; 2016b).

From Opportunistic to Strategic Policy Networks

It would have become clear from the above that our local health policy development research, up to that point, was prominently driven by the need to develop *social* (rather than *policy*) network analysis as expressed by local policy stakeholders. The fact that we looked, in the perception of stakeholders, at "tangible" social network issues (communication; collaborative action; and strategy) was in retrospect perhaps not the wisest option. The result was, as we showed, that stagnant, single, "independent" social networks were described. Reflecting on the constructed network configurations, we noticed a certain dynamic undertow when looking at the networks simultaneously, influencing the same process of policy making. The position and possible (coordinative) activities of actors in the communication network for instance would be of interest for taking an influential position in the action or strategic network. With the data from our inquiry we were at the time not yet able to really grasp and underpin this observation, although we were curious how such dynamics could be stimulated further and be visualised; especially to create better possibilities for community groups to get such positions in policy networks that enable their participation also in policy decision-making.

Practical Validation

Only when we discussed these findings with policymakers, and put them in the context of the theory that drove our inquiry, it dawned on us that an altogether different approach might well have contributed to policy change. The intent was—as in so much political research— to describe the processes that would lead to change. In this endeavor, we made an effort to distance ourselves as "objective" and "value-free" researchers from the actual engagement in potential change. Our policy and practice colleagues, it turned out, were less interested in the process descriptions, and much more in tactical process prompts: "So what could we *do* to be more policy-relevant?" It turned out that combining the network perspective with Kingdon's Streams made for appealing narratives that instantly rang true to those involved in (health) policy networks. Looking back, there may have been more of a need to act ourselves as policy entrepreneurs than we ever anticipated—and our adoption of a Participatory Action Research perspective would possibly have had an impact on the local policy games (e.g., Quoss, Cooney, and Longhurst 2000). We also learned an important lesson on choosing and applying theory: adopting hybrid frameworks in which several commensurate and complementary theories are applied may yield important new insights (see also, for instance, Greenhalgh and Stones 2010).

Based on our theoretical, methodological and empirical foundations we thus developed IMPolS: the Interactive Mapping of Policy Streams tool. In a number of sessions with practitioners, policymakers and academics we presented and tested the dummy version, which evolved as a consequence. IMPolS operates, still in its alpha version, on a secure internet URL. One of the key considerations in possible implementation is that its management and operation is essentially driven by the end users themselves, and that very little "theoretical debris" or "text ballast"

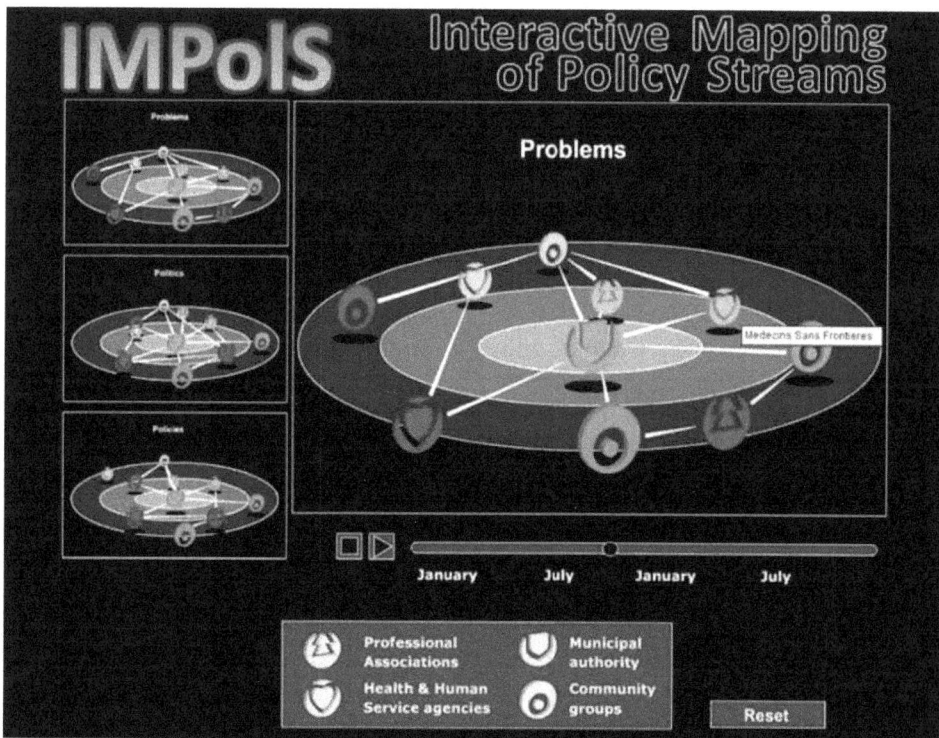

Figure 2: IMPolS main visualisation screen with switchable problems, politics and policies networks. Actor/stakeholder descriptions visualise when the cursor is hovered over the actor icon (in this case "Medecins Sans Frontieres")

should be present on the site. End users would self-identify as actor-stakeholders in a specific policy domain, either by directly signing up to a specific (self-defined) URL within IMPolS and then nominating network colleagues (the tool will then send e-invites), or by initiating an IMPolS instance during a network meeting (for instance, an Annual General Meeting) at which a first round of network data is entered.

At this stage, actor/stakeholders also choose a representative icon (categories in Figure 2 shown in the red box at the bottom of the screen, but fully adaptable to other specific policy domains), and may define and select categories of participants. Actors may continue to be added; the expectation is that from the initiation stage onward actors will regularly access their domain and answer about a dozen questions relating to their position and connection in the network. These data will then be added to the database and first, the network visualization algorithm will recalculate the three network configurations, *and*, second, notify other members of the network that an actor has updated their position and connection (thus prompting others to do the same). Over time, with more data added, the network mapping visualizations (and possibly actor behavior, about which more below) will gain intricacy, and will allow for a dynamically animated, pulsing set of network configurations. Further sophistication could be added, either by the self-selected network members or by a network manager (again, see below), through the refinement of the timeline with critical events, such as described by Kingdon above (e.g., elections, climactic events, policy change or press release, etc.).

In our alpha testing of the IMPolS tool we have found a number of things: first, a visually attractive and transparent architecture of both the input screens (user identification and network variable entry) and the network screens would increase the likelihood of actors engaging with the tool. This is precisely what the developers of the Gephi software platform (Gephi is an interactive visualization and exploration platform for all kinds of networks and complex systems, dynamic and hierarchical graphs—see gephi.org) found: applying visualization principles from the gaming sector enhances the attractiveness of the application (Bastian, Heymann, and Jacomy 2009). Second, and in full concordance with both the propositions by Kingdon and our initial research, virtually all actors in their "face-value analysis" of the network outputs focused more on the problem stream than on either of the other streams. They found that problem stream graphic network visualizations provided them with arguments and impulses to (re)consider

a) the nature of the problem they are engaging with;

b) their framing of the problem, and how it might link with other actors if reframed (Kingdon's "alternative specification"); and

c) how to seek alliances with actors found to be similar (sometimes called "homophilic network relations," for example, Monge and Contractor 2003, and Provan and Kenis 2008), either in their position in the problem network (in terms of connectedness and centrality), or in perceived similarities in mission or vision of the institutional characteristics of the actor.

Also in their reflections on the problem stream, most alpha testers were curious how changes in problem framing and perception would impact

    I. on reconfigurations of the problem network (e.g., would they come closer to central actors?); and
    II. on their capacity and capability of reconfiguring the policy and politics streams.

Answers to such questions would be theory-informed, but relatively speculative until we have accumulated enough data to develop an algorithm that might suggest such outcomes.

    Third, we were interested in the question whether the nodes in our network visualizations should be seen as individuals-operating-in-organizations or as actors-representing-institutions. Although we feel that this issue can ultimately only be resolved empirically (when, over time, large amounts of data have been input into a range of policy domain IMPolS instances, and changes in policy have been mapped onto the resulting network configurations), our alpha testers felt that the tool would work at both levels: individuals engaging in policy change "a la Kingdon," but also institutional actors assessing their positions in network configurations.

Reflection

We set out to find Kingdon's "policy entrepreneurs" and did not find any (Hoeijmakers et al. 2007). We also identified, in our own research and elsewhere, "policy inertia" or "a stagnant policy environment." Whether or not the policy inertia was a consequence of the absence of entrepreneurs could not unequivocally be ascertained. However, our alpha testing of IMPolS suggested that participants in this policy domain may have been connected and activated to the problems, politics and policies discourse if they would have had insight in their own and others" network positions. The question whether this would have led to stronger policy entrepreneurial activity, although speculative, seems to have to be answered in the affirmative. Further theoretical thinking about network governance may shed light on this.

    Provan and Kenis (2008) and Kenis and Provan (2009) have proposed some interesting theory-based postulates on network performance and effectiveness. This is not the place to reflect comprehensively on their material, but in light of our quest for policy entrepreneurs in networks we find that the views on "network management" are valuable. Are policy entrepreneurs network managers? If they are, what are the conditions for them to operate effectively, and do they have the ability to create those conditions when absent? Ultimately—what would be the tools they need to play such roles affectively?

    Based on the postulates by Provan and Kenis we could suggest theoretical and empirical—and tentative practical— approaches that would enhance the functionality of IMPolS. The two network scholars suggest the following typology (see Table 1) for predictors of forms of network governance (Provan and Kenis 2008, 237).

    Network governance in complex policy environments (such as the health field), according to this typology, requires a collective "Network

Table 1: Provan and Kenis' key predictors of effectiveness of network governance forms

Governance Forms	Trust	Number of Participants	Goal Consensus	Need for Network-Level Competencies
Shared governance	High density	Few	High	Low
Lead organization	Low density, highly centralized	Moderate number	Moderately low	Moderate
Network Administrative Organization (NAO)	Moderate density, NAO monitored by members	Moderate to many	Moderately high	High

Administrative Organization" that is capable of simultaneous monitoring and management of the many dimensions, actors, and connections in the policy environment. Such a role would require the capacity to dynamically engage at many different levels of governance and many elements of the policy process simultaneously. This inference resonates with Laumann and Knoke's (1987) finding that effective policy intervention is predicated by larger teams of media and communication monitors based in influential (public and private) organizations.

Juggling

This issue touches on the very nature of theories of the policy process. Theories applied in *behavioral* research are typically linear, at best with a feedback loop: a number of inputs (say, "attitudes" and "beliefs") are transformed through a number of conditioners (say, "social norm" and "self-efficacy") to produce intermediary ("intention") and final (behavioral) change (e.g., the theory of planned behavior and the theory of reasoned action, Madden, Ellen, and Ajzen1992). In more complex behavioral systems there may be iterative and more incremental steps, and sometimes the models may take the shape of a cycle.

This, then, is also how policy development is typically modeled. A policy cycle can variably exist of as little as three steps (problem—solution—evaluation), four stages (agenda setting—policy formation—policy implementation—policy review) with as many as 15 subprocesses, to retrospective policy analyses that yield dozens of policy development instances, phases, and events. In Figure 3, we can see the Google image yield for the search term "policy cycle."

All of these represent the policy process as displaying a curved linearity in which one stage—sometimes under conditions—necessarily leads to the next stage, just like the behavioral theories

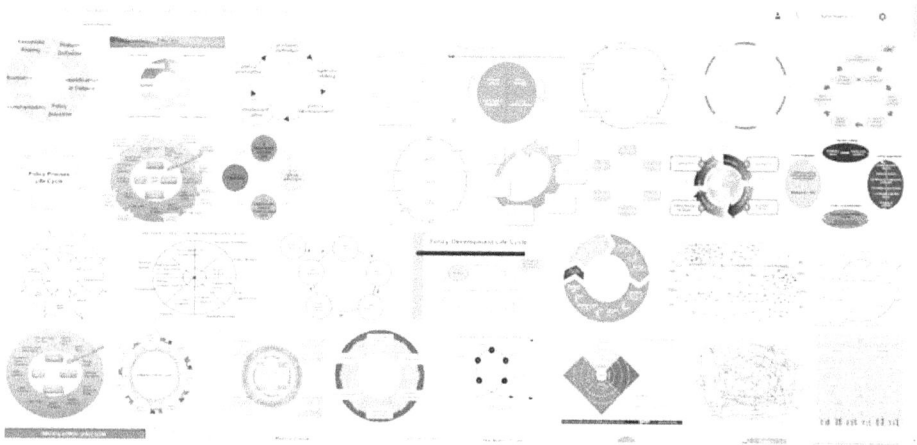

Figure 3: The first 32 "hits" when performing a Google Image search for "policy cycle" (8 March 2016)

introduced above. Although this cyclic metaphor may be useful for analytical purposes, the notion that there is a linear logic to policy processes may cloud and hamper the actions of actors at the policy development coalface.

It is not just that one stage or step coincides with another (for instance, the specification of policy alternatives may interface with the selection of policy instruments/interventions). In fact, often a step that comes "later" in the stages heuristic in fact precedes an earlier phase in the cycle. A "real life" example would be policy implementation. Implementation is driven by a wide array of contextual factors, including shifting power relations. Even when the policy problem is debated (as a first "agenda setting" exercise), actors in the system implicitly, or by default, know that some implementation strategies will be impossible to develop. Regardless of how well planned and analytical

earlier stages in the policy process are, only certain types of interventions can be favored (Pressman and Wildavsky 1983). In a comprehensive review of the literature on policy instruments and interventions, Bemelmans-Videc, Rist, and Vedung (1998) formulate the "least coercion rule": policy-makers favor the intervention that is least intrusive into individual choice (as evidenced for obesity policy by, for instance, Allender et al. (2012)). Thus, despite following the policy planning process conscientiously, the outcome in implementation terms favors communicative over facilitative or regulatory interventions. Steps in the cycle are therefore in reality rarely sequential or with feedback loops between sequential stages: often the process jumps a few steps ahead, to return to a previous step, or it finds itself going both clockwise *and* counter-clockwise for only sections of the cycle.

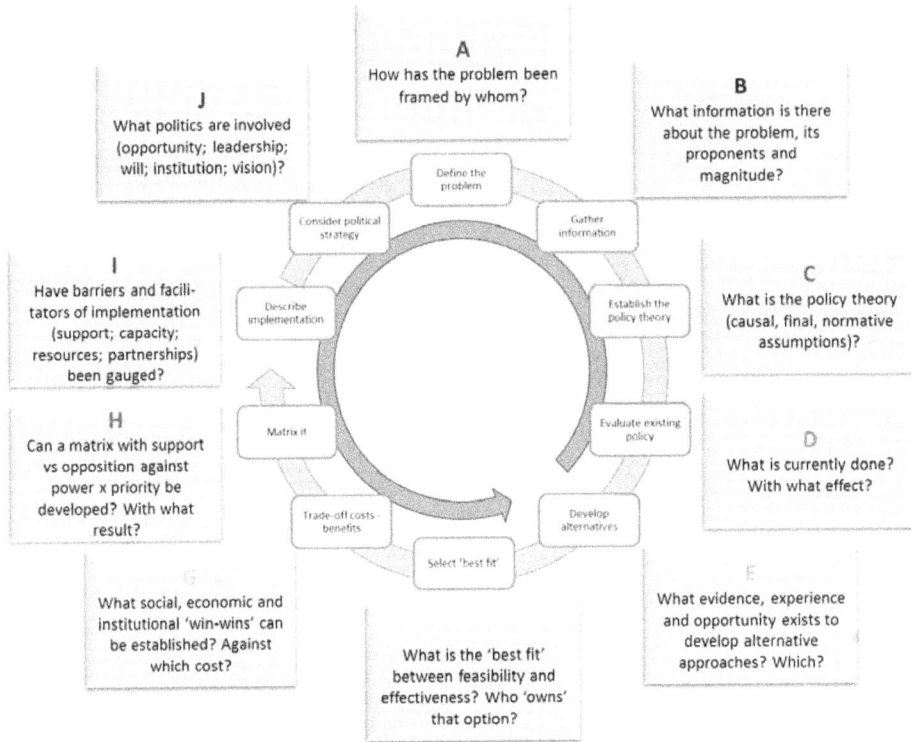

Figure 4. Ten issues in developing Health in All Policies (de Leeuw and Peters 2014)

We were commissioned by the World Health Organization to develop a tool that would guide the development and application of Health in All Policies (de Leeuw and Peters 2014). Through discussions with key stakeholders around the world we identified 10 issues that need to be analysed and mapped in order to enhance the feasibility of HiAP development. We drafted a HiAP cycle (Figure 4) for discussion with HiAP experts, showing both the clockwise and counterclockwise sequential options for considering these options. The feedback on the figure demonstrated that the intuitive response to the graph was to diligently follow each of the stages,

assuming there was a progressive logic to them. At the same time, our panel agreed that the reality is that "*everything happens at the same time.*"

This is the essence of the critique that has been voiced by political scientist on the "stages heuristic" (Nowlin 2011; Sabatier1999;2007a; 2007b)—that there is no causality between the different stages, and therefore stages heuristic models defy theoretical testing mechanisms. The stages heuristic is useful as a mnemonic and an analytical visualization of elements of the policy process, but does not describe the complex interactions within, between and beyond its different features. Hassenteufel (2011) furthermore argued that the analytical linearity of the stages heuristic clouds the symbolic nature of policymaking in society as a sense-making activity rather than a purely methodical enterprise.

We sought an alternative to the linearity or cyclical nature of the policy process, and found that the best visual metaphor is that of juggling. The juggling metaphor appears to ring true to policy entrepreneurs and activists at the coal face of policy development and change. It recognizes that, although keeping all balls in the air virtually simultaneously creates an apparently hugely chaotic scene, systematic and disciplined action is required at all times. We contend that the mastery of perspicacious language (either by rigorous application of the Frame Theory and standard rhetorical repertoire, or purely grounded in a charismatic talent for words) is one of the most critical tools in this process.

Juggling is decidedly not the same as the idea of policy making as a garbage-can process (most profoundly professed by March and Olsen 1984)—the application of theories highlighted above would aim at structuring and making sense of the logic, diligence and structure of managing a chaotic process. Theory-led discussions between academics and practitioners have been suggested to work towards this end (Cairney 2014).

Policy entrepreneurs who want to make an impact in the art of juggling should consider:

- The complexity of the policy domain at hand, in terms of problems, policies and politics streams;
- The identification of actor–stakeholders, their relations and perceptions in these streams;

- The potential for further, bespoke, "alternative specifications" for bringing in actor–stakeholders from the periphery to the center of, particularly, the problem stream network;
- Considerations for the development, deployment and necessary morphing of rhetorical tools that resonate with different (cliques of) stakeholders, for example, compelling narratives, synecdoche, metaphor, and ambiguous statements (Stone 2002)
- The identification and empowerment of as yet disconnected actor–stakeholders to connect to the policy discourse (de Leeuw and Clavier 2011);
- The identification (and we would speculate that strategies of "naming and shaming" might have utility) of actor–stakeholders who sustain policies and politics streams inertia, thereby pointing to issues of trust, network membership and joint purpose;
- The analysis and description of critical agents in network governance; and
- The identification and enabling of new skills and competencies required for network governance.

It will be clear that such roles, objectives, and techniques require a certain degree of mastery of the theoretical foundations for network mapping, management, and operations as quite tentatively outlined above. The professionals and activists engaging in these entrepreneurial roles will also have to possess great skills and knowledge around issues of knowledge utilisation (de Leeuw et al. 2008). Mostly, throughout our analyses we have seen the importance of mastery of language, and rhetorical tools to mobilise and frame policy agendas. Those agendas, we found (de Leeuw 2016a; 2016b), are shaped in sub-populations, cliques, and specific actor networks. For policy entrepreneurs it will help if they can speak with a certain authority and resonance on health (equity) issues to those that are directly affected (i.e., disadvantaged communities), but also to those that may not feel directly affected. Equity and the social gradient of health (Marmot 2005) by their very nature have two sides: the lower end and the upper end, the have-nots and the haves. Developing a public policy for all (no matter through which mechanisms, e.g., Carey, Crammond, and de Leeuw 2015) must, at least in its framing and rhetorical tools, embrace all.

Conclusion

The dynamics in policies for health development processes can be better understood by applying hybrid theoretical lenses. And by the use of interactive techniques in analyzing network development and its efficiency as first order effects. Furthermore, techniques such as IMPoIS provide participants in the network with necessary insights to further aim their actions and strengthen their position to communicate, collaborate and make (joint) decisions in making policies for health. This is of utmost importance for community groups to better integrate in health policy networks. Network development then needs the explicit attention of stakeholders in health policy making.

Policy entrepreneurs should be active in raising this attention and awareness. There is an emerging body of work that demonstrates that appropriate policy network management practices enhance the outcomes of policy development (Klijn, Steijn, and Edelenbos 2010) and that the juggling extends quite beyond the agenda setting "phase" (Pump 2011) or the role of government administration (Baumgartner et al. 2009; to add another—punctuated equilibrium—theoretical perspective to the mix). This suggests that effective policy entrepreneurs should be able to glean their strategies from our hybrid theoretical gaze. Such a perspective holds promise for two future paths: one where a more specific and guided policy network management toolbox can be made available to the aspiring entrepreneur, and another where our juggling metaphor is linked with network management ideas in an exciting new research program. Clearly the emerging practice of such policy entrepreneurship should be intertwined with the research agenda.

References

Allender, S., E. Gleeson, B. Crammond, G. Sacks, M. Lawrence, A. Peeters, and. B. Swinburn. 2012. "Policy Change to Create Supportive Environments for Physical Activity and Healthy Eating: which Options are the most Realistic for Local Government?" *Health Promotion International* 27 (2): 261–274.

Bastian, M., S. Heymann, and M. Jacomy.2009. *Gephi: An Open Source Software for Exploring and Manipulating Networks.* International AAAI Conference on Weblogs and Social Media.

Baumgartner, F.R., C. Breunig, C. Green-Pedersen, B.D. Jones, P.B. Mortensen, M. Nuytemans, and S. Walgrave. 2009. "Punctuated Equilibrium in Comparative Perspective." *American Journal of Political Science* 53 (3): 603–620.

Bemelmans-Videc, M.-L., R.C. Rist, and E. Vedung, eds. 1998. *Carrots, Sticks &Sermons: Policy Instruments and Their Evaluation*. New Brunswick, NJ, USA: Transaction Publishers.

Bernier, J., M. Rock, M. Roy, R. Bujold, and L. Potvin. 2006. "Structuring an Inter-Sector Research Project. A Negotiated Zone." *Sozial-und Präventivmedizin* 51: 335–344.

Blum, H.L. 1974. *Planning for Health Development and Application of Social Change Theory*. New York: Human Sciences Press.

Börzel, T. A. 1998. Organizing Babylon: On the different conceptions of policy networks. *Public Administration* 76: 253–273

Brass, D.J., J. Galaskiewicz, H.R. Greve, and W. Tsai. 2004. "Taking Stock of Networks and Organizations: A Multilevel Perspective." *Academy of Management Journal* 47: 795–818.

Brugha, R., and Z. Varvasovszky. 2000. "Stakeholder Analysis: A Review." *Health Policy and Planning* 15: 239–246.

Cairney, P. 2014. "How can Policy Theory have an Impact on Policy making? The Role of Theory-Led Academic–Practitioner Discussions." *Teaching Public Administration.* doi: 10.1177/0144739414532284.

Carey, G., B. Crammond, and E. de Leeuw. 2015."Towards Health Equity: A Framework for the Application of Proportionate Universalism." *International Journal for Equity in Health* 14:81.doi:10.1186/s12939-015-0207-6.

de Goede, J., K.Putters, T. van der Grinten, and H.A.M. van Oers. 2010. "Knowledge in Process? Exploring Barriers between Epidemiological Research and Local Health Policy Development." *Health Research Policy and Systems* 8: 26.

de Goede, J., K. Putters, and H.A.M. van Oers. 2012. "Utilization of Epidemiological Research during the Development of Local Public Health Policy in the Netherlands: A Case Study Approach." *Social Science & Medicine* 74: 707–714.

de Leeuw, E. 1999. "Healthy Cities: Urban Social Entrepreneurship for Health." *Health Promotion International* 14 (3): 261–269.

de Leeuw, E. 2016a. *The Nature of the Silent Arrow*. Blog 14 March 2016 http://glocalhealthconsultants.com/the-nature-of-the-silent-arrow/.

de Leeuw, E. 2016b."We Need Action on Social Determinants of Health—but Do We Want It, too? Comment on "Understanding the Role of Public Administration in Implementing Action on the Social Determinants of Health and Health Inequities." *International Journal of Health Policy and Management* 5 (x): 1–4.doi:10.15171.

de Leeuw, E., and C. Clavier. 2011. "Healthy Public in all Policies. The Ottawa Charter for Health Promotion 25 Years On. The Move towards a new Public Health Continues." *Health Promotion International* 26 (Supplement 2): ii237–ii244.

de Leeuw, E., and D. Peters. 2014. "Nine Questions to Guide Development and Implementation of Health in All Policies." *Health Promotion International* 30: 987-997

de Leeuw, E., and L. Polman. 1995. "Health Policy making: The Dutch Experience." *Social Science & Medicine* 40 (3): 331–338.

de Leeuw, E., A. McNess, B. Crisp, and K. Stagnitti. 2008. "Theoretical Reflections on the Nexus between Research, Policy and Practice." *Critical Public Health* 18 (1): 5–20.

de Leeuw, E., C. Clavier, and E. Breton. 2014."Health Policy—why Research it and how: Health Political Science." *Health Research Policy and Systems* 12 (1): 55.

Greenhalgh, T., and R. Stones. 2010. "Theorising Big IT Programmes in Healthcare: Strong Structuration Theory Meets Actor-Network Theory." *Social Science & Medicine* 70: 1285–1294.

Gusfield, J. 1981. *The Culture of Public Problems: Drinking-Driving and the Symbolic Order.* Chicago: University of Chicago Press.

Gusfield, J.R. 1989. "Constructing the Ownership of Social Problems: Fun and Profit in the Welfare State." *Social Problems* 36 (5): 431–441. DOI: http:// dx.doi.org/10.2307/3096810.

Harting, J., A.E. Kunst, A. Kwan, and K. Stronks. 2010. "A 'Health Broker' Role as a Catalyst of Change to Promote Health: An Experiment in Deprived Dutch Neighbourhoods." *Health Promotion International* 26 (1): 65–81.

Hassenteufel, P. 2011. *Sociologiepolitique: l'actionpublique*, 2ème édition. Paris: Armand-Colin.

Hill, M., and P. Hupe. 2006. "Analysing Policy Processes as Multiple Governance: Accountability in Social Policy." *Policy & Politics* 34 (3): 557–573.

Hoeijmakers, M. 2005. Local health policy development processes: health promotion and network perspectives on local health policy-making in the Netherlands (Doctoral dissertation, Maastricht University).

Hoeijmakers, M., E., de Leeuw, P. Kenis, and N.K. de Vries. 2007. "Local Health Policy Development Processes in the Netherlands: An Expanded Toolbox for Health Promotion." *Health Promotion International* 22 (2): 112–121.

Hoeijmakers, M., J. Raab, and M. Jansen. 2012. "Academische werkplaatsen ter versterking van kennisontwikkeling en kennisuitwisseling in de publieke gezondheidszorg. Resultaten van netwerkanalyses in de Limburgse werkplaats." *Tijdschrift voor Gezondheidswetenschappen* 90: 442-450.

Howlett, M. 2002. "Do Networks Matter? Linking Policy Network Structure to Policy Outcomes: Evidence from Four

Canadian Policy Sectors 1990–2000." *Canadian Journal of Political Science* 35 (2): 235–267.

International Conference on Primary Health Care. 1978.Declaration of Alma-Ata. Geneva: World Health Organization. Jansen, M.W.J., H.A.M. van Oers, G.Kok, and N.K. de Vries. 2010. "Public Health: Disconnections between Policy, Practice and Research." *Health Research Policy and Systems* 8: 37–49.

Jones, M.D., H.L. Peterson, J.J. Pierce, N. Herweg, A. Bernal, H. Lamberta Raney, and N. Zahariadis. 2016. "A River Runs Through It: A Multiple Streams Meta-Review." *Policy Studies Journal* 44 (1): 13–36. DOI: 10.1111/psj.12115

Kenis, P., and K.G. Provan. 2009."Towards an Exogenous Theory of Public Network Performance." *Public Administration* 87 (3): 440–456.

Kenis, P., and J. Raab. 2003."Wanted: A Good Network Theory of Policy Making." *National Public Management Conference, Proceedings*. Washington DC.

Kickbusch, I. 2010. "Health in All Policies: The Evolution of the Concept of Horizontal Health Governance." In *Implementing Health in All Policies*, eds. I. Kickbusch, and K. Buckett. Adelaide: Government of South Australia, 11–23.

Kingdon, J.W. 1995. *Agenda's, Alternatives, and Public Policies*. Michigan: Harper Collins College Publishers.

Klijn, E.H., B.Steijn, and J. Edelenbos.2010. "The Impact of Network Management on Outcomes in Governance Networks." *Public Administration* 88 (4): 1063-1082.

Laframboise, H.L. 1973. "Health Policy: Breaking the Problem Down into more Manageable Segments." *Canadian Medical Association Journal* 108: 388–393.

Lalonde, M. 1974. *Nouvelle perspective sur la santé des Canadiens/A new perspective on the health of Canadians*.Ottawa: Gouvernement du Canada.

Lasswell, H.D. 1936. *Politics: Who Gets What, When, How*. New York: McGraw-Hill.

Laumann, E.O., and D. Knoke.1987. *The Organizational State. Social Choice in National Policy*. Wisconsin: The University of Wisconsin Press.

Laumann, E.O., P.V. Marsden, and D. Prensky. 1989. "The Boundary Specification Problem in Network Analysis." In *Research Methods in Social Network Analysis*, eds. L.C. Freeman, D.R. White, and A.K. Romney. Fairfax: George Mason University Press, 61–87.

Lecy, J.D., I.A. Mergel, and H.P. Schmitz. 2014. "Networks in Public Administration: Current Scholarship in Review." *Public Management Review* 16 (5): 643–665.

Lemstra, W.C. 1996. *Gemeentelijk Gezondheidsbeleid. Beter op zijn Plaats*. [Municipal Health Policy. Better placed]. Den Haag: Commissie Versterking Collectieve Preventie [Committee Reinforcement Collective Prevention].

Löfgren, H., M. Leahy, and E. de Leeuw. 2011. "Participation and Democratization in Health and Health Care. In

Democratising Health: Consumer Groups in the Policy Process, eds. H. Löfgren, E. De Leeuw, and M. Leahy. Cheltenham: Edward Elgar Publishing, 1–14.

Madden, T.J., P.S.Ellen, and I. Ajzen. 1992. "A Comparison of the Theory of Planned behavior and the Theory of Reasoned Action." *Personality and Social Psychology Bulletin* 18 (1): 3–9.

March, J.G., and Olsen, J.P. 1984. "The New Institutionalism: Organizational Factors in Political Life." *American Political Science Review* 78 (3): 734–749.

Marmot, M. 2005."Social Determinants of Health Inequalities." *The Lancet* 365 (9464): 1099–1104.

Ministerie van Volksgezondheid Welzijn en Sport [Ministry of Health, Welfare and Sports]. 2000. *Spelen op de Winst. Een visie op de openbare gezondheidszorg [Go for Victory. A vision on public health]*. Den Haag: Ministerie van Volksgezondheid, Welzijn en Sport [Ministry of Health, Welfare and Sports].

Ministerie van Volksgezondheid Welzijn en Sport [Ministry of Health, Welfare and Sports], GGD Nederland [Association of Dutch Public Health Services], VNG [Association of Dutch Municipalities] and Ministerie van BinnenlandseZaken [MinistryofHomeAffairs].2001.*Nationaal Contract Openbare Gezondheidszorg [National Public Health Contract]*. Leiden: Platform Openbare Gezondheidszorg (Public Health Council).

Monge, P.R., and N.S. Contractor. 2003. *Theories of Communication Networks*. New York: Oxford University Press.

Navarro, V. 1986. *Crisis, Health, and Medicine: A Social Critique*. New York: Tavistock.

Nowlin, M.C. 2011. "Theories of the Policy Process: State of the Research and Emerging Trends." *Policy Studies Journal* 39 (S1): 41–60. doi: 10.1111/j.1541-0072.2010.00389_4.x

Peters, D.T.J.M., J. Harting, H. Van Oers, J. Schuit, N. De Vries, and K. Stronks. 2014. "Manifestations of Integrated Public Health Policy in Dutch Municipalities." *Health Promotion International.* doi: 10.1093/heapro/dau104 (Online First).

Pressman, J.L., and A. Wildavsky. 1983. Implementation. How great expectations in Washington are dashed in Oakland; or why it's amazing that federal programs work at all, this being a saga of the economic development administration as told by two sympathetic observers who seek to build morals on a foundation of ruined hopes. Berkeley, Los Angeles, London: University of California Press.

Provan, K.G., and P. Kenis. 2008. "Modes of Network Governance: Structure, Management, and Effectiveness." *Journal of Public Administration Research and Theory* 18 (2): 229–257.

Provan, K.G., and H.B. Milward. 2001."Do Networks Really Work?" A Framework for Evaluating Public-Sector Organizational Networks. *Public Administration Review* 61 (4):414-423.

Pump, B. 2011. "Beyond Metaphors: New Research on Agendas in the Policy Process1." *Policy Studies Journal* 39 (S1): 1–12.

Putland, C., F.E. Baum, and A.M. Ziersch.2011. "From Causes to Solutions—Insights from Lay Knowledge about Health Inequalities." *BMC Public Health* 11:67.

Robert Wood Johnson Foundation, E. Carger, and D. Westen. 2010. *A New Way to Talk about the Social Determinants of Health.* Princeton: Robert Wood Johnson Foundation, http://www.rwjf.org/en/library/research/2010/01/a-new-way-to-talk-about-the-social-determinants-of-health.html(accessed March7, 2016).

Quoss, B., M.Cooney, and T. Longhurst. 2000. "Academics and Advocates: Using Participatory Action Research to Influence Welfare Policy." *Journal of Consumer Affairs* 34 (1): 47–61.

Sabatier, P.A.,ed. 1999. *Theories of the Policy Process. Theoretical Lenses on Public Policy.* Boulder, CO: Westview Press.

Sabatier, P.A. 2007a. "The Need for Better Theories." In *Theories of the Policy Process*, ed. P.A. Sabatier. Cambridge, MA: Westview Press, 3–17.

Sabatier, P.A., ed. 2007b. *Theories of the Policy Process.* Boulder, CO: Westview Press.

Salganik, M.J., and D.D. Heckathorn. 2004. "Sampling and Estimation in Hidden Populations Using Respondent-Driven Sampling." *Sociological Methodology* 34: 193–239.

Schön, D.A., and M. Rein. 1995. *Frame Reflection: Toward the Resolution of Intractable Policy Controversies.* New York: Basic Books.

Skok, J.E. 1995. "Policy Issue Networks and the Public Policy Cycle: A Structural-Functional Framework for Public Administration." *Public Administration Review* 55 (4): 325–332.

Stone, D. 2002. Policy Paradox. *The Art of Political Decision Making*, Revised Edition. New York: WW Norton & Company.

Van Bon-Martens, M.J.H., P.W. Achterberg, I.A.M. van de Goor, and H.A.M. van Oers. 2011. "Towards Quality Criteria for Regional Public Health Reporting: Concept Mapping with Dutch Experts." *European Journal of Public Health* 22 (3): 337–342.

Waddell, S. 1995. "Lessons from the Healthy Cities Movement for Social Indicator Development." *Social Indicators Research* 34 (2): 213–235.

Wasserman, S., and K. Faust. 1994. *Social Network Analysis: Methods and Applications.* Cambridge, UK: Cambridge University Press.

World Health Organisation, Canadian Public Health Association and Health Canada. 1986. "The Ottawa Charter for Health Promotion." *Health Promotion* 1 (4): i–v.

World Health Organization Commission on Social Determinants of Health. 2009. *Closing the Gap in a Generation: Health Equity through Action on the Social Determinants of Health.* http://www.who.int/social_determinants/thecommission/finalreport/en/index.html (accessed November 21, 2012).

Why You Should Read My Book

Sager, Fritz, and Patrick Overeem, eds. The European Public Servant: A Shared Administrative Identity? Colchester: ECPR Press.2015. ISBN: 9781907301742.

Patrick Overeem, *Universiteit Leiden, Campus Den Haag*

O ur book departs from the basic idea, promoted by the European Union, that European public policy needs to be embedded in a European administrative space. So far, however, no one seems to know exactly whether there is a shared European administrative identity and what it looks like. The various contributions in this volume set out to explore indications of family traits of the European public servant. And indeed, while there is no clear-cut overall identity, there are many characteristics shared across various European countries. This book helps you understand, from both historical and comparative perspectives, the heterogeneous phenomenon of the European public servant.

doi: 10.18278/epa.2.1.11

Reimut Zohlnhöfer and Friedbert W. Rüb, eds. Decision Making under Ambiguity and Time Constraints. Assessing the Multiple-Streams Framework.Colchester: ECPR Press. (ISBN 9781785521256)

Friedbert Rüb, *Humboldt University Berlin, Germany*

O ur book assesses the analytical clout of Kingdon's Multiple-Streams Framework, which is widely used and well established in policy studies. High-ranking experts and talented junior researchers apply the Framework in their theoretically and empirically profound contributions.

Different national contexts, such as Germany, Greece, Spain, Sweden, the United Kingdom, and United States, are covered and a wide variety of policy areas such as abortion, climate change, foreign policy, healthcare, internal security, nonsmoking regulations, social policy, and tax policy are investigated.

This coherently edited book offers an excellent overview of key comparative issues and will fascinate you, especially if you work with the now-classic Multiple-Streams Framework.

doi: 10.18278/epa.2.1.12

www.ingramcontent.com/pod-product-compliance
Lightning Source LLC
Chambersburg PA
CBHW081653270326
41933CB00017B/3160